ITALIAN

PHRASEBOOK

Compiled by

LEXUS

ROUGH
GUIDES

www.roughguides.com

Credits

Compiled by Lexus with Michela Masci
Lexus Series Editor: Sally Davies
Rough Guides Reference Director: Andrew Lockett
Rough Guides Series Editor: Mark Ellingham

First edition published in 1995.
Reprinted in 1995, 1996, 1998 and 2004.
This updated edition published in 2006 by
Rough Guides Ltd,
80 Strand, London WC2R 0RL
345 Hudson St, 4th Floor, New York 10014, USA
Email: mail@roughguides.co.uk.

Distributed by the Penguin Group.

Penguin Books Ltd, 80 Strand, London WC2R 0RL
Penguin Putnam, Inc., 375 Hudson Street, NY 10014, USA
Penguin Group (Australia), 250 Camberwell Road, Camberwell,
Victoria 3124, Australia
Penguin Books Canada Ltd, 10 Alcorn Avenue, Toronto,
Ontario, Canada M4V 1E4
Penguin Group (New Zealand), Cnr Rosedale and Airborne Roads,
Albany, Auckland, New Zealand

Typeset in Bembo and Helvetica to an original design by Henry Iles.
Printed in Italy by LegoPrint S.p.A

British Library Cataloguing in Publication Data
A catalogue for this book is available from the British Library.

ISBN 13: 978-1-84353-630-7
ISBN 10: 1-84353-630-7

The publishers and authors have done their best to ensure the
accuracy and currency of all information in The Rough Guide
Italian Phrasebook however, they can accept no responsibility for
any loss or inconvenience sustained by any reader using the book.

Online information about Rough Guides can be found at our website www.
roughguides.com

CONTENTS

Introduction 5

Basic Phrases 8

Scenarios 13

English - Italian 31

Italian - English 124

Menu Reader

Food 204

Drink 228

How the Language Works

Pronunciation 237

Abbreviations 237

Nouns 238

Articles 241

Prepositions 243

Adjectives and Adverbs 243

Possessive Pronouns 248

Personal Pronouns 248

Verbs 252

Questions 263

Dates 263

Days 263

Months 264

Time 264

Numbers 265

Conversion Tables 268

Introduction

The Rough Guide Italian phrasebook is a highly practical introduction to the contemporary language. Laid out in clear A-Z style, it uses key-word referencing to lead you straight to the words and phrases you want – so if you need to book a room, just look up 'room'. The Rough Guide gets straight to the point in every situation, in bars and shops, on trains and buses, and in hotels and banks.

The main part of the Rough Guide is a double dictionary: English-Italian then Italian-English. Before that, there's a section called **Basic Phrases** and to get you involved in two-way communication, the Rough Guide includes, in this new edition, a set of **Scenario** dialogues illustrating questions and responses in key situations such as renting a car and asking directions. You can hear these and then download them free from **www.roughguides.com/phrasebooks** for use on your computer or MP3 player.

Forming the heart of the guide, the **English-Italian** section gives easy-to-use transliterations of the Italian words wherever pronunciation might be a problem. Throughout this section, cross-references enable you to pinpoint key facts and phrases, while asterisked words indicate where further information can be found in a section at the end of the book called **How the Language Works**. This section sets out the fundamental rules of the language, with plenty of practical examples. You'll also find here other essentials like numbers, dates, telling the time and basic phrases. In the **Italian-English** dictionary, we've given you not just the phrases you'll be likely to hear (starting with a selection of slang and colloquialisms) but also many of the signs, labels, instructions and other basic words you may come across in print or in public places.

Near the back of the book too the Rough Guide offers an extensive **Menu Reader**. Consisting of food and drink sections (each starting with a list of essential terms), it's indispensable whether you're eating out, stopping for a quick drink, or browsing through a local food market.

buon viaggio!
have a good trip!

Basic
Phrases

yes
sì

no
no

OK
d'accordo

hello
(in the daytime) buongiorno
bwonjorno
(late afternoon, in the evening)
buonasera
bwonasaira

good night
buonanotte bwonanot-tay

goodbye
arrivederci
ar-reevedairchee

please
per favore
pair favoray

yes please
sì, grazie
see gratzee-ay

thanks, thank you grazie
gratzee-ay

thank you very much
grazie mille
meel-lay

no thanks
no grazie

that's OK, don't mention it
prego
praygo

how do you do?
piacere
p-yachairay

how are you?
come sta?
komay

fine, thanks, and you?
bene, grazie e tu/lei?
baynay gratzee-ay ay tay/lay?

pleased to meet you
piacere di conoscerla
p-yachairay dee konoshairla

excuse me
(to get past) permesso
pairmes-so
(to get attention) mi scusi
mee skoozee
(to say sorry) chiedo scusa
k-yaydo skooza

sorry: (I'm) sorry
scusa/mi scusi
skooza/mee skoozee

sorry? (didn't understand)
prego?
praygo

I understand
capisco

I don't understand
non capisco

do you understand?
capisci/capisce?
kap**ee**shee/kap**ee**shay

do you speak English?
parla inglese?
eengl**ay**zay

I don't speak Italian
non parlo italiano
  XXXcheck please

could you say it slowly?
puoi/può dirlo più
  lentamente?
pwoy/pwo d**ee**rlo p-yoo

could you repeat that?
può ripetere?
pwo reep**e**tairay

could you write it down?
può scrivermelo?
pwo skr**ee**vairmelo

I'd like ...
vorrei ...
vor-r**ay**

would you like ...?
vuoi/vuole ...
vwoy/vw**o**lay

can I have a ...?
vorrei ...
vor-r**ay**

do you have ...?
avete ...?
av**ay**tay

how much is it?
quanto costa?
kw**a**nto

cheers!
(toast) alla salute!
sal**oo**tay
(thanks) grazie
gr**a**tzee-ay

it is ...
è...
ay

where is ...?
dov'è ...?
dov**ay**

is it far from here?
è lontano da qui?
ay – kwee

Scenarios

1. Accommodation

is there an inexpensive hotel you can recommend?
▶ mi può consigliare un albergo economico?
[mee pwo konseel-yaray oon albairgo ekonomeeko]

mi dispiace, sembrano tutti al completo ◀
[mee deesp-yachay sembrano toot-tee al komplayto]
I'm sorry, they all seem to be fully booked

can you give me the name of a good middle-range hotel?
▶ mi può dare il nome di un buon albergo a prezzo medio?
[mee pwo daray eel nomay dee oon bwon albairgo a pretzo mayd-yo]

vediamo: vuol essere al centro? ◀
[ved-yamo vwol es-sairay al chentro]
let me have a look; do you want to be in the centre?

if possible
▶ se possibile
[say pos-seebeelay]

le dà fastidio essere un po' fuori città? ◀
[lay da fasteed-yo es-sairay oon po fworee cheet-ta]
do you mind being a little way out of town?

not too far out
▶ non troppo fuori
[non trop-po fworee]

where is it on the map?
▶ dove si trova sulla piantina?
[dovay see trova sool-la p-yanteena]

can you write the name and address down?
▶ mi può scrivere il nome e l'indirizzo?
[mee pwo skreevairay eel nomay ay leendeereetzo]

I'm looking for a room in a private house
▶ cerco una stanza in una casa privata
[chairko oona stanza een oona kaza preevata]

13

2. Banks

bank account	il conto bancario	[konto bankar-yo]
to change money	cambiare dei soldi	[kamb-yaray day soldee]
cheque	l'assegno	[as-sen-yo]
to deposit	depositare	[daypozeetaray]
euro	l'euro	[ay-ooro]
pin number	il pin	[peen]
pound	la sterlina	[stairleena]
to withdraw	ritirare	[reeteeraray]

can you change this into euros?
▶ mi può cambiare questi in euro?
[mee pwo kamb-yaray kwestee een ay-ooroo]

come preferisce i soldi? ◀
[komay prefaireeshay ee soldee]
how would you like the money?

small notes
▶ banconote di piccolo taglio
[bankonotay dee peek-kolo tal-yo]

big notes
▶ banconote di grosso taglio
[bankonotay dee gros-so tal-yo]

do you have information in English about opening an account?
▶ ha informazioni in inglese su come aprire un conto?
[a eenformatz-yonee een eenglayzay soo komay apreeray oon konto]

▶ sì, che tipo di conto vuole?
[see kay teepo dee konto vwolay]
yes, what sort of account do you want?

I'd like a current account
vorrei un conto corrente ◀
[vor-ray oon konto kor-rentay]

▶ il suo passaporto, per favore
[eel soo-o pas-saporto pair favoray]
your passport, please

can I use this card to draw some cash?
▶ posso usare questa carta per ritirare dei soldi?
[pos-so oozaray kwesta karta pair reeteeraray day soldee]

▶ deve andare alla cassa
[dayvay andaray al-la kas-sa]
you have to go to the cashier's desk

I want to transfer this to my account at the Banco di Roma
▶ voglio trasferire questi soldi nel mio conto presso il Banco di Roma
[vol-yo trasfaireeray kwestee soldee nel mee-o konto pres-so eel banko dee roma]

va bene, ma le dobbiamo addebitare la telefonata ◀
[va baynay ma lay dob-byamo ad-debeetaray la telefonata]
OK, but we'll have to charge you for the phonecall

14

3. Booking A Room

shower	la doccia	[docha]
telephone in the room	telefono in stanza	[telefono een stanza]
payphone in the lobby	telefono pubblico nella hall	[telefono poob-bleeko nel-la oll]

do you have any rooms?
▶ avete stanze libere?
[avaytay stanzay leebairay]

▶ per quante persone?
[pair kwantay pairsonay]
for how many people?

for one/for two
per una/per due ◀
[pair oona/pair doo-ay]

▶ si, abbiamo delle stanze libere
[see ab-byamo del-lay stanzay leebairay]
yes, we have rooms free

▶ per quante notti?
[pair kwantay not-tee]
for how many nights?

just for one night
solo per una notte ◀
[solo pair oona not-tay]

how much is it?
▶ quanto costa?
[kwanto kosta]

90 euro col bagno e 70 euro senza bagno ◀
[novanta ay-ooro kol ban-yo ay set-tanta ay-ooro sentza ban-yo]
90 euros with bathroom and 70 euros without bathroom

does that include breakfast?
▶ la colazione è compresa?
[la kolatz-yonay ay komprayza]

can I see a room with bathroom?
▶ posso vedere una stanza col bagno?
[pos-so vedairay oona stanza kol ban-yo]

ok, I'll take it
va bene. la prendo ◀
[va baynay la prendo]

when do I have to check out?
▶ quando devo lasciare la stanza?
[kwando dayvo lasharay la stanza]

is there anywhere I can leave luggage?
▶ posso lasciare i bagagli da qualche parte?
[pos-so lasharay ee bagal-yee da kwalkay partay]

4. Car hire

automatic	con il cambio automatico	[kon eel **kamb**-yo owto-**mateeko**]
full tank	il serbatoio pieno	[sairbato**y**-o p-y**ay**no]
manual	con il cambio manuale	[kon eel **kamb**-yo manoo-**alay**]
rented car	l'automobile a noleggio	[owtom**obeelay** a nol**ej**-jo]

I'd like to rent a car
▶ vorrei noleggiare un'automobile
[vor-**ray** nol**ej**-jaray oon owtom**obeelay**]

per quanti giorni? ◀
[pair kw**antee jornee**]
for how long?

two days
▶ due giorni
[**doo**-ay j**ornee**]

I'll take the ...
▶ prendo la ...
[pr**endo** la ...]

is that with unlimited mileage?
▶ il chilometraggio è illimitato?
[eel keelometr**aj**-jo ay eel-leemeet**ato**]

sì ◀
[see]
it is

mi fa vedere la patente per favore? ◀
[mee fa ved**air**ay la pat**entay** pair fav**oray**]
can I see your driving licence?

e il passaporto ◀
[ay eel pas-sap**orto**]
and your passport

is insurance included?
▶ l'assicurazione è compresa?
[as-seekooratz-y**o**nay ay kompr**ayza**]

sì, ma deve pagare i primi 100 euro ◀
[see ma d**ay**vay pag**aray** ee pr**eemee** chento **ay-oo**ro]
yes, but you have to pay the first 100 euros

può lasciare una caparra di 100 euro? ◀
[pwo lash**aray oo**na kap**ar**-ra dee chento **ay-oo**ro]
can you leave a deposit of 100 euros?

and if this office is closed, where do I leave the keys?
▶ e se quest'ufficio è chiuso, dove posso lasciare le chiavi?
[ay say kwest oof-f**ee**cho ay k-y**oo**zo d**o**vay pos-so lash**aray** lay k-y**avee**]

le infili in quella cassetta ◀
[lay eenf**ee**lee een kwel-la kas-s**et**-ta]
you drop them in that box

5. Communications

ADSL modem	il modem ADSL	[modem a-dee-es-say-el-lay]
at	chiocciola	[koch-chola]
dial-up modem	il modem a linea commutata	[modem a leenay-a kom-mootata]
dot	punto	[poonto]
Internet	l'Internet	[eentairnet]
mobile (phone)	il cellulare	[chel-loolaray]
password	la password	
telephone socket adaptor	l'adattatore del telefono	[adat-tatore del telefono]
wireless hotspot	il punto di accesso wireless a Internet	[poonto dee achayso wireless a eentairnet]

is there an Internet café around here?
▶ c'è un Internet café da queste parti?
[chay oon eentairnet kafay da kwestay partee]

can I send email from here?
▶ posso mandare delle mail da qui?
[pos-so mandaray del-lay mail da kwee]

where's the at sign on the keyboard?
▶ dov'è la chiocciola sulla tastiera?
[dovay la koch-chola sool-la tast-yaira]

can you switch this to a UK keyboard?
▶ si può cambiare la tastiera in britannica?
[see pwo kamb-yaray la tast-yaira een breetan-neeka]

can you help me log on?
▶ mi può aiutare a fare il log in?
[mee pwo a-yootaray a faray eel log een]

I'm not getting a connection, can you help?
▶ non riesco a collegarmi, mi può aiutare?
[non ree-esko a kol-legarmee mee pwo a-yootaray]

where can I get a top-up card for my mobile?
▶ dove posso comprare una ricarica per il mio cellulare?
[dovay pos-so kompraray oona reekareeka pair eel mee-o chel-loolaray]

can you put me through to ...?
▶ mi può passare ...?
[mee pwo pas-saray ...]

zero	five
zero	cinque
[tzairo]	[cheenk way]
one	six
uno	sei
[oono]	[say]
two	seven
due	sette
[doo-ay]	[set-tay]
three	eight
tre	otto
[tray]	[ot-to]
four	nine
quattro	nove
[kwat-tro]	[no-vay]

6. Directions

hi, I'm looking for the via Messina
▶ salve, cerco via Messina
[salvay chairko vee-a mes-seena]

mi dispiace, mai sentita ◀
[mee deesp-yachay ma-ee senteeta]
sorry, never heard of it

hi, can you tell me where the via Messina is?
▶ salve, mi sa dire dove si trova via Messina?
[salvay mee sa deeray dovay see trova vee-a mes-seena]

anch'io non sono di qui ◀
[ankee-o non sono dee kwee]
I'm a stranger here too

hi, the via
Messina,
do you
know
where it is?
▶ salve, via
Messina, sa
dov'è?
[salvay vee-a
mes-seena sa
dovay]

where?
dove?
[dovay]

which direction?
in quale direzione?
[een kwalay deeks-yonay]

▶ a sinistra al secondo semaforo
[a seeneestra al sekondo semaforo]
left at the second traffic lights

▶ all'angolo
[al-langolo]
around the corner

poi è la prima strada a destra ◀
[poy ay la preema strada a destra]
then it's the first street on the right

appena dopo [ap-payna dopo] just after	indietro [eend-yaytro] back	sempre dritto [sempray dreet-to] straight ahead	svoltare [zvoltaray] turn off
davanti a [davantee a] in front of	lì [lee] over there	strada [strada] street	vicino [veecheeno] near
di fronte [dee frontay] opposite	più avanti [p-yoo avantee] further	sulla destra [sool-la destra] on the right	
dopo il ... [dopo eel ...] past the ...	prossimo [pros-seemo] next	sulla sinistra [sool-la seeneestra] on the left	

7. Emergencies

accident	l'incidente	[eencheedentay]
ambulance	l'ambulanza	[amboolantza]
consul	il console	[konsolay]
embassy	l'ambasciata	[ambashata]
fire brigade	i vigili del fuoco	[veejeelee del fwoko]
police	la polizia	[poleetzee-a]

help!
▸ aiuto!
[a-yooto]

can you help me?
▸ può aiutarmi?
[pwo a-yootarmee]

please come with me! it's really very urgent
▸ per favore venga con me! è davvero molto urgente
[pair favoray venga kon may ay dav-vairo molto oorjentay]

I've lost (my keys)
▸ ho perso (le chiavi)
[o pairso (lay k-yavay)]

(my car) is not working
▸ (la mia automobile) non funziona
[(la mee-a owtomobeelay) non foontz-yona]

(my purse) has been stolen
▸ (il mio borsellino) è stato rubato
[(eel mee-o borsel-leeno) ay stato roobato]

I've been mugged
▸ sono stato aggredito
[sono stato ag-gredeeto]

---

come si chiama? ◂
[komay see k-yama]
what's your name?

---

mi può mostrare il passaporto? ◂
[mee pwo mostraray eel pas-saporto]
I need to see your passport

I'm sorry, all my papers have been stolen
▸ mi dispiace, mi hanno rubato tutti i documenti
[mee deesp-yachay mee an-no roobato toot-tee ee dokoomentee]

8. Friends

hi, how're you doing?
▶ ciao, come va?
[chow **ko**may va]

bene, e tu? ◀
[**bay**nay ay too]
OK, and you?

---

yeah, fine
▶ bene
[**bay**nay]

not bad
▶ non c'è male
[non chay **ma**lay]

---

d'you know Marco?
▶ conosci Marco?
[kon**o**shee **ma**rco]

---

and this is Hannah
▶ e questa è Hannah
[ay **kwe**sta ay **han**-nah]

sì, ci conosciamo già ◀
[see chee konosh-**ya**mo ja]
yeah, we know each other

---

where do you know each other from?
▶ dove vi siete conosciuti?
[**do**vay vee s-**yay**tay konosh**oo**tee]

---

we met at Luca's place
▶ ci siamo conosciuti da Luca
[chee s-**ya**mo konosh**oo**tee da **loo**ka]

---

that was some party, eh?
▶ che festa quella, vero?
[kay **fe**sta kw**el**-la **vai**ro]

fantastica ◀
[fant**a**steeka]
the best

---

are you guys coming for a beer?
▶ venite a prendere una birra?
[ven**ee**tay a pr**en**dairay **oo**na beer-ra]

▶ grande, andiamo
[gr**an**day and-**ya**mo]
cool, let's go

no, mi vedo con Luisa ◀
[no mee **vay**do kon loo-**ee**sa]
no, I'm meeting Luisa

---

see you at Luca's place tonight
▶ ci vediamo da Luca stasera
[chee ved-**ya**mo da **loo**ka stas**ai**ra]

ciao ◀
[chow]
see you

9. Health

I'm not feeling very well
▶ non mi sento bene
[non mee sento baynay]

can you get a doctor?
▶ può chiamare un dottore?
[pwo k-yamaray oon dot-toray]

▶ dove le fa male?
[dovay lay fa malay]
where does it hurt?

it hurts here
mi fa male qui ◀
[mee fa malay kwee]

▶ il dolore è continuo?
[eel doloray ay konteenoo-o]
is the pain constant?

it's not a constant pain
non è un dolore continuo ◀
[non ay oon doloray konteenoo-o]

can I make an appointment?
▶ posso prendere un appuntamento?
[pos-so prendairay oon ap-poontamento]

can you give me something for ...?
▶ mi può dare qualcosa per ...?
[mee pwo daray kwalkoza pair ...]

yes, I have insurance
sì, sono assicurato ◀
[see sono as-seekoorato]

antibiotics	gli antibiotici	[anteebioteechee]
antiseptic ointment	la pomata antisettica	[pomata anteeset-teeka]
cystitis	la cistite	[cheesteetay]
dentist	il/la dentista	[denteesta]
diarrhoea	la diarrea	[dee-aray-a]
doctor	il dottore	[dot-toray]
hospital	l'ospedale	[ospedalay]
ill	malato/a	[malato]
medicine	la medicina	[medeecheena]
painkillers	gli analgesici	[analjayseechee]
pharmacy	la farmacia	[farmachee-a]
to prescribe	prescrivere	[preskreevairay]
thrush	la candida	[kandeeda]

10. Language difficulties

a few words	qualche parola	[kwalkay parola]
interpreter	l'interprete	[eentairpretay]
to translate	tradurre	[tradoor-ray]

la sua carta di credito è stata respinta ◀
[la soo-a karta dee kraydeeto ay stata respeenta]
your credit card has been refused

what, I don't understand; do you speak English?
▶ come, non capisco; parla inglese?
[komay non kapeesko parla eenglayzay]

non è valida ◀
[non ay valeeda]
this isn't valid

could you say that again?   slowly
▶ può ripetere?   lentamente ◀
[pwo reepetairay]   [lentamentay]

I understand very little Italian
▶ capisco solo un po' d'italiano
[kapeesko solo oon po deetal-yano]

I speak Italian very badly
▶ parlo italiano molto male
[parlo eetal-yano molto malay]

non può usare questa carta per pagare ◀
[non pwo oozaray kwesta karta pair pagaray]
you can't use this card to pay

▶ capisce?   sorry, no
[kapeeshay]   no, mi dispiace ◀
do you understand?   [no mee deesp-yachay]

is there someone who speaks English?
▶ c'è qualcuno che parla inglese?
[chay kwalkoono kay parla eenglayzay]

oh, now I understand   **is that ok now?**
▶ oh, ora capisco   ▶ va bene ora?
[oh ora kapeesko]   [va baynay ora]

download these scenarios as MP3s from:

11. Meeting people

hello
▸ salve
[salvay]

salve, mi chiamo Anna ◂
[salvay mee k-yamo an-na]
hello, my name's Anna

Graham, from England, Thirsk
▸ io sono Graham, di Thirsk, in Inghilterra
[ee-o sono graham dee thirsk een eengeeltair-ra]

non conosco questo posto, dove si trova? ◂
[non konosko kwesto posto dovay see trova]
don't know that, where is it?

not far from York, in the North; and you?
▸ non lontano da York, nel nord; e lei di dov'è?
[non lontano da york nel nord ay lay dee dovay]

▸ io sono di Milano; è qui da solo?
[ee-o sono dee meelano ay kwee da solo]
I'm from Milan; here by yourself?

no, I'm with my wife and two kids
▸ no, sono qui con mia moglie e i miei due figli
[no sono kwee kon mee-a mol-yay ay ee m-yay-ee doo-ay feel-yee]

what do you do?
▸ che lavoro fa?
[kay lavoro fa]

mi occupo di computer ◂
[mee ok-koopo dee 'computer']
I'm in computers

me too
▸ anch'io
[ankee-o]

here's my wife now
▸ ecco mia moglie
[ek-ko mee-a mol-yay]

piacere ◂
[p-yachairay]
nice to meet you

12. Post offices

airmail	la posta aerea	[posta a-airay-a]
post card	la cartolina	[kartoleena]
post office	la posta	[posta]
stamp	il francobollo	[frankobol-lo]

what time does the post office close?
▶ a che ora chiude la posta?
[a kay ora k-yooday la posta]

◀ alle cinque dal
lunedì al venerdì
**[al-lay cheenkway dal
loonedee al venairdee]
five o'clock weekdays**

is the post office open on Saturdays?
▶ la posta è aperta il sabato?
[la posta ay apairta eel sabato]

◀ fino a mezzogiorno
**[feeno a metzojorno]
until midday**

I'd like to send this registered to England
▶ vorrei spedire questo in Inghilterra per raccomandata
[vor-ray spedeeray kwesto een eenghleetair-ra pair rak-komandata]

◀ sì, sono 10 euro
**[see sono dee-aychee ay-ooro]
certainly, that will cost 10 euros**

and also two stamps for England, please
▶ e anche due francobolli per l'Inghilterra, per favore
[ay ankay doo-ay frankobol-lee pair leenghleetair-ra pair favoray]

do you have some airmail stickers?
▶ ha degli adesivi di posta aerea?
[a dayl-yee adeseevee dee posta a-airay-a]

do you have any mail for me?
▶ c'è posta per me?
[chay posta pair may]

estero	international
pacchi	parcels
fermo posta	poste restante

24

13. Restaurants

bill	il conto	[konto]
menu	il menù	[menoo]
table	il tavolo	[tavolo]

can we have a non-smoking table?
▶ vorremmo un tavolo per non fumatori
[vor-**raym**-mo oon **t**avolo pair non foomat**o**ree]

there are two of us
▶ siamo in due
[s-y**a**mo een d**oo**-ay]

there are four of us
▶ siamo in quattro
[s-y**a**mo een kw**a**t-tro]

what's this?
▶ questo cos'è?
[kw**e**sto koz**ay**]

è un tipo di pesce ◀
[ay oon **tee**po dee p**e**shay]
it's a type of fish

è una specialità del posto ◀
[ay **oo**na spech-yal**ee**ta del p**o**sto]
it's a local speciality

entri e le faccio vedere ◀
[**e**ntree ay lay **f**acho ved**air**ay]
come inside and I'll show you

we would like two of these, one of these, and one of those
▶ vorremmo due di questi, uno di questi, e uno di questi
[vor-**raym**-mo d**oo**-ay dee kw**e**stee **oo**no dee kw**e**stee ay **oo**no dee kw**e**stee]

▶ e da bere?
[ay da b**air**ay]
and to drink?

red wine
▶ vino rosso
[v**ee**no r**o**s-so]

white wine
▶ vino bianco
[v**ee**no b-y**a**nko]

a beer and two orange juices
▶ una birra e due succhi d'arancia
[**oo**na b**ee**r-ra ay d**oo**-ay s**oo**k-kee dar**a**ncha]

some more bread please
▶ ancora pane, per favore
[ank**o**ra p**a**nay pair fav**o**ray]

▶ è andata bene?
[ay and**a**ta b**a**ynay]
how was your meal?

excellent!, very nice!
▶ ottimo!, molto buono!
[**o**t-teemo m**o**lto bw**o**no]

▶ desiderano altro?
[dezeed**e**rano **a**ltro]
will there be anything else?

just the bill thanks
▶ solo il conto, grazie
[s**o**lo eel k**o**nto gr**a**tzee-ay]

14. Shopping

posso esserle d'aiuto? ◄
[**pos**-so **es**-sairlay da-**yoo**to]
can I help you?

can I just have a look around?
▶ posso dare uno sguardo?
[**pos**-so d**a**ray **oo**no zg**wa**rdo]

yes, I'm looking for ...
▶ sì, cerco ...
[see ch**air**ko ...]

how much is this?
▶ quanto costa questo?
[k**wa**nto k**o**sta k**we**sto]

trentadue euro ◄
[trentad**oo**-ay **ay-oo**ro]
thirty-two euros

OK, I think I'll have to leave it; it's a little too expensive for me
▶ lasciamo stare; è un po' troppo caro per me
[lash-**ya**mo st**a**ray ay oon po tr**op**-po k**a**ro pair may]

e questo? ◄
[ay k**we**sto]
how about this?

can I pay by credit card?
▶ posso pagare con una carta di credito?
[**pos**-so pag**a**ray kon **oo**na k**a**rta dee kr**ay**deeto]

it's too big
▶ è troppo grande
[ay tr**op**-po gr**a**nday]

it's too small
▶ è troppo piccolo
[a ay tr**op**-po p**ee**k-kolo]

it's for my son – he's about this high
▶ è per mio figlio: è alto più o meno così
[ay pair m**ee**-o f**ee**l-yo ay **a**lto p-yoo o m**ay**no koz**ee**]

▶ altro?
[**a**ltro]
will there be anything else?

that's all thanks
▶ è tutto, grazie
[ay t**oo**t-to gr**a**tzee-ay]

make it twenty euros and I'll take it
▶ se me lo dà a venti euro, lo prendo
[say may lo dà a v**e**ntee **ay-oo**ro lo pr**e**ndo]

fine, I'll take it
▶ bene lo prendo
[b**ay**nay lo pr**e**ndo]

aperto	open	chiuso	closed
cambiare	to exchange	svendita	sale
la cassa	cash desk		

download these scenarios as MP3s from:

15. Sightseeing

art gallery	la galleria d'arte	[gal-lairee-a dartay]
bus tour	la gita in autobus	[jeeta een owtobooss]
city centre	il centro della città	[chentro del-la cheet-ta]
closed	chiuso	[k-yoozo]
guide	la guida	[gweeda]
museum	il museo	[moozay-o]
open	aperto	[apairto]

I'm interested in seeing the old town
▶ mi piacerebbe vedere la città vecchia
[mee p-yachaireb-bay vedairay la cheet-ta vek-ya]

are there guided tours?　　　　mi dispiace, siamo al completo ◀
▶ ci sono visite guidate?　　　[mee deesp-yachay al komplayto]
[chee sono veezeetay gweedatay]　　I'm sorry, it's fully booked

how much would you charge to drive us around for four hours?
▶ quanto vorrebbe per portarci in giro in automobile per quattro ore?
[kwanto vor-reb-bay pair portarchee een jeero een owtomobeelay pair kwat-tro oray]

can we book tickets for the concert here?
▶ possiamo prenotare qui i biglietti per il concerto?
[poss-yamo prenotaray kwee ee beel-yet-tee pair eel konchairto]

▶ sì, a che nome?　　　　　quale carta di credito? ◀
[see a kay nomay]　　　[kwalay karta dee kraydeeto]
yes, in what name?　　　　which credit card?

where do we get the tickets?　　potete ritirarli all'entrata ◀
▶ dove possiamo ritirare i biglietti?　[potaytay reeteerarlee al-lentrata]
[dovay poss-yamo reeteeraray ee beel-yet-tee]　just pick them up at the
　　　　　　　　　entrance

is it open on Sundays?　　how much is it to get in?
▶ apre la domenica?　　▶ quanto costa l'ingresso?
[apray la domayneeka]　[kwanto kosta leengres-so]

are there reductions for groups of 6?
▶ ci sono sconti per gruppi di 6 persone?
[chee sono skontee pair groop-pee dee say pairsonay]

that was really impressive!
▶ era davvero straordinario!
[aira dav-vairo stra-ordeenaree-o]

16. Trains

to change trains	cambiare	[kamb-yaray]
platform	il binario	[beenaree-o]
return	andata e ritorno	[andata ay reetorno]
single	sola andata	[sola andata]
station	la stazione	[statz-yonay]
stop	la fermata	[fairmata]
ticket	il biglietto	[beel-yet-to]

how much is ...?
▶ quanto costa ...?
[kwanto kosta ...]

a single, second class to ...
▶ un biglietto di seconda classe, di sola andata per ...
[oon beel-yet-to dee sekonda klas-say dee sola andata pair ...]

two returns, second class to ...
▶ due biglietti di seconda classe, andata e ritorno per ...
[doo-ay beel-yet-tee dee sekonda klas-say andata ay reetorno pair ...]

for today	for tomorrow	for next Tuesday
▶ per oggi	▶ per domani	▶ per martedì prossimo
[pair oj-jee]	[pair domanee]	[pair martedee pros-seemo]

c'è un supplemento per l'Intercity ◀
[chay oon soop-plemento pair leentairseetee]
there's a supplement for the Intercity

vuole prenotare un posto? ◀
[vwolay prenotaray oon posto]
do you want to make a seat reservation?

deve cambiare a Bologna ◀
[dayvay kamb-yaray a bologna]
you have to change at Bologna

is this seat free?
▶ è libero questo posto?
[ay leebairo kwesto posto]

excuse me, which station are we at?
▶ scusi, che stazione è questa?
[skoozee kay statz-yonay ay kwesta]

is this where I change for Pisa?
▶ è qui che devo cambiare per Pisa?
[ay kwee kay dayvo kamb-yaray pair pisa]

English

→

Italian

A

a, an* uno/una [**oo**no/**oo**na]

about: about 20 circa venti [**cheer**ka]

it's about 5 o'clock sono le cinque circa

a film about Italy un film sull'Italia

above di sopra

above ... sopra a...

abroad all'estero [al-le**stai**ro]

absolutely (I agree) senz'altro [sentz**al**tro]

accelerator l'acceleratore m [achelaira**to**ray]

accept accettare [achet-**ta**ray]

accident l'incidente m [eenchee**day**ntay]

there's been an accident c'è stato un incidente [chay]

accommodation l'alloggio m [al-**loj**-jo]

accurate accurato [ak-koo**ra**to]

ache (verb) fare male [**fa**ray **ma**lay]

my back aches mi fa male la schiena

across: across the road dall'altra parte della strada [**par**tay]

adapter il riduttore [reedoot-**to**ray]

address l'indirizzo m [eendee**reet**zo]

what's your address? qual è il suo indirizzo? [kwal**ay** ay eel **soo**-o]

address book la rubrica

admission charge il prezzo d'ingresso [**pret**zo deen**gres**-so]

Adriatic il mare Adriatico [**ma**ray]

adult l'adulto m [a**dool**to]

advance: in advance in anticipo [een an**tee**cheepo]

aeroplane l'aeroplano m [a-airo**pla**no]

after dopo

after you dopo di lei [lay]

after lunch dopo pranzo

afternoon il pomeriggio [pomai**reej**-jo]

in the afternoon nel pomeriggio

this afternoon questo pomeriggio

aftershave il dopobarba

aftersun cream la crema doposole [dopo**so**lay]

afterwards dopo

again di nuovo [dee **nwo**vo]

against contro

age l'età f [ay**ta**]

ago: a week ago una settimana fa

an hour ago un'ora fa

agree: I agree sono d'accordo

AIDS l'aids m [a-**eeds**]

air l'aria f

by air per via aerea [pair **vee**-a a-**ai**ray-a]

air-conditioning l'aria condizionata [kondeetz-yo**na**ta]

airmail: by airmail per via aerea [a-**ai**ray-a]

airmail envelope la busta per
posta aerea [**boo**sta pair]
airport l'aeroporto m
[a-airop**or**to]
to the airport, please
all'aeroporto, per favore [pair
fav**o**ray]
airport bus l'autobus
dell'aeroporto m [**low**toboos]
aisle seat il posto vicino al
corridoio [veech**ee**no al kor-
reed**o**-yo]
alarm clock la sveglia [zvel-ya]
Albania l'Albania f
Albanian (adj) albanese
[alban**ay**zay]
alcohol l'alcool m [**al**kol]
alcoholic alcolico [al**ko**leeko]
all: all the boys tutti i ragazzi
[**toot**-tee ee]
all the girls tutte le ragazze
[**toot**-tay lay]
all of it tutto [**toot**-to]
all of them tutti
that's all, thanks è tutto,
grazie [ay – gr**a**tzee-ay]
allergic: I'm allergic to ... sono
allergico a... [al-l**air**jeeko]
allowed: is it allowed? è
permesso? [ay pairm**e**s-so]
all right (I agree) va bene,
d'accordo [b**e**nay]
I'm all right sto bene
are you all right? stai/sta
bene? [sty/sta]
almond la mandorla
almost quasi [kw**a**zee]
alone solo
alphabet l'alfabeto m

a a   j ee-**loo**nga   s **e**s-say
b bee   k **kap**-pa   t tee
c chee   l **el**-lay   u oo
d dee   m **em**-may   v voo
e ay   n **en**-nay   w voo **dop**-yo
f **ef**-fay   o o   x **eeks**
g jee   p pee   y **eep**seelon
h **ak**-ka   q koo   z **tzay**-ta
i ee   r **air**-ray

Alps le Alpi
already già [ja]
also anche [**ank**ay]
although anche se [say]
altogether in tutto [een t**oot**-to]
always sempre [**sem**pray]
am*: I am sono
a.m.: at seven a.m. alle sette
del mattino [**al**-lay]
amazing (surprising)
sorprendente [sorprend**en**tay]
(very good) eccezionale [echetz-
yon**a**lay]
ambulance l'ambulanza f
[amboo**la**ntza]
call an ambulance! chiamate
un'ambulanza! [k- yam**a**tay]
America l'America f
[am**ai**reeka]
American americano
[amairee**ka**no]
I'm American (man/woman)
sono americano/americana
among tra, fra
amount la quantità
(money) la somma
amp: a 13 amp fuse un
fusibile da tredici ampere
[foozee**bee**lay da – amp**ai**ray]

amphitheatre l'anfiteatro m
[anfeetay-atro]
ancient antico
and e [ay]
angry arrabbiato [ar-rab-yato]
animal l'animale m [aneemalay]
ankle la caviglia [kaveel-ya]
anniversary (wedding)
l'anniversario di
matrimonio m
**annoy: this man's annoying
me** quest'uomo mi sta
importunando [kwestwomo
mee sta eemportoonando]
annoying seccante [sek-kantay]
another un altro, un'altra [oon]
can we have another room?
potremmo avere un'altra
stanza? [avairay]
another beer, please ancora
una birra, per favore
antibiotics gli antibiotici
[anteebee-oteechee]
antifreeze l'antigelo m
[anteejelo]
antihistamine l'antistaminico m
antique: is it an antique? è un
pezzo d'antiquariato? [ay oon
petzo danteekwar-yato]
antique shop il negozio di
antiquariato [negotz-yo dee
antiseptic l'antisettico m
**any: have you got any bread/
tomatoes?** avete del pane/dei
pomodori? [avetay del – /day]
do you have any change?
ha degli spiccioli? [a dayl-yee
speecholee]
sorry, I don't have any mi

dispiace, non ne ho [mee
deesp-yachay non nay o]
anybody qualcuno [kwalkoono]
**does anybody speak
English?** c'è qualcuno che
parla inglese? [chay – kay parla
eenglayzay]
there wasn't anybody there
non c'era nessuno lì [non
chaira nes-soono]
anything qualcosa [kwalkoza]

dialogues

anything else? altro?
nothing else, thanks
nient'altro, grazie
[n-yentaltro]

**would you like anything
to drink?** vuole qualcosa
da bere? [vwolay kwalkoza
da bairay]
**I don't want anything,
thanks** non voglio niente,
grazie [non vol-yo n-yentay]

apart from a parte [partay]
apartment l'appartamento m
aperitif l'aperitivo m
[apaireeteevo]
apology le scuse [skoozay]
Apennines gli Appennini
appendicitis l'appendicite f
[ap-pendeecheetay]
appetizer l'antipasto m
apple la mela [mayla]
appointment l'appuntamento
m [ap-poontamento]

dialogue

good morning, how can I help you? buongiorno, mi dica

I'd like to make an appointment vorrei fissare un appuntamento [vor-**ray** fees-**sa**ray]

what time would you like? per che ora? [pair kay]

three o'clock le tre

I'm afraid that's not possible; is four o'clock all right? mi dispiace, non è possibile: va bene alle quattro? [mee deesp-**ya**chay, non ay pos-**see**beelay: va **bay**nay]

yes, that will be fine sì, va bene

the name was ...? il suo nome, per favore? [**soo**-o **no**may]

apricot l'albicocca f [albeekok-ka]

April aprile [apreelay]

are*: we are siamo [s-**ya**mo]

you are siete [s-**yay**tay]

they are sono

area la zona

area code il prefisso

arm il braccio [**bra**cho]

arrange: will you arrange it for us? può organizzarlo per noi? [pwo organeetz**a**rlo pair noy]

arrival l'arrivo m [ar-**ree**vo]

arrive arrivare [ar-reev**a**ray]

when do we arrive? quando arriviamo? [**kwa**ndo ar-reev-**ya**mo]

has my fax arrived yet? è arrivato il mio fax?

we arrived today siamo arrivati oggi [s-**ya**mo]

art l'arte f [**a**rtay]

art gallery la galleria d'arte [gal-lair**ee**-a]

artist l'artista m/f

as: as big as (così) grande come [koz**ee** gra**nd**ay k**o**may]

as soon as possible al più presto possibile [p-yoo – pos-**see**beelay]

ashtray il portacenere [portach**e**nairay]

ask chiedere [k-y**ay**dairay]

I didn't ask for this non ho chiesto questo [non o k-y**e**sto kw**e**sto]

could you ask him to ...? può chiedergli di...? [pwo k-y**ay**dairl-yee dee]

asleep: she's asleep dorme [**do**rmay]

aspirin l'aspirina f

asthma l'asma f

astonishing stupefacente [stoopay-fach**e**ntay]

at: at the hotel in albergo

at the station alla stazione

at six o'clock alle sei [**al**-lay]

at Giovanni's da Giovanni

athletics l'atletica f [atla**y**teeka]

attractive attraente [at-tra-**e**ntay]

aubergine la melanzana [melantz**a**na]

August agosto
aunt la zia [tzee-a]
Australia l'Australia f [owstral-ya]
Australian australiano [owstral-yano]
  I'm Australian (man/woman) sono australiano/australiana
Austria l'Austria f [owstree-a]
Austrian austriaco [owstree-ako]
automatic automatico [owtomateeko]
  (car) l'automobile con il cambio automatico f [owtomobeelay kon eel kamb-yo]
automatic teller il bancomat®
autumn l'autunno m [owtoon-no]
  in the autumn in autunno
avenue il viale [vee-alay]
average (not good) mediocre [med-yokray]
  (ordinary) ordinario [ordeenar-yo]
  on average in media [mayd-ya]
awake: is he awake? è sveglio? [ay zvayl-yo]
away: go away! vattene! [vat-tenay]
  is it far away? è lontano?
awful terribile [tair-reebeelay]
axle l'asse m [as-say]

B

baby (male/female) il bambino, la bambina
baby food gli alimenti per bambini

baby's bottle il biberon
baby-sitter il/la baby-sitter
back (of body) la schiena [sk-yayna]
  (back part) la parte posteriore [partay postair-yoray]
  at the back dietro [d-yetro]
  can I have my money back? posso riavere i miei soldi? [ree-avairay ee mee-yay soldee]
  to come/go back tornare [tornaray]
backache il mal di schiena [sk-yayna]
bacon la pancetta [panchet-ta]
bad cattivo [kat-teevo]
  a bad headache un brutto mal di testa [broot-to]
badly male [malay]
bag la borsa
  (handbag) la borsetta
  (suitcase) la valigia [valeeja]
baggage i bagagli [bagal-yee]
baggage check (US) il deposito bagagli
baggage claim il ritiro bagagli
bakery la panetteria [panet-tairee-a], il panificio [paneefeecho]
balcony il balcone [balkonay]
  a room with a balcony una stanza con balcone
bald calvo
ball (large) la palla
  (small) la pallina
ballet il balletto
banana la banana
band (musical) il gruppo [groop-po]

bandage la fasciatura [fashatoora]

Bandaids® i cerotti [chairot-tee]

bank (money) la banca

bank account il conto in banca

bar il bar

a bar of chocolate una tavoletta di cioccolato [chokkolato]

barber's il barbiere [barb-yairay]

basket il cestino [chesteeno] (in shop) il cestello [chestel-lo]

bath il bagno [ban-yo]

can I have a bath? posso fare un bagno? [faray]

bathroom il bagno, la stanza da bagno [stantza]

with a private bathroom con bagno

bath towel l'asciugamano da bagno m [ashoogamano]

bathtub la vasca da bagno

battery la batteria [bat-tairee-a]

bay la baia [ba-ya]

be* essere [es-sairay]

beach la spiaggia [spee-aj-ja]

beach mat la stuoia [stwo-ya]

beach umbrella l'ombrellone m [ombrel-lonay]

beans i fagioli [fajolee]

French beans i fagiolini [fajoleenee]

broad beans le fave [favay]

beard la barba

beautiful bello

because perché [pairkay]

because of ... a causa di... [kowza]

bed il letto

I'm going to bed vado a letto

bed and breakfast camera con prima colazione [preema kolatz-yonay]

bedroom la camera da letto

beef il manzo [mantzo]

beer la birra [beer-ra]

two beers, please due birre, per favore [doo-ay beer-ray]

before prima di [preema]

begin cominciare [komeencharay]

when does it begin? quando comincia? [kwando komeencha]

beginner il/la principiante [preencheep-yantay]

beginning: at the beginning all'inizio [al-eeneetz-yo]

behind dietro (a) [d-yetro]

behind me dietro di me [may]

beige beige

believe credere [kraydairay]

bell (church) la campana (doorbell) il campanello

below sotto (a)

belt la cintura [cheentoora]

bend (in road) la curva [koorva]

berth la cuccetta [koochet-ta]

beside: beside the ... accanto a... [ak-kanto]

best il migliore [meel-yoray]

better meglio [mayl-yo]

are you feeling better? ti senti/si sente meglio? [see sentay]

between tra, fra
beyond oltre [oltray]
bicycle la bicicletta [beecheeklet-ta]
big grande [granday]
  too big troppo grande
  it's not big enough non è abbastanza grande [ay ab-bastantza]
bike la bici [beechee]
  (motorbike) la moto(cicletta) [motocheeklet-ta]
bikini il bikini
bill il conto
  could I have the bill, please? il conto, per favore
bin la pattumiera [pat-toom-yaira]
bin liners i sacchetti per la pattumiera [sak-ket-tee pair la pat-toom-yaira]
binding (ski) l'attacco m
bird l'uccello m [oochel-lo]
biro® la biro
birthday il compleanno [komplay-an-no]
  happy birthday! buon compleanno! [bwon]
biscuit il biscotto
bit: a little bit un po'
  a big bit un grosso pezzo [petzo]
  a bit of ... un pezzetto di... [petzet-to dee]
  a bit expensive un po' caro
bite (by insect) la puntura [poontoora]
  (by dog) il morso
bitter amaro

black nero [nairo]
blanket la coperta [kopairta]
blast! accidenti! [acheedentee]
bleach (for toilet) la varechina [varekeena]
bless you! salute! [salootay]
blind cieco [chee-ayko]
blinds gli avvolgibili [av-voljeebeelay]
blister la vescica [vesheeka]
blocked (road, pipe) bloccato
  (sink) intasato [eentazato]
block of apartments il caseggiato [kasej-jato]
blond biondo [b-yondo]
blood il sangue [sangway]
  high blood pressure la pressione alta [press-yonay]
blouse la camicetta [kameechet-ta]
blow-dry l'asciugatura col fon f [ashoogatoora]
  I'd like a cut and blow-dry vorrei taglio e piega con il fon [vor-ray tal-yo ay p-yayga]
blue blu [bloo]
  blue eyes gli occhi azzurri [ok-kee adzoor-ree]
blusher il fard
boarding house la pensione [pens-yonay]
boarding pass la carta d'imbarco [eembarko]
boat la barca
  (for passengers) il battello [bat-tel-lo]
body il corpo
boil (verb: of water) bollire [bol-leeray]

(water, potatoes etc) far bollire
boiled egg l'uovo sodo m
[wovo]
boiler lo scaldabagno
[skaldaban-yo]
bone l'osso m
bonnet (of car) il cofano
book il libro
(verb) prenotare [prenotaray]
can I book a seat? posso
prenotare un posto?

dialogue

I'd like to book a table for
two vorrei prenotare un
tavolo per due [vor-ray
prenotaray – pair doo-ay]
what time would you like it
booked for? per che ora lo
vuole? [kay – vwolay]
half past seven per le sette
e mezza
that's fine va bene [baynay]
and your name? il suo
nome, per favore [soo-o
nomay]

bookshop/bookstore la
libreria [leebrairee-a]
boot (footwear) lo stivale
[steevalay]
(of car) il bagagliaio [bagal-ya-
yo]
border (of country) il confine
[konfeenay]
bored: I'm bored mi sto
annoiando [an-noy-ando]
boring noioso [noy-ozo]

born: I was born in
Manchester sono nato/nata a
Manchester
I was born in 1960 sono
nato/nata nel millenove-
centosessanta
borrow prendere a prestito
[prendairay]
may I borrow ...? posso
prendere a prestito...?
both tutti e due [toot-tee ay doo-
ay], tutte e due [toot-tay]
bother: sorry to bother you mi
scusi il disturbo [skoozee eel
deestoorbo]
bottle la bottiglia [bot-teel-ya]
a bottle of house red una
bottiglia di (vino) rosso della
casa
bottle-opener il cavatappi
bottom (of person) il sedere
[sedairay]
at the bottom of ... (hill etc) ai
piedi di... [a-ee p-yaydee]
(street, sea etc) in fondo a...
box la scatola
(wooden) la cassetta
box office il botteghino [bot-
tegeeno]
boy il ragazzo [ragatzo]
boyfriend il ragazzo
bra il reggiseno [rej-jeesayno]
bracelet il braccialetto
[brachalet-to]
brake il freno [frayno]
brandy il brandy
bread il pane [panay]
white bread il pane bianco
[b-yanko]

brown bread il pane nero
[nairo]

wholemeal bread il pane
integrale [eentegralay]

break (verb) rompere
[rompairay]

I've broken the ... ho rotto
il/la... [o rot-to]

I think I've broken my wrist
credo di essermi rotto il
polso [kraydo dee es-sairmee]

break down (car) rimanere in
panne [reemanairay een pan-nay]

I've broken down sono
rimasto in panne

breakdown il guasto [gwasto]

breakdown service il servizio
riparazioni [sairveetz-yo
reeparatz-yonee]

breakfast la (prima) colazione
[kolatz-yonay]

break-in: I've had a break-in
mi sono entrati i ladri in casa

breast il seno [sayno], il petto

breathe respirare [respeeraray]

breeze la brezza [bretza]

bridge (over river) il ponte
[pontay]

brief breve [brayvay]

briefcase la cartella

bright (light etc) brillante [breel-
lantay]

bright red rosso acceso
[achayzo]

brilliant (idea, person) brillante
[breel-lantay]

bring portare [portaray]

I'll bring it back later
lo riporterò più tardi

[reeportairo]

Britain la Gran Bretagna
[bretan-ya]

British britannico

brochure l'opuscolo m
[opooskolo]

broken rotto [rot-to]

bronchitis la bronchite
[bronkeetay]

brooch la spilla

broom la scopa

brother il fratello

brother-in-law il cognato
[kon-yato]

brown marrone [mar-ronay]

brown hair i capelli castani

brown eyes gli occhi castani
[ok-kee]

bruise il livido

brush (for hair) la spazzola
[spatzola]

(artist's) il pennello

(for cleaning) la scopa

bucket il secchio [sek-yo]

buffet car il vagone ristorante
[vagonay reestorantay]

buggy (for child) il passeggino
[pas-sej-jeeno]

building l'edificio m
[edeefeecho]

bulb (light bulb) la lampadina

bumper il paraurti [para-oortee]

bunk la cuccetta [koochet-ta]

bureau de change l'agenzia
di cambio f [ajentzee-a dee
kamb-yo]

burglary il furto [foorto]

burn la bruciatura
[broochatoora]

(verb) bruciare [broocharay]
burnt: this is burnt questo è
bruciato [kwesto ay
broochato]
burst: a burst pipe una
tubatura scoppiata [toobatoora
skop-yata]
bus l'autobus m [owtoboos]
what number bus is it to ...?
che numero va a...? [kay
noomairo]
when is the next bus to ...?
quando parte il prossimo
autobus per...? [kwando partay]
what time is the last bus?
a che ora parte l'ultimo
autobus?
could you let me know when
we get there? mi può dire
quando siamo arrivati? [pwo
deeray kwando s-yamo]

dialogue

does this bus go to ...?
questo autobus va a...?
[kwesto]
no, you need a number
... no, deve prendere il...
[dayvay prendairay]

business gli affari
bus station la stazione degli
autobus [statz-yonay dayl-yee
owtoboos]
bus stop la fermata
dell'autobus [fairmata]
bust il busto [boosto]
busy (restaurant etc) animato

I'm busy tomorrow domani
ho da fare [o da faray]
but ma
butcher's il macellaio [machel-
la-yo]
butter il burro [boor-ro]
button il bottone [bot-tonay]
buy comprare [kompra-ray]
where can I buy ...? dove
vendono...?
by: by bus/car in autobus/
macchina [een]
written by ... scritto da...
by the window vicino al
finestrino [veecheeno]
by the sea sul mare [sool]
by Thursday per giovedì
[pair]
bye ciao [chow]

C

cabbage il cavolo
cabin (on ship) la cabina
cable car la funivia [fooneevee-
a]
café il caffè [kaf-fay]
cagoule la giacca a vento
[jak-ka]
cake la torta
cake shop la pasticceria
[pasteechairee-a]
call (verb) chiamare
[k-yamaray]
(to phone) telefonare
[telefonaray]
what's it called? come si
chiama? [komay see k-yama]

40

he/she/it is called ... si chiama...

please call the doctor chiamate un medico, per favore [k-yamatay oon maydeeko]

please give me a call at 7.30 a.m. tomorrow domani mattina, mi svegli alle sette e mezza, per favore [mee zvayl-yee al-lay]

please ask him to call me gli chieda di chiamarmi, per favore [l-yee kee-yayda dee]

call back: I'll call back later (phone back) richiamerò più tardi [reek-yamairo p-yoo]

call round: I'll call round tomorrow passerò domani

camcorder la videocamera

camera la macchina fotografica [mak-keena]

camera shop il negozio del fotografo [negotz-yo del]

camp (verb) campeggiare [kampej-jaray]

can we camp here? possiamo accamparci qui? [pos-yamo ak-kamparchee kwee]

camping gas il gas liquido [leekweedo]

campsite il campeggio [kampej-jo]

can la lattina

a can of beer una lattina di birra

can*: can you ...? puoi/può...? [pwoy/pwo]

can I have ...? posso avere...? [avairay]

I can't ... (am not able to) non posso...

(don't know how to) non so...

Canada il Canada

Canadian canadese [kanadayzay]

I'm Canadian sono canadese

canal il canale [kanalay]

cancel annullare [an-nool-laray]

candies le caramelle [karamel-lay]

candle la candela [kandayla]

canoe la canoa [kano-a]

canoeing la canoa

can opener l'apriscatole **m** [apreeskatolay]

cap (hat) il berretto [bair-ret-to]

(of bottle) il tappo

car la macchina [mak-keena], l'auto(mobile) **f** [owtomobeelay]

by car in macchina

carafe la caraffa

a carafe of house white, please una caraffa di (vino) bianco della casa, per favore [kaza]

caravan la roulotte [roolot]

caravan site il campeggio per roulotte [kampej-jo pair]

carburettor il carburatore [karbooratoray]

card (birthday etc) il biglietto [beel-yet-to]

my (business) card il mio biglietto da visita [veezeeta]

cardigan il cardigan

cardphone il telefono a scheda [telayfono a skayda]

Ca

41

careful attento
be careful! fa'/faccia
attenzione! [facha at-tentz-yonay]
caretaker il portinaio
[porteena-yo]
car ferry la nave traghetto
[navay]
car hire l'autonoleggio m
[owtonolej-jo]
carnival il carnevale
[karnevalay]
car park il parcheggio [parkej-jo]
carpet il tappeto [tap-payto]
(wall to wall) la moquette
[moket]
carriage (of train) la carrozza
[kar-rotza]
carrier bag il sacchetto [sak-ket-to]
carrot la carota
carry portare [portaray]
carry-cot il porte-enfant [port-onfan]
carton il tetrapack®, la
scatola di cartone
carwash l'autolavaggio m
[owtolavaj-jo]
case (suitcase) la valigia
[valeeja]
cash il contante [kontantay]
(verb) riscuotere [reeskwotairay]
will you cash this cheque
for me? mi cambia questo
assegno? [kwesto as-sen-yo]
cash desk la cassa
cash dispenser il bancomat®
cashier (man/woman) il cassiere

[kas-yairay], la cassiera
cassette la cassetta
cassette recorder il
registratore a cassette
[rejeestratoray a kas-set-tay]
castle il castello
casualty department il pronto
soccorso
cat il gatto
catch (verb) prendere
[prendairay]
where do we catch the bus
to ...? dove prendiamo
l'autobus per...? [dovay prend-yamo]
cathedral la cattedrale [kat-tedralay], il duomo [dwomo]
Catholic cattolico
cauliflower il cavolfiore [kavolf-yoray]
cave la grotta
ceiling il soffitto
celery il sedano [saydano]
cellar (for wine) la cantina
cemetery il cimitero
[cheemeetairo]
Centigrade* centigrado
[chenteegrado]
centimetre* il centimetro
[chenteemetro]
central centrale [chentralay]
central heating il
riscaldamento autonomo
[owtonomo]
centre il centro [chentro]
how do we get to the city
centre? come si arriva in
centro? [komay]
cereal i cereali [chairay-alee]

certainly certamente
[chairtamentay]
certainly not certamente no
chair la sedia [sayd-ya]
chair lift la seggiovia [sej-jovee-a]
change (money) gli spiccioli
[speecholee]
(verb: money, trains) cambiare
[kamb-yaray]
can I change this for ...?
posso cambiarlo con...?
[kamb-yarlo]
I don't have any change non
ho spiccioli [o]
can you give me change
for a 50 euro note? mi può
cambiare cinquanta euro?
[mee pwo – cheenkwanta ay-ooro]

dialogue

do we have to change
(trains)? dobbiamo
cambiare? [dob-yamo]
yes, change at Rome/
no it's a direct train sì,
cambiate a Roma/no, è
diretto [kamb-yatay – ay]

changed: to get changed
cambiarsi [kamb-yarsee]
chapel la cappella
charge il prezzo [pretzo]
(verb) far pagare [pagaray]
what is the charge per night?
quant'è a notte? [kwantay]
charge card la carta di

addebito
cheap a buon mercato [bwon
mairkato]
do you have anything
cheaper? ha qualcosa di
meno caro? [kwalkoza]
check (verb) controllare
[kontrol-laray]
(US: noun) l'assegno m [as-sen-yo]
see cheque
(US: bill) il conto
see bill
could you check the ...,
please? può controllare...,
per favore? [pwo]
checkbook il libretto degli
assegni [dayl-yee as-sen-yee]
check-in il check-in
check in (at airport) fare il
check-in [faray]
where do we have to check
in? dove dobbiamo fare il
check-in? [dovay dob-yamo]
cheek la guancia [gwancha]
cheerio! ciao! [chow]
cheers! (toast) alla salute!
[salootay]
cheese il formaggio [formaj-jo]
chemist's la farmacia
[farmachee-a]
cheque l'assegno m [as-sen-yo]
do you take cheques?
accettate assegni? [achet-tatay
as-sen-yee]
cheque book il libretto degli
assegni [dayl-yee]
cheque card la carta assegni
cherry la ciliegia [cheel-yay-ja]

chess gli scacchi [skak-kee]
chest il petto
chewing gum il chewing gum
chicken il pollo
chickenpox la varicella [varee-chel-la]
child (male/female) il bambino, la bambina
child minder la bambinaia [bambeena-ya]
children's pool la piscina per bambini [peesheena pair]
children's portion la porzione per bambini [portz-yonay]
chin il mento
china la porcellana [porchel-lana]
Chinese cinese [cheenayzay]
chips le patatine fritte [patateenay freet-tay]
chocolate il cioccolato [chok-kolato]
  milk chocolate il cioccolato al latte [al lat-tay]
  plain chocolate il cioccolato fondente [fondentay]
  a hot chocolate una cioccolata calda
choose scegliere [shayl-yairay]
Christian name il nome di battesimo [nomay dee bat-tayzeemo]
Christmas il Natale [natalay]
  Christmas Eve la vigilia di Natale [veejeel-ya]
  merry Christmas! Buon Natale! [bwon]
church la chiesa [k-yayza]
cider il sidro

cigar il sigaro
cigarette la sigaretta
cigarette lighter l'accendino m [achendeeno]
cinema il cinema [cheenema]
circle il cerchio [chairk-yo]
  (in theatre) la galleria
city la città [cheet-ta]
city centre il centro [chentro]
clean (adj) pulito [pooleeto]
  can you clean these for me? me li/le può pulire? [may lee/lay pwo pooleeray]
cleaning solution (for contact lenses) la soluzione per la pulizia delle lenti a contatto [solootz-yonay pair la pooleetzee-a]
cleansing lotion la lozione detergente [lotz-yonay detairjentay]
clear chiaro [k-yaro]
clever intelligente [eentel-leejentay]
cliff la scogliera [skol-yaira]
climbing l'alpinismo m
cling film la pellicola trasparente [trasparentay]
clinic la clinica
cloakroom il guardaroba [gwardaroba]
clock l'orologio m [orolojo]
close (verb) chiudere [k-yoodairay]

dialogue

what time do you close? a che ora chiudete? [kay – k-yoodaytay]

we close at 8 pm
chiudiamo alle otto
[k-yood-yamo]
do you close for lunch?
chiudete per pranzo?
yes, between 1 and 3.30
pm sì, dall'una alle tre e
mezza

closed chiuso [k-yoozo]
cloth (fabric) la stoffa
(for cleaning etc) lo straccio
[stracho]
clothes gli abiti
clothes line la corda del
bucato
clothes peg la molletta da
bucato
cloud la nuvola [noovola]
cloudy nuvoloso [noovolozo]
clutch la frizione
[freetz-yonay]
coach (bus) la corriera [kor-
yaira], il pullman
(on train) la carrozza [kar-rotza]
coach station la stazione dei
pullman [statz-yonay day]
coach trip la gita in pullman
[jeeta]
coast la costa
on the coast sulla costa [sool-
la]
coat (long coat) il cappotto
(jacket) la giacca [jak-ka]
coat hanger la gruccia
[groocha]
cockroach lo scarafaggio
[skarafaj-jo]
cocoa il cacao [kaka-o]

code (for telephoning) il prefisso
[prayfees-so]
what's the (dialling) code for
Florence? qual è il prefisso di
Firenze? [kwalay]
coffee il caffè [kaf-fay]
two coffees, please due
caffè, per favore
coin la moneta [monayta]
Coke® la Coca-Cola
cold (adj) freddo
I'm cold ho freddo [o]
I have a cold ho il
raffreddore [raf-fred-doray]
collapse: he's collapsed ha
avuto un collasso [a avooto]
collar il colletto
collect prendere [prendairay]
I've come to collect ... sono
venuto a prendere...
collect call la telefonata a
carico del destinatario
college l'istituto superiore m
[eesteetooto soopair-yoray]
colour il colore [koloray]
do you have this in other
colours? ce l'ha in altri
colori? [chay la]
colour film la pellicola a colori
comb il pettine [pet-teenay]
come venire [veneeray]

dialogue

where do you come from?
di dov'è? [dee dovay]
I come from Edinburgh
sono di Edimburgo

come back ritornare
[reetornaray]

I'll come back tomorrow
tornerò domani [tornairo]

come in entrare [entraray]

comfortable comodo

compact disc il compact disc

company (business) la ditta

compartment (on train) lo
scompartimento

compass la bussola [boos-sola]

complain lamentarsi

complaint il reclamo [reklamo]

I have a complaint voglio
fare un reclamo [vol-yo faray]

completely completamente
[kompleta-mentay]

computer il computer

concert il concerto [konchairto]

concussion la commozione
cerebrale [kom-motz-yonay
chairay-bralay]

conditioner (for hair) il balsamo

condom il preservativo
[prezairvateevo]

conference la conferenza
[konfairentza]

confirm dare conferma [daray
konfairma]

congratulations!
congratulazioni!
[kongratoolatz-yonee]

connecting flight la
coincidenza [ko-eenchee-
dentza]

connection la coincidenza

conscious cosciente
[koshentay]

constipation la stitichezza

[steeteeketza]

consulate il consolato

contact mettersi in contatto
con

contact lenses le lenti a
contatto

contraceptive il
contraccettivo [kontrachet-
teevo]

convenient comodo

that's not convenient non
(mi) va bene [baynay]

cook (verb) cucinare
[koocheenaray]

it's not cooked non è
abbastanza cotto [ay ab-
bastanza]

cooker la cucina
[koocheena]

cookie il biscotto

cooking utensils gli utensili da
cucina [koocheena]

cool fresco

cork il tappo

corkscrew il cavatappi

corner: on the corner
all'angolo

in the corner nell'angolo

cornflakes i fiocchi di
granturco [f-yok-kee dee
grantoorko]

correct (right) esatto

corridor il corridoio [kor-
reedo-yo]

cosmetics i cosmetici
[kosmeteechee]

cost costare [kostaray]

how much does it cost?
quanto costa? [kwanto]

cot il lettino

cotton il cotone [kotonay]

cotton wool l'ovatta f

couch (sofa) il divano

couchette la cuccetta [koochet-ta]

cough la tosse [tos-say]

cough medicine lo sciroppo per la tosse [sheerop-po pair]

could: could you ...? potresti/ potrebbe...? [potrayb-bay]

could I have ...? vorrei... [vor-ray]

I couldn't ... (wasn't able to) non ho potuto... [o potooto]

country il paese [pa-ayzay] (countryside) la campagna [kampan-ya]

couple (two people) la coppia [kop-ya]

a couple of ... un paio di... [pa-yo dee]

courgette il zucchino [zook-keeno]

courier la guida turistica [gweeda]

course (main course etc) la portata

of course naturalmente [natooralmentay]

of course not no di certo [dee chairto]

cousin (male/female) il cugino [koojeeno], la cugina

cow la mucca [mook-ka]

crab il granchio [grank-yo]

cracker il cracker [krekair]

craft shop il negozio di artigianato [nay-gotz-yo dee arteejanato]

crash l'incidente m [eencheedentay]

I've had a crash ho avuto un incidente [o avooto]

crazy pazzo [patzo]

cream (on milk, in cake) la panna (lotion) la crema [krayma] (colour) crema

crèche l'asilo nido m

credit card la carta di credito [kraydeeto]

do you take credit cards? prendete carte di credito? [prendaytay kartay]

dialogue

can I pay by credit card? posso pagare con una carta di credito? [pagaray]

which card do you want to use? con quale carta vuole pagare? [kwalay – vwolay]

Access/Visa

yes, sir sì, signore [seen-yoray]

what's the number? qual è il numero? [kwal ay eel noomairo]

and the expiry date? e la data di scadenza? [ay – skadentza]

crisps le patatine [patateenay]

crockery il vasellame [vazel-lamay]

crossing (by sea) la traversata [travair-sata]

crossroads l'incrocio **m** [eenkrocho]

crowd la folla

crowded affollato

crown (on tooth) la capsula [kapsoola]

cruise la crociera [krochaira]

crutches le stampelle [stampel-lay]

cry (verb) piangere [p-yanjairay]

cucumber il cetriolo [chetree-olo]

cup la tazza [tatza]

a cup of ..., please una tazza di..., per favore

cupboard l'armadio **m** [armad-yo]

(in kitchen) la credenza [kredentza]

cure la cura [koora]

curly riccio [reecho]

current la corrente [kor-rentay]

curtains le tende [tenday]

cushion il cuscino [koosheeno]

custom il costume [kostoomay]

Customs la dogana

cut il taglio [tal-yo]

(verb) tagliare [tal-yaray]

I've cut myself mi sono tagliato [tal-yato]

cutlery le posate [pozatay]

cycling il ciclismo [cheekleesmo]

cyclist il ciclista [cheekleesta]

D

dad il papà

daily ogni giorno [on-yee jorno]

(adj) quotidiano [kwoteed-yano]

damage (verb) danneggiare [dan-nej-jaray]

damaged danneggiato [dan-nej-jato]

I'm sorry, I've damaged this mi dispiace, l'ho danneggiato [mee deesp-yachay lo]

damn! accidenti! [acheedentee]

damp (adj) umido [oomeedo]

dance il ballo

(verb) ballare [bal-laray]

would you like to dance? balla?

dangerous pericoloso [paireekolozo]

Danish danese [danayzay]

dark (adj: colour) scuro [skooro]

(hair) bruno [broono]

it's getting dark si sta facendo buio [fachendo boo-yo]

date*: what's the date today? che giorno è oggi? [kay jorno ay oj-jee]

let's make a date for next Monday possiamo fissare un appuntamento per lunedì prossimo? [pos-yamo fees-saray oon ap-poontamento]

dates (fruit) i datteri [dat-tairee]

daughter la figlia [feel-ya]

daughter-in-law la nuora [nwora]

dawn l'alba f
at dawn all'alba
day il giorno [jorno]
the day after il giorno dopo
the day after tomorrow
dopodomani
the day before il giorno
prima
the day before yesterday
l'altroieri m [altro-yairee]
every day ogni giorno [on-
yee]
all day? tutto il giorno?
in two days' time tra due
giorni
have a nice day! buona
giornata! [bwona jornata]
day trip la gita (di un giorno)
[jeeta dee oon jorno]
dead morto
deaf sordo
deal (business) l'affare m [af-
faray]
it's a deal affare fatto
death la morte [mortay]
decaffeinated coffee il caffè
decaffeinato [kaf-fay dekaf-fee-
aynato]
December dicembre
[deechembray]
decide decidere
[decheedairay]
we haven't decided yet non
abbiamo ancora deciso [ab-
yamo – decheezo]
decision la decisione [decheez-
yonay]
deck (on ship) il ponte (di
coperta) [pontay dee kopairta]

deckchair la sedia a sdraio
[sayd-ya a zdra-yo]
deep profondo
definitely certamente
[chairtamentay]
definitely not assolutamente
no [as-solootamentay]
degree (qualification) la laurea
[lowray-a]
delay il ritardo
deliberately volutamente
[voolootamentay]
delicatessen (shop) la
gastronomia
delicious delizioso [deleetz-
yozo]
deliver consegnare [konsen-
yaray]
delivery (of mail) la consegna
[konsen-ya]
Denmark la Danimarca
dental floss il filo interdentale
[eentairdentalay]
dentist il dentista m/f

dialogue

it's this one here è questo
qui [ay kwesto kwee]
this one? questo?
no that one no, quello
[kwel-lo]
here? qui?
yes sì

dentures la dentiera [dent-
yaira]
deodorant il deodorante [day-
odorantay]

department il reparto

department store il grande magazzino [granday magatzeeno]

departure la partenza [partentza]

departure lounge la sala d'attesa (delle partenze) [attayza del-lay partentzay]

depend: it depends dipende [deependay]

it depends on ... dipende da...

deposit (on bottle) la cauzione [kowtz-yonay]
(for reservation) la caparra
(as part payment) l'acconto **m**

description la descrizione [deskreetz-yonay]

dessert il dessert [des-sair]

destination la destinazione [desteenatz-yonay]

develop sviluppare [zveeloop-paray]

dialogue

could you develop these films? può sviluppare queste pellicole? [pwo – kwestay pel-leekolay]

yes certainly sì, certo [chairto]

when will they be ready? quando sono pronte? [kwando – prontay]

tomorrow afternoon domani pomeriggio [pomaireej-jo]

how much is the 24-hour service? quanto costa lo sviluppo in giornata? [kwanto – jornata]

diabetic (man/woman) il diabetico [dee-abayteeko], la diabetica

diabetic foods gli alimenti per diabetici [dee-abayteechee]

dial (verb) comporre il numero (di...) [kompor-ray eel noomairo dee]

dialling code il prefisso telefonico [prefees-so]

diamond il diamante [dee-amantay]

diarrhoea la diarrea [dee-aray-a]

diary (business etc) l'agenda **f** [ajenda]
(for personal experiences) il diario [dee-ar-yo]

dictionary il dizionario [deetz-yonario]

didn't*
see not

die morire [moreeray]

diesel il gasolio [gaz-ol-yo]

diet la dieta [d-yayta]

I'm on a diet sono a dieta

I have to follow a special diet devo seguire una dieta speciale [dayvo segweeray – spechalay]

difference la differenza [deeffairentza]

what's the difference? qual è la differenza? [kwalay]

different diverso [deevairso]
  this one is different questo è
  diverso [kwesto ay]
  a different table un altro
  tavolo
difficult difficile [deef-
  feecheelay]
difficulty la difficoltà
dinghy il gommone
  [gommonay]
dining room la sala da pranzo
  [prantzo]
dinner (evening meal) la cena
  [chayna]
  to have dinner cenare
  [chenaray]
direct (adj) diretto [deeretto]
  is there a direct train? c'è un
  treno diretto? [chay]
direction la direzione [deeretz-
  yonay]
  which direction is it? in quale
  direzione è [kwalay – ay]
  is it in this direction? è in
  questa direzione? [ay een
  kwesta]
directory enquiries
  informazioni elenco
  abbonati [eenformatz-yonee]
dirt lo sporco
dirty sporco
disabled invalido
  **is there access for the
  disabled?** c'è un accesso per
  gli invalidi? [chay oon aches-so
  pair]
disappear scomparire
  [skompareeray]
  it's disappeared è sparito [ay]

disappointed deluso [deloozo]
disappointing deludente
  [deloodentay]
disaster il disastro
disco la discoteca
discount lo sconto
  is there a discount? c'è uno
  sconto? [chay]
disease la malattia [malat-tee-a]
disgusting (taste, food)
  disgustoso [deesgoostozo]
dish (meal) il piatto [p-yat-to]
  (bowl) la scodella
dishes i piatti
dishcloth lo strofinaccio per i
  piatti [strofeenacho pair]
disinfectant il disinfettante
  [deeseenfet-tantay]
disk (for computer) il dischetto
  [deesket-to]
disposable diapers i pannolini
  (usa e getta) [ooza ay jet-ta]
disposable nappies i
  pannolini (usa e getta)
distance la distanza
  [deestantza]
  in the distance in lontananza
  [lontanantza]
distilled water l'acqua
  distillata f [akwa]
district la zona
disturb disturbare
  [deestoobaray]
diversion (detour) la deviazione
  [dev-yatz-yonay]
diving board il trampolino
divorced divorziato [deevortz-
  yato]
dizzy: I feel dizzy mi gira la

testa [mee jeera]
do fare [faray]
what shall we do? che
facciamo? [kay fachamo]
how do you do it? come si fa?
[komay]
will you do it for me? lo può
fare lei per me? [pwo faray lay
pair may]

dialogues

how do you do? piacere
[p-yachairay]
nice to meet you molto
lieto [l-yayto]
what do you do? (work) che
lavoro fa? [kay]
I'm a teacher, and you?
sono insegnante, e lei?
[eensen-yantay, ay lay]
I'm a student sono
studente [stoodentay]
what are you doing this
evening? che cosa fa
questa sera? [kay koza fa
kwesta saira]
we're going out for a drink;
do you want to join us?
andiamo a bere qualcosa:
vuole venire con noi?
[and-yamo a bairay kwalkoza:
vwolay veneeray kon noi]

do you want cream? con
panna?
I do, but she doesn't per
me sì, ma non per lei [pair
may – lay]

doctor il medico [maydeeko]
we need a doctor abbiamo
bisogno di un medico [ab-
yamo beezon-yo dee]
please call a doctor può
chiamare un medico, per
favore? [pwo k-yamaray]

dialogue

where does it hurt? dove le
fa male? [dovay lay fa malay]
right here proprio qui
[kwee]
does that hurt more? così
le fa male di più? [lay
– malay dee p-yoo]
yes sì
take this to a chemist porti
questo in farmacia [kwesto
een farmachee-a]

document il documento
[dokoomento]
dog il cane [kanay]
doll la bambola
domestic flight il volo
nazionale [natz-yonalay]
donkey l'asino m
don't!: don't do that! non
farlo!
see not
door (of room) la porta
(of train, car) lo sportello
doorman il portiere [port-
yairay]
double doppio [dop-yo]
double bed il letto a due
piazze [doo-ay p-yatzay]

double room la camera doppia [dop-ya]

doughnut il krapfen

down giù [joo]

down here quaggiù [kwaj-joo]

put it down over there lo/la metta giù lì

it's down there on the right è giù di lì sulla destra

it's further down the road è più avanti su questa strada [ay p-yoo – soo kwesta]

downhill skiing la discesa libera [deeshayza leebaira]

downmarket (restaurant etc) scadente [skadentay]

downstairs di sotto

dozen la dozzina [dotzeena]

half a dozen mezza dozzina [metza]

drain lo scarico

draught beer la birra alla spina [beer-ra]

draughty: it's draughty c'è corrente [chay kor-rentay]

drawer il cassetto

drawing il disegno [deesayn-yo]

dreadful terribile [tair-reeb-beelay]

dream il sogno [son-yo]

dress il vestito

dressed: to get dressed (oneself) vestirsi

dressing (for cut) la fasciatura [fasha-toora]

salad dressing il condimento

dressing gown la vestaglia [vestal-ya]

drink (alcoholic) la bevanda alcolica

(non-alcoholic) la bibita analcolica

(verb) bere [bairay]

a cold drink una bevanda fredda

can I get you a drink? posso offrirti qualcosa da bere? [kwalkoza da bairay]

what would you like (to drink)? cosa vuoi bere? [koza vwoy]

no thanks, I don't drink no, grazie, non bevo alcolici [bayvo alkoleechee]

I'll just have a drink of water posso avere solo un po' d'acqua? [avairay – dakwa]

drinking water l'acqua potabile [akwa potabeelay]

is this drinking water? è potabile quest'acqua? [ay – kwest]

drive (verb) guidare [gweedaray]

can you drive? sa guidare?

we drove here siamo venuti in macchina [s-yamo venootee een mak-keena]

I'll drive you home ti/la accompagno a casa in macchina [ak-kompan-yo]

driver (of car) l'autista m/f [owteesta]

(of bus) il/la conducente [kondoochentay]

driving licence la patente [patentay]

drop: just a drop, please (of drink) solo una goccia [gocha]

drug la medicina [medeecheena]

drugs (narcotics) la droga

drunk (adj) ubriaco [oobree-ako]

drunken driving la guida in stato di ebbrezza [gweeda – eb-bretza]

dry (adj) asciutto [ashoot-to]
(wine) secco

dry-cleaner il lavasecco

duck l'anatra f

due: he was due to arrive yesterday doveva arrivare ieri [dovayva ar-reevaray]
when is the train due? a che ora dovrebbe arrivare il treno? [a kay ora dovreb-bay]

dull (pain) sordo
(weather) uggioso [uj-joso]
(boring) noioso [noy-ozo]

dummy (baby's) il succhiotto [sook-yot-to]

during durante [doorantay]

dust la polvere [polvairay]

dusty polveroso

dustbin la pattumiera [pat-toom-yaira]

duty-free (goods) merci esenti da dazio [mairchee esentee da datz-yo]

duty-free shop il duty free

duvet il piumone [p-yoo-monay]

E

each (every) ciascuno [chaskoono]
how much are they each? quanto vengono l'uno/l'una? [kwanto]

ear l'orecchio m [orek-yo]

earache: I have earache ho mal d'orecchi [o mal dorek-kee]

early presto
early in the morning di mattina presto
I called by earlier sono passato/passata prima

earrings gli orecchini [orek-keenee]

east l'est m
in the east ad est

Easter la Pasqua [paskwa]

easy facile [facheelay]

eat mangiare [manjaray]
we've already eaten, thanks abbiamo già mangiato, grazie [ab-yamo ja manjato]

eau de toilette l'eau de toilette f

EC la CE [chay]

economy class la classe turistica [klas-say]

Edinburgh Edimburgo

egg l'uovo m [wovo]

eggplant la melanzana [melantzana]

Eire la Repubblica d'Irlanda [repoob-bleeka deerlanda]

either: either ... or ... o... o...
either of them o l'uno/l'una o l'altro/l'altra

elastic l'elastico m

elastic band l'elastico m

elbow il gomito

electric elettrico

electrical appliances gli elettrodomestici [elet-trodomesteechee] electric fire la stufa elettrica [st**oo**fa]

electrician l'elettricista **m** [elet-treech**ee**sta]

electricity l'elettricità **f** [elet-treech**ee**ta]

elevator l'ascensore **m** [ashens**o**ray]

else: something else qualcos'altro [kwalk**o**z]

somewhere else da qualche altra parte [kw**a**lkay – p**a**rtay]

dialogue

> would you like anything else? altro?
>
> no, nothing else, thanks nient'altro, grazie [n-yent**a**ltro]

email la mail

embassy l'ambasciata **f** [ambash**a**ta]

emergency l'emergenza **f** [emair**j**entza]

this is an emergency! è un'emergenza! [ay]

emergency exit l'uscita di sicurezza **f** [oosh**ee**ta dee seekoor**e**tza]

empty vuoto [vw**o**to]

end la fine [f**ee**nay]

(verb) finire [feen**ee**ray]

at the end of the street in fondo alla strada

when does it end? quando finisce? [kw**a**ndo feen**ee**shay]

engaged (toilet, telephone)

occupato [ok-koop**a**to]

(to be married) fidanzato [feedantz**a**to]

engine (car) il motore [mot**o**ray]

England l'Inghilterra **f** [eengheelt**ai**r-ra]

English inglese [eengl**ay**zay]

I'm English sono inglese

do you speak English? parla inglese?

enjoy: to enjoy oneself divertirsi

dialogue

> how did you like the film? ti/le è piaciuto il film? [lay ay p-yach**oo**to]
>
> I enjoyed it very much; did you enjoy it? mi è piaciuto molto; e a te/lei? [ay a tay/lay]

enjoyable piacevole [p-yach**ay**volay]

enlargement (of photo) l'ingrandimento **m**

enormous enorme [en**o**rmay]

enough abbastanza [ab-bast**a**ntza]

there's not enough ... non c'è abbastanza... [non chay]

it's not big enough non è grande abbastanza [ay]

that's enough basta

entrance l'entrata **f**

envelope la busta [b**oo**sta]

epileptic epilettico

equipment l'attrezzatura f [attretzatoora]

error l'errore m [er-roray]

especially specialmente [spechalmentay]

essential essenziale [es-sentzyalay]

it is essential that ... è essenziale che... [ay – kay]

EU l'UE f [oo ay]

euro l'euro m [ay-ooro]

Eurocheque l'eurocheque m [ay-oorochek]

Eurocheque card la carta eurocheque

Europe l'Europa f [ay-ooropa]

European europeo [ay-ooropay-o]

even perfino [pairfeeno]

even if ... anche se... [ankay say]

evening la sera [saira]

this evening questa sera [kwesta]

in the evening di sera

evening meal la cena [chayna]

eventually alla fine [feenay]

ever mai [my]

dialogue

have you ever been to Padua? è mai stato a Padova? [ay]

yes, I was there two years ago sì, ci sono stato due anni fa [chee]

every ogni [on-yee]

every day ogni giorno

everyone ognuno [on-yoono]

everything tutto [toot-to]

everywhere dappertutto [dappairtoot-to]

exactly! esattamente! [esattamentay]

exam l'esame m [esamay]

example l'esempio m [esempyo]

for example per esempio [pair]

excellent eccellente [echelentay]

excellent! ottimo!

except eccetto [echet-to]

excess baggage il bagaglio in eccesso [bagal-yo een eches-so]

exchange rate il tasso di cambio [kamb-yo]

exciting emozionante [emotz-yonantay]

excuse me (to get past) permesso [pairmes-so]

(to get attention) mi scusi [mee skoozee]

(to say sorry) chiedo scusa [k-yaydo skooza]

exhaust (pipe) il tubo di scappamento [toobo]

exhausted (tired) esausto [esowsto]

exhibition la mostra

exit l'uscita f [oosheeta]

where's the nearest exit? dov'è l'uscita più vicina? [dovay – p-yoo veecheena]

expect aspettare [aspet-taray]

expensive caro

experienced esperto [espairto]

explain spiegare [sp-yegaray]

can you explain that? me lo puoi/può spiegare? [may lo pwoy/pwo]

express (mail, train) l'espresso m

extension (telephone) l'interno m [eentairno]

extension 221, please interno duecentoventuno, per favore

extension lead la prolunga

extra: can we have an extra one? possiamo averne uno/una in più? [poss-yamo avairnay – p-yoo]

do you charge extra for that? si paga in più per questo? [pair kwesto]

extraordinary straordinario [stra-ordeenar-yo]

extremely estremamente [estrema-mentay]

eye l'occhio m [ok-yo]

will you keep an eye on my suitcase for me? mi tiene d'occhio la valigia, per favore? [mee t-yaynay]

eyebrow pencil la matita per le sopracciglia [pair lay sopra-cheel-ya]

eye drops il collirio [kol-leer-yo]

eyeglasses (US) gli occhiali [ok-yalee]

eyeliner l'eye-liner m

eye make-up remover lo struccante per gli occhi [strook-kantay pair l-yee ok-kee]

eye shadow l'ombretto m

F

face la faccia [facha]

factory la fabbrica

Fahrenheit* Fahrenheit

faint (verb) svenire [sveneeray]

she's fainted è svenuta [ay svenoota]

I feel faint mi sento venir meno [mayno]

fair (funfair) il luna park [loona]

(trade) la fiera [f-yaira]

(adj) giusto [joosto]

fairly abbastanza [ab-bastantza]

fake il falso

fall l'autunno m [owtoon-no]

fall (verb) cadere [kadairay]

she's had a fall è caduta [ay kadoota]

false falso

family la famiglia [fameel-ya]

famous famoso

fan (electrical) il ventilatore [venteelato-ray]

(hand held) il ventaglio [vental-yo]

(sports: man/woman) il tifoso, la tifosa

fan belt la cinghia della ventola [cheeng-ya]

fantastic fantastico

far lontano

dialogue

is it far from here? è lontano da qui? [ay – kwee]
no, not very far no, non è molto lontano
well how far? quant'è lontano? [kwantay]
it's about 20 kilometres circa venti chilometri [cheerka]

fare il prezzo del biglietto [pretzo del beel-yet-to]
farm la fattoria [fat-toree-a]
fashionable di moda
fast veloce [velochay]
fat (person) grasso
  (on meat) il grasso
father il padre [padray]
father-in-law il suocero [swochairo]
faucet il rubinetto
fault il difetto
  sorry, it was my fault mi dispiace, è stata colpa mia [mee deesp-yachay ay – mee-a]
  it's not my fault non è colpa mia
faulty difettoso [deefet-tozo]
favourite preferito [prefaireeto]
fax il fax
  (verb: person) mandare un fax a [mandaray]
  (document) mandare per fax
February febbraio [feb-bra-yo]
feel sentire [senteeray]
  I feel hot sento caldo
  I feel unwell non mi sento

bene [baynay]
  I feel like going for a walk ho voglia di fare una passeggiata [o vol-ya dee faray oona pas-sej-jata]
how are you feeling? come si sente? [komay see sentay]
I'm feeling better mi sento meglio [mayl-yo]
felt-tip (pen) il pennarello
fence lo steccato
fender il paraurti [para-oortee]
ferry il traghetto [traget-to]
festival (music, arts) il festival
fetch (andare a) prendere [prendairay]
  I'll fetch him vado a prenderlo [prendairlo]
  will you come and fetch me later? passi/passa a prendermi più tardi? [prendairmee p-yoo]
feverish febbricitante [feb-breecheetantay]
few: a few alcuni/alcune [alkoonee/alkoonay]
  a few days alcuni giorni
fiancé il fidanzato [feedantzato]
fiancée la fidanzata
field il campo
fight la lite [leetay]
figs i fichi [feekee]
fill riempire [r-yempeeray]
fill in riempire
  do I have to fill this in? devo riempire questo? [dayvo – kwesto]
fill up fare il pieno [faray eel p-yayno]

fill it up, please il pieno, per favore

filling (in cake, sandwich) il ripieno [reep-**yay**no]
(in tooth) l'otturazione **f** [ot-tooratz-**yo**nay]

film (movie) il film [**feelm**]
(for camera) la pellicola

dialogue

do you have this kind of film? avete questo tipo di pellicola? [a**vay**tay **kwes**to]
yes; how many exposures? sì, da quante pose? [**kwan**tay **po**zay]
36 trentasei

film processing lo sviluppo della pellicola [zveel**oop**-po]
filthy lurido [**loo**reedo]
find (verb) trovare [tro**va**ray]
I can't find it non lo/la trovo
I've found it l'ho trovato/trovata
find out scoprire [sko**pree**ray]
could you find out for me? può informarsi per me? [pwo – pair may]
fine (weather) bello
(punishment) la multa

dialogues

how are you? come sta? [**ko**may]
I'm fine, thanks bene, grazie [**bay**nay **grat**zee-ay]

is that OK? va bene?
that's fine, thanks va bene, grazie

finger il dito [**dee**to]
finish (verb) finire [fee**nee**ray]
I haven't finished yet non ho ancora finito [o]
when does it finish? quando finisce? [**kwan**do fee**nee**shay]
fire: fire! al fuoco! [**fwo**ko]
can we light a fire here? si possono accendere fuochi qui? [a**chen**dairay **fwo**kee kwee]
it's on fire è in fiamme [ay een f-**yam**-may]
fire alarm l'allarme antincendio **m** [al-**lar**may anteen**chen**d-yo]
fire brigade i vigili del fuoco [**vee**jeelee del **fwo**ko]
fire escape l'uscita di sicurezza [oo**shee**ta dee seekoo**retz**a]
fire extinguisher l'estintore **m** [esteen-**to**ray]
first primo [**pree**mo]
I was first c'ero prima io [**chai**ro – **ee**-o]
at first all'inizio [eeneetz-yo]
the first time la prima volta
first on the left la prima a sinistra
first aid il pronto soccorso
first aid kit la cassetta del pronto soccorso
first class (travel etc) in prima classe [**klas**say]
first floor (UK) il primo piano (US) il piano terra [**tair**-ra]

first name il nome di battesimo [**no**may dee bat-**tay**seemo]

fish il pesce [**pe**shay]

fishing village il villaggio di pescatori [veel-**laj**-jo]

fishmonger's la pescheria [peskair**ee**-a]

fit (attack) l'attacco m

it doesn't fit me non mi sta

fitting room il camerino di prova

fix (verb) riparare [reepar**a**ray]
(arrange) fissare [fees-**sa**ray]

can you fix this? può ripararlo? [pwo]

fizzy frizzante [freetz**a**ntay]

flag la bandiera [band-**ya**ira]

flannel la pezza di spugna [**pe**tza dee sp**oo**n-ya]

flash (for camera) il flash

flat (noun: apartment) l'appartamento m
(adj) piatto [p-**yat**-to]

I've got a flat tyre ho una gomma a terra [o – **tair**-ra]

flavour il sapore [sap**o**ray]

flea la pulce [**pool**chay]

flight il volo

flight number il numero del volo [**noo**mairo]

flippers le pinne [**peen**-nay]

flood l'inondazione f [eenondatz-**yo**nay]

floor (of room) il pavimento
(of building) il piano

on the floor sul pavimento [sool]

Florence Firenze [feer**en**tzay]

Florentine (adj) fiorentino

florist il fioraio [f-**yo**ra-yo]

flour la farina

flower il fiore [f-**yo**ray]

flu l'influenza f

fluent: he speaks fluent Italian parla l'italiano correntemente [eetal-**ya**no kor-rentem**ent**ay]

fly la mosca
(verb) volare [vol**a**ray]

fly in arrivare in aereo [ar-reev**a**ray een a-**airy**-o]

fly out partire in aereo [part**ee**ray]

fog la nebbia

foggy: it's foggy c'è nebbia [chay]

folk dancing le danze folk [**dant**zay]

folk music la musica folk [m**oo**zeeka]

follow seguire [segw**ee**ray]

follow me mi segua [mee **say**-gwa]

food il cibo [**chee**bo]

food poisoning l'intossicazione alimentare f [eentos-seekatz-**yo**nay alim**ent**aray]

food shop/store il negozio di generi alimentari [neg**otz**-yo dee j**ay**nairee]

foot* il piede [p-**yay**day]

on foot a piedi

football il calcio [**kal**cho]
(ball) il pallone [pal-**lo**nay]

football match la partita di calcio

for per [pair], da

do you have something for ...? (headache/diarrhoea etc) avete qualcosa contro...? [avaytay kwalkoza]

dialogues

who's the ice cream for? per chi è il gelato? [pair kee ay]

that's for me è per me [may]

and this one? e questa? [ay kwesta]

that's for her quella è per lei [kwel-la – lay]

where do I get the bus for San Pietro? dove si prende l'autobus per San Pietro? [dovay see prenday low-toboos pair]

the bus for San Pietro leaves from Termini Station l'autobus per San Pietro parte dalla Stazione Termini [partay – statz-yonay]

how long have you been here for? da quanto è qui? [kwanto ay kwee]

I've been here for two days, how about you? sono qui da due giorni, e lei? [jornee, ay lay]

I've been here for a week sono qui da una settimana

forehead la fronte [frontay]

foreign straniero [stran-yairo]

foreigner (man/woman) lo straniero [stran-yairo], la straniera

forest la foresta

forget dimenticare [deementeekaray]

I forget non ricordo

I've forgotten ho dimenticato

fork la forchetta [forket-ta] (in road) la biforcazione [beeforkatz-yonay]

form (document) il modulo [modoolo]

formal (dress) da cerimonia [chaireemon-ya]

fortnight quindici giorni [kweendeechee jornee]

fortunately fortunatamente [fortoonata-mentay]

forward: could you forward my mail? potrebbe inoltrare la mia corrispondenza? [potreb-bay eenoltraray la mee-a kor-reespondentza]

forwarding address il nuovo recapito [nwovo]

foundation cream il fondotinta

fountain la fontana

foyer (of hotel) l'atrio m (theatre) il foyer

fracture la frattura [frat-toora]

France la Francia [francha]

free libero [leebairo] (no charge) gratuito [gratoo-eeto]

is it free (of charge)? è gratis?

freeway l'autostrada f
[owtostrada]
freezer il freezer [freetzair]
French francese [franchayzay]
French fries le patatine fritte
[patatee-nay freet-tay]
frequent frequente
[frekwentay]
how frequent is the bus to
Perugia? ogni quanto passa
l'autobus per Perugia? [on-
yee kwanto – pair]
fresh fresco
fresh orange juice il succo
d'arancia [sook-ko darancha]
Friday venerdì [venairdee]
fridge il frigo
fried fritto
fried egg l'uovo al tegamino
m [wovo]
friend (male/female) l'amico m,
l'amica f
friendly cordiale [kord-yalay]
from da
when does the next train from
Rome arrive? quando arriva
il prossimo treno da Roma?
[kwando]
from Monday to Friday dal
lunedì al venerdì
from next Thursday da
giovedì prossimo

dialogue

where are you from? di
dov'è? [dovay]
I'm from Slough sono di
Slough

front il davanti
in front davanti
in front of the hotel davanti
all'albergo
at the front sul davanti [sool]
frost il gelo [jaylo]
frozen ghiacciato [g-yachato]
frozen food i cibi surgelati
[cheebee soor-jelatee]
fruit la frutta [froot-ta]
fruit juice il succo di frutta
[sook-ko dee froot-ta]
fry friggere [freej-jairay]
frying pan la padella
full pieno [p-yayno]
it's full of ... è pieno/piena
di... [ay]
I'm full sono pieno/piena
full board la pensione
completa [pens-yonay komplayta]
fun: it was fun è stato
divertente [deevairtentay]
funeral il funerale [foonairalay]
funny (strange) strano
(amusing) buffo [boof-fo]
furniture i mobili
further più avanti [p-yoo]
it's further down the road è
più avanti su questa strada

dialogue

how much further is it to
San Gimignano? quanto
manca a San Gimignano?
[kwanto]
about 5 kilometres circa
cinque chilometri [cheerka
– keelometree]

fuse il fusibile [foozeebeelay]
the lights have fused sono
saltate le valvole [saltatay lay
valvolay]
fuse box i fusibili [foozeebeelee]
fuse wire il filo fusibile
[-beelay]
future il futuro [footooro]
in future in futuro

G

gallon* il gallone [gal-lonay]
game (cards etc) il gioco [jo-ko]
(match) la partita
(meat) la selvaggina [selvaj-
jeena]
garage (for fuel) il distributore
di benzina [deestreebootoray dee
bentzeena]
(for repairs) l'autofficina f
[owtof-feecheena]
(for parking) l'autorimessa f
[owtoreemes-sa]
garden il giardino [jardeeno]
garlic l'aglio m [al-yo]
gas il gas
gas cylinder (camping gas) la
bombola del gas
gas permeable lenses le lenti
semirigide [semeereejeeday]
gasoline (US) la benzina
[bentzeena]
gas station la stazione di
servizio [statz-yonay dee
sairveetz-yo]
gate il cancello [kanchel-lo]
(at airport) l'uscita f [oosheeta]

gay il gay
gay bar il bar gay
gear la marcia [marcha]
gearbox la scatola del cambio
[kamb-yo]
gear lever la leva del cambio
general generale [jenairalay]
Genoa Genova [jaynova]
gents (toilet) la toilette (degli
uomini) [twalet dayl-yee wo-
meenee]
genuine (antique etc) autentico
[owtenteeko]
German (adj) tedesco
German measles la rosolia
Germany la Germania
get (fetch) prendere
[prendairay]
will you get me another one,
please? me ne porta un
altro/un'altra, per favore?
[may nay]
how do I get to ...? come si
arriva a...? [komay]
do you know where I can get
them? sa dove posso trovarli/
trovarle? [dovay – trovarlay]

dialogue

can I get you a drink?
posso offrirle qualcosa da
bere? [of-freerlay kwalkoza da
bairay]
no, I'll get this one, what
would you like? no, offro
io questa volta, cosa
prende? [ee-o kwesta – koza
prenday]

a glass of red wine un bicchiere di vino rosso [beek-k-yairay]

get back (return) tornare [tornaray]

get in (arrive) arrivare [ar-reevaray]

get off scendere [shendairay]
where do I get off? dove devo scendere? [dovay dayvo]

get on (to train etc) salire [saleeray]

get out (of car etc) scendere [shendairay]

get up (in the morning) alzarsi [altzarsee]

gift il regalo

gift shop il negozio di articoli da regalo [negotz-yo]

gin il gin
a gin and tonic, please un gin tonic, per favore

girl la ragazza [ragatza]

girlfriend la ragazza

give dare [daray]
can you give me some change? mi può dare degli spiccioli? [mee pwo – dayl-yee]
I gave it to him l'ho dato a lui [lo – loo-ee]
will you give this to ...? puoi/ può dare questo a...? [pwoy/ pwo – kwesto]

dialogue

how much do you want for this? quanto vuole per questo? [kwanto vwolay pair kwesto]
20 euros venti euro [ventee ay-ooro]
I'll give you 18 euros gliene do diciotto [l-yee-aynee – deechot-to]

give back restituire [resteetweeray]

glad contento

glass (material) il vetro (tumbler) il bicchiere [beek-yairay]
(wine glass) il bicchiere da vino
a glass of wine un bicchiere di vino

glasses (spectacles) gli occhiali [ok-yalee]

gloves i guanti [gwantee]

glue la colla

go (verb) andare [andaray]
we'd like to go to the Roman Forum vorremmo andare al Foro Romano [vor-rem-mo]
where are you going? dove stai andando? [dovay sty]
where does this bus go? dove va questo autobus? [dovay va kwesto]
let's go! andiamo! [and-yamo]
she's gone (left) se n'è andata [say nay]
where has he gone? dov'è andato? [dovay]
I went there last week ci sono andato la settimana scorsa [chee]

pizza to go una pizza da

portare via [portaray **vee**-a]

go away andare via [an**dar**ay]

go away! vattene! [**vat**-tenay]

go back (return) tornare
[tor**nar**ay]

go down (the stairs etc) scendere
[**shen**dairay]

go in entrare [en**trar**ay]

go out (in the evening) uscire
[oo**sheer**ay]

**do you want to go out
tonight?** vuoi/vuole uscire
stasera? [vwoy/**vwol**ay]

go through attraversare [at-
travair**sar**ay]

go up (stairs) salire [sa**leer**ay]

goat la capra

goats' cheese il caprino

God Dio [**dee**-o]

goggles (for skiing) gli occhiali
da sci [ok-**yal**ee da shee]
(for swimming) gli occhiali da
nuoto [**nwo**to]

gold l'oro **m**

golf il golf

golf course il campo di golf

gondola la gondola

gondolier il gondoliere
[gondol-**yair**ay]

good buono [**bwo**no]

good! bene! [**bay**nay]

it's no good non va bene

goodbye arrivederci [ar-
reeve**dair**chee]

good evening buonasera
[bwona**sair**a]

Good Friday Venerdì Santo
[venair**dee** **san**to]

good morning buongiorno

[bwon**jor**no]

good night buonanotte
[bwona**not**-tay]

goose l'oca **f**

got: we've got to leave
dobbiamo partire [dob-**ya**mo
par**tee**ray]

have you got any ...? avete...?
[a**vay**tay]

government il governo
[go**vair**no]

gradually gradualmente
[gradoo-al**men**tay]

grammar la grammatica

gram(me) il grammo

granddaughter la nipote
[neepo**tay**]

grandfather il nonno

grandmother la nonna

grandson il nipote [neepo**tay**]

grapefruit il pompelmo

grapefruit juice il succo di
pompelmo [**sook**-ko]

grapes l'uva **f** [**oo**va]

grass l'erba **f** [**air**ba]

grateful grato

gravy il sugo [**soo**go]

great (excellent) fantastico

that's great! magnifico!

a great success un gran
successo [soo**ches**-so]

Great Britain la Gran Bretagna
[bretan-**ya**]

Greece la Grecia [**gre**cha]

greedy goloso

Greek (adj) greco

green verde [**vair**day]

green card (car insurance) la
carta verde

greengrocer's il fruttivendolo [froot-teevendolo]

grey grigio [greejo]

grill la griglia [greel-ya]

grilled alla griglia

grocer's il negozio di alimentari [negotz-yo]

ground la terra [tair-ra]
  on the ground per terra [pair]

ground floor il piano terra [tair-ra]

group il gruppo [groop-po]

guarantee la garanzia [garantzee-a]
  is it guaranteed? è garantito? [ay]

guest l'ospite m/f [ospeetay]

guesthouse la pensione [pens-yonay]

guide la guida [gweeda]

guidebook la guida

guided tour la visita guidata [veezeeta gweedata]

guitar la chitarra [keetar-ra]

gum (in mouth) la gengiva [jen-jeeva]

gun il fucile [foocheelay]

gym la palestra

H

hair i capelli

hairbrush la spazzola per capelli [spatzola pair]

haircut il taglio di capelli [tal-yo]

hairdresser (men's) il barbiere [barb-yairay]

(women's: man/woman) il parrucchiere [par-rook-yairay], la parrucchiera

hairdryer il fon

hair gel il gel per capelli [jel pair]

hairgrips i fermacapelli

hair spray la lacca per capelli

half la metà
  half an hour mezz'ora [metzora]
  half a litre mezzo litro [metzo]
  about half that una metà di quello [kwel-lo]

half board la mezza pensione [metza pens-yonay]

half bottle mezza bottiglia [bot-teel-ya]

half fare mezzo biglietto [metzo beel-yet-to]

half price metà prezzo [pretzo]

ham il prosciutto [proshoot-to]

hamburger l'hamburger m [amboorgair]

hammer il martello

hand la mano

handbag la borsetta

handbrake il freno a mano [frayno]

handkerchief il fazzoletto [fatzolet-to]

handle (on door, suitcase) la maniglia [maneel-ya]
  (on handbag) il manico

hand luggage il bagaglio a mano [bagal-yo]

hang-gliding il deltaplano

hangover i postumi della sbornia [zborn-ya]

I've got a hangover soffro per i postumi di una sbornia

happen succedere [soochaydairay]

what's happening? che succede? [kay soochayday]

what has happened? che è successo? [ay soochays-so]

happy felice [feleechay]

I'm not happy about this non ne sono convinto [nay]

harbour il porto

hard duro [dooro]

(difficult) difficile [deef-feecheelay]

hard-boiled egg l'uovo sodo m [wovo]

hard lenses le lenti rigide [reejeeday]

hardly a mala pena

hardly ever quasi mai [kwazee my]

hardware shop il negozio di ferramenta [negotz-yo dee fair-ramenta]

hat il cappello

hate (verb) detestare [detestaray]

have* avere [avairay]

can I have ...? vorrei... [vor-ray]

do you have ...? hai/ha...? [a-ee/a]

what'll you have? cosa prendi/prende? [koza prendee/prenday]

I have to leave now devo andarmene adesso [dayvo andarmenay]

do I have to ...? devo...?

can we have some ...? vorremmo un po' di... [vor-rem-mo]

hayfever la febbre da fieno [feb-bray da f-yayno]

hazelnuts le nocciole [nocholay]

he* lui [loo-ee]

head la testa

headache il mal di testa

headlights i fari

headphones la cuffia [koof-ya]

health food shop il negozio di cibi naturali [negotz-yo dee cheebee]

healthy sano

hear sentire [senteeray]

dialogue

can you hear me? mi sente? [sentay]

I can't hear you, could you repeat that? non la sento, può ripetere? [pwo reepetairay]

hearing aid l'apparecchio acustico m [ap-parek-yo akoosteeko]

heart il cuore [kworay]

heart attack l'infarto m

heat il caldo

heater (in room) il radiatore [rad-yatoray]

(in car) il riscaldamento

heating il riscaldamento

heavy pesante [pezantay]

heel (of foot) il tallone [tal-lonay]

(of shoe) il tacco

could you heel these? può rifare i tacchi a queste scarpe? [pwo reefaray ee tak-kee a kwestay skarpay]

heelbar riparazione scarpe [reeparatz-yonay]

height l'altezza f [altetza]

helicopter l'elicottero m [eleekot-tairo]

hello (in the daytime) buongiorno [bwonjorno]
(late afternoon, in the evening) buonasera [bwonasaira]
(answer on phone) pronto

helmet (for motorcycle) il casco

help l'aiuto m [a-yooto]
(verb) aiutare [a-yootaray]

help! aiuto!

can you help me? mi può aiutare? [pwo]

thank you very much for your help grazie dell'aiuto [gratzee-ay]

helpful disponibile [deesponeebeelay]

hepatitis l'epatite f [epateetay]

her*: I haven't seen her non l'ho vista [lo]
to her a lei [lay], le [lay]
with her con lei, con sé [say]
for her per lei
that's her è lei
that's her towel è il suo asciugamano [ay eel soo-o]

herbal tea la tisana [teezana]

herbs le erbe [airbay]

here qui [kwee]
here is/are ... ecco...

here you are ecco a te/lei [tay/lay]

hers*: that's hers quello è suo [kwel-lo ay soo-o]

hey! ehi! [ay-ee]

hi! (hello) ciao! [chow], salve! [salvay]

hide (verb) nascondere [naskondairay]

high alto

highchair il seggiolone [sej-jolonay]

highway l'autostrada f [owtostrada]

hill la collina

him*: I haven't seen him non l'ho visto [lo]
to him a lui [loo-ee], gli [l-yee]
with him con lui, con sé [say]
for him per lui [pair]
that's him è lui [ay]

hip il fianco [f-yanko]

hire noleggiare [nolej-jaray]
for hire a nolo
where can I hire a bike? dove posso noleggiare una bicicletta? [dovay]

his*: it's his car è la sua macchina [ay la soo-a]
that's his quello è suo [kwel-lo ay soo-o]

hit (verb) colpire [kolpeeray]

hitch-hike fare l'autostop [faray lowtostop]

hobby l'hobby m

hockey l'hockey m

hold (verb) tenere [tenairay]

hole il buco [booko]

holiday la vacanza [vakantza]

on holiday in vacanza
home la casa [kaza]
  at home (in my house etc) a casa
  (in my country) in patria
  we go home tomorrow
  torniamo in patria domani
  [torn-yamo]
honest onesto
honey il miele [m-yaylay]
honeymoon la luna di miele
  [loona dee]
hood (US) il cofano
hope la speranza [spairantza]
  I hope so spero di sì [spairo]
  I hope not spero di no
hopefully se tutto va bene [say
  toot-to va baynay]
horn (of car) il clacson
horrible orribile [or-reebeelay]
horse il cavallo
horse riding l'equitazione f
  [ekweetatz-yonay]
hospital l'ospedale m
  [ospedalay]
hospitality l'ospitalità f
  thank you for your hospitality
  grazie dell'ospitalità
hot caldo
  (spicy) piccante [peek-kantay]
  I'm hot ho caldo [o]
  it's hot today fa caldo oggi
  [oj-jee]
hotel l'albergo m [albairgo]
hotel room la camera d'albergo
hour l'ora f
house la casa [kaza]
house wine il vino della casa
hovercraft l'hovercraft m
how come [komay]

how many? quanti? [kwantee]
how much? quanto?

dialogues

how are you? come stai/
sta? [komay sty]
fine, thanks, and you?
bene, grazie, e lei? [baynay
– ay lay]

how much is it? quanto
costa? [kwanto]
... euros ... euro [ay-ooro]
I'll take it lo/la prendo

humid umido [oomeedo]
humour l'umorismo m
  [oomoreezmo]
hungry: I'm hungry ho fame
  [o famay]
  are you hungry? ha fame? [a]
hurry (verb) sbrigarsi
  I'm in a hurry ho fretta [o]
  there's no hurry non c'è fretta
  [non chay]
  hurry up! sbrigati! [zbreegatee]
hurt far male [malay]
  it really hurts mi fa proprio
  male
husband il marito [mareeto]
hydrofoil l'aliscafo m
hypermarket l'ipermercato m

I

I io [ee-o]
ice il ghiaccio [g-yacho]

with ice con ghiaccio

no ice, thanks niente ghiaccio, grazie [n-yentay]

ice cream il gelato [jelato]

ice-cream cone il cono gelato

iced coffee il caffè freddo [kaf-**fay**]

ice lolly il ghiacciolo [g-yacholo]

ice rink la pista di pattinaggio (sul ghiaccio) [pat-teenaj-jo sool g-yacho]

ice skates i pattini da ghiaccio

idea l'idea f [eeday-a]

idiot l'idiota m/f [eed-yota]

if se [say]

ignition l'accensione m [achens-yonay]

ill malato

I feel ill mi sento male [malay]

illness la malattia [malat-tee-a]

imitation (leather etc) l'imitazione f [eemeetatz-yonay]

immediately immediatamente [eem-med-yatamentay]

important importante [eemportantay]

it's very important è molto importante [ay]

it's not important non ha importanza [non a eemportantza]

impossible impossibile [eempos-seebeelay]

impressive notevole [notay-volay]

improve migliorare [meel-yoraray]

I want to improve my Italian voglio migliorare il mio italiano [vol-yo – eel mee-o]

in: it's in the centre è in centro [chentro]

in my car con la mia macchina

in Florence a Firenze

in two days from now tra due giorni

in five minutes tra cinque minuti

in May a maggio

in English in inglese [een]

in Italian in italiano

is he in? c'è? [chay]

inch* il pollice [pol-leechay]

include comprendere [komprendairay]

does that include meals? sono compresi i pasti? [komprayzee]

is that included? questo è compreso? [kwesto ay]

inconvenient scomodo

incredible incredibile [eenkredeebeelay]

Indian indiano [eend-yano]

indicator la freccia [frecha]

indigestion l'indigestione f [eendeejest-yonay]

indoor pool la piscina coperta [pee-sheena kopairta]

indoors all'interno [eentairno]

inexpensive a buon mercato [bwon mairkato]

see cheap

infection l'infezione f [eenfetz-yonay]

infectious contagioso
[kontajozo]

inflammation l'infiammazione
f [eenf-yam-matz-yonay]

informal informale
[eenformalay]

information l'informazione f
[eenformatz-yonay]

do you have any information
about ...? ha informazioni
su...?

information desk il banco
(delle) informazioni [del-lay]

injection l'iniezione f [een-yetz-
yonay]

injured ferito [faireeto]

she's been injured è rimasta
ferita [ay]

in-laws i suoceri [swochairee]

inner tube (for tyre) la camera
d'aria

innocent innocente [een-
nochentay]

insect l'insetto m

insect bite la puntura
d'insetto [poon-toora]

do you have anything for
insect bites? ha qualcosa
per le punture d'insetto? [a
kwalkoza pair lay poon-tooray]

insect repellent l'insettifugo m
[eenset-teefoogo]

inside dentro

inside the hotel nell'albergo

let's sit inside sediamoci
dentro [sed-yamochee]

insist insistere [eenseestairay]

I insist insisto

insomnia l'insonnia f

instant coffee il caffè solubile
[kaf-fay soloobeelay]

instead invece [eenvaychay]

give me that one instead mi
dia quello, invece [kwel-lo]

instead of ... invece di...

insulin l'insulina f [eensooleena]

insurance l'assicurazione f [as-
seekooratz-yonay]

intelligent intelligente [eentel-
leejentay]

interested: I'm interested in
... mi interesso di... [mee
eentaires-so]

interesting interessante
[eentaires-santay]

that's very interesting è molto
interessante [ay]

international internazionale
[eentairnatz-yonalay]

Internet Internet [eentairnet]

interpret interpretare
[eentairpretaray]

interpreter l'interprete m/f
[eentairpretay]

intersection l'incrocio m
[eenkrocho]

interval (at theatre) l'intervallo
m [eentairval-lo]

into in

I'm not into ... non
m'interesso di...

introduce presentare
[presentaray]

may I introduce ...? posso
presentarle...? [presentarlay]

invitation l'invito m

invite invitare [eenveetaray]

Ireland l'Irlanda f [eerlanda]

Irish irlandese [eerlandayzay]
  I'm Irish sono irlandese
iron (for ironing) il ferro da stiro
  [fair-ro]
  can you iron these for me?
  me li può stirare? [may lee pwo
  steeraray]
is* è [ay]
island l'isola f [eezola]
it esso
  it is ... è... [ay]
  is it ...? è...?
  where is it? dov'è? [dovay]
  it's him è lui [loo-ee]
  it was ... era... [aira]
Italian (adj) italiano
  [eetal-yano]
  (language, man) l'italiano m
  (woman) l'italiana f
  the Italians gli Italiani
Italy l'Italia f [eetal-ya]
itch: it itches mi prude
  [prooday]

J

jack (for car) il cric
jacket la giacca [jak-ka]
jar il vasetto
jam la marmellata
jammed: it's jammed si è
  inceppato [ay eenchep-pato]
January gennaio [jen-na-yo]
jaw la mascella [mashel-la]
jazz il jazz [jetz]
jealous geloso [jelozo]
jeans i jeans
jellyfish la medusa [medooza]

jersey la maglia [mal-ya]
jetty il molo
Jewish ebreo [ebray-o]
jeweller's la gioielleria
  [joy-el-lairee-a]
jewellery i gioielli [joy-el-lee]
job l'impiego m [eemp-yaygo]
jogging il jogging
  to go jogging andare a fare
  jogging [andaray a faray]
joke lo scherzo [skairtzo]
  (story) la barzelletta [bartzel-let-
  ta]
journey il viaggio [vee-aj-jo]
  have a good journey! buon
  viaggio! [bwon]
jug la brocca
  a jug of water una brocca
  d'acqua [dakwa]
juice il succo [sook-ko]
July luglio [lool-yo]
jump (verb) saltare [saltaray]
jumper il maglione
  [mal-yonay]
jump leads il cavo per
  collegare due batterie [pair
  kol-legaray doo-ay bat-tairee-ay]
junction il bivio [beev-yo]
June giugno [joon-yo]
just (only) solo
  just two soltanto due
  just for me solo per me [pair
  may]
  just here proprio qui [kwee]
  not just now non ora
  we've just arrived siamo
  appena arrivati [s-yamo ap-
  payna]

K

keep tenere [ten**ai**ray]
 keep the change tenga il resto
 can I keep it? posso tenerlo? [ten-**ai**rlo]
 please keep it puoi/può tenerlo [pwoy/pwo]
ketchup il ketchup
kettle il bollitore [bol-leet**o**ray]
key la chiave [k-y**a**vay]
 the key for room 201, please (la chiave del) duecentuno, per favore
key ring il portachiavi [portak-y**a**vee]
kidneys (in body) i reni [**ray**nee]
 (food) il rognone [ron-y**o**nay]
kill (verb) uccidere [ooch**ee**dairay]
kilo* il chilo [**kee**lo]
kilometre* il chilometro [keel**o**metro]
 how many kilometres is it to ...? a quanti chilometri da qui è...? [kw**a**ntee – kwee ay]
kind (generous) gentile [jent**ee**lay]
 that's very kind of you è molto gentile da parte tua/sua [ay – partay t**oo**-a/s**oo**-a]

dialogue

 which kind do you want? che tipo vuole? [kay – vw**o**lay]

 I want this/that kind questo/quel tipo [kw**e**sto/kwel]

king il re [ray]
kiosk il chiosco [kee-**o**sko]
 (selling newspapers) l'edicola f
kiss il bacio [b**a**cho]
 (verb) baciare [bach**a**ray]
kitchen la cucina [kooch**ee**na]
kitchenette il cucinino [koocheen**ee**no]
Kleenex® i fazzolettini di carta [fatzolet-t**ee**nee]
knee il ginocchio [jeen**o**k-yo]
knickers le mutande [moot**a**nday]
knife il coltello
knitwear la maglieria [mal-yee- air**ee**-a]
knock (verb: on door) bussare [boos-s**a**ray]
knock down: he's been knocked down è stato investito [ay]
knock over (object) far cadere [kad**ai**ray]
 (pedestrian) investire [eenvest**ee**ray]
know (somebody, a place) conoscere [kon**o**-shairay]
 (something) sapere [sap**ai**ray]
 I don't know non lo so
 I didn't know that non lo sapevo [sap**ay**vo]
 do you know where I can find ...? sai/sa dove posso trovare...? [s**a**-ee/sa d**o**vay posso trov**a**ray]

L

label l'etichetta f [eteeket-ta]

ladies' (toilets) la toilette (delle donne) [twalet del-lay don-nay]

ladies' wear l'abbigliamento da donna m [ab-beel-yamento]

lady la signora [seen-yora]

lager la birra chiara [beer-ra k-yara]

lake il lago

lamb l'agnello m [an-yel-lo]

lamp la lampada

lane (motorway) la corsia (small road) la stradina

language la lingua [leengwa]

language course un corso di lingua

large grande [granday]

last ultimo [oolteemo]

what time is the last train to Trieste? a che ora parte l'ultimo treno per Trieste? [kay – partay]

last week la settimana scorsa

last Friday venerdì scorso

last night la notte scorsa

late tardi

sorry I'm late mi scuso del ritardo [mee skoozo]

the train was late il treno era in ritardo

we must go – we'll be late dobbiamo andare – altrimenti faremo tardi [dob-yamo andaray – faraymo]

it's getting late si sta facendo tardi [fachendo]

later più tardi [p-yoo]

I'll come back later torno più tardi

see you later ci vediamo dopo [chee ved-yamo]

later on poi, più tardi [poy]

latest ultimo [oolteemo]

by Wednesday at the latest … entro mercoledì al più tardi [p-yoo]

laugh (verb) ridere [reedairay]

launderette la lavanderia automatica [lavandairee-a owto-mateeka]

laundromat la lavanderia automatica

laundry (clothes) il bucato (place) la lavanderia

lavatory il gabinetto

law la legge [lej-jay]

lawn il prato all'inglese [eenglayzay]

lawyer l'avvocato m

laxative il lassativo

lazy pigro

lead (electrical) il filo (verb) condurre [kondoor-ray], guidare [gweedaray]

where does this lead to? dove porta questo? [dovay – kwesto]

leaf la foglia [fol-ya]

leaflet il dépliant [daypleeay-an]

leak la perdita [pairdeeta] (verb) perdere [pairdairay]

the roof leaks gocciola acqua dal tetto [gochola akwa]

learn imparare [eempararay]

least: not in the least per
niente [n-yentay]
 at least come minimo
 [komay]
leather il cuoio [kwo-yo], la
 pelle [pel-lay]
leave (verb: depart) partire
 [parteeray]
 (leave behind) lasciare [lasharay]
 I am leaving tomorrow parto
 domani
 he left yesterday è partito ieri
 [ay – yairee]
 may I leave this here? posso
 lasciarlo qui? [lasharlo kwee]
 I left my coat in the bar ho
 lasciato il cappotto al bar [o]
 when does the bus for
 Venice leave? a che ora parte
 l'autobus per Venezia [kay
 – partay lowtoboos pair]
leek il porro
left la sinistra [seeneestra]
 on the left, to the left a
 sinistra
 turn left giri a sinistra [jeeree]
 there's none left non ce n'è
 più nessuno/nessuna [chay nay
 p-yoo nes-soono]
left-handed mancino
 [mancheeno]
left luggage (office) il deposito
 bagagli [bagal-yee]
leg la gamba
lemon il limone [leemonay]
lemonade la gassosa [gas-soza]
lemon tea un tè al limone [tay
 al leemonay]
lend prestare [prestaray]

will you lend me your ...
? può prestarmi il suo/la
sua...? [pwo – soo-o/soo-a]
lens (of camera) l'obiettivo m
[ob-yet-teevo]
lesbian la lesbica
less meno [mayno]
 less than meno di
 less expensive più a buon
 mercato [p-yoo]
lesson la lezione [letz-yonay]
let (allow) permettere [pairmet-
 tairay]
 will you let me know? mi
 faccia sapere [mee facha
 sapairay]
 I'll let you know ti/le farò
 sapere [lay]
 let's go for something to
 eat andiamo a mangiare
 qualcosa [and-yamo a manjaray
 kwalkoza]
 let off far scendere [shendairay]
 will you let me off at ...? può
 farmi scendere a...? [pwo]
letter la lettera [let-taira]
 do you have any letters for
 me? ci sono lettere per me?
 [chee sono let-tairay pair may]
letterbox la buca delle lettere
 [booka del-lay]
lettuce la lattuga [lat-tooga]
lever la leva [layva]
library la biblioteca [beeblee-
 otayka]
licence il permesso [pairmes-so]
lid il coperchio [kopairk-yo]
lie (verb: tell untruth) mentire
 [menteeray]

75

lie down stendersi [stendairsee]

life la vita

lifebelt il salvagente [salvajentay]

lifeguard (man/woman) il bagnino [ban-yeeno], la bagnina

life jacket il giubbotto di salvataggio [joob-bot-to dee salva-taj-jo]

lift (in building) l'ascensore m [ashensoray]

could you give me a lift? mi puoi/può dare un passaggio? [mee pwoy/pwo daray oon pas-saj-jo]

would you like a lift? vuoi/vuole un passaggio? [vwoy/vwolay]

lift pass lo skipass

a daily/weekly lift pass uno skipass giornaliero/settimanale

light la luce [loochay]

(not heavy) leggero [lej-jairo]

do you have a light? (for cigarette) puoi/può farmi accendere? [pwoy/pwo farmee achendairay]

light green verde chiaro [k-yaro]

light bulb la lampadina

I need a new light bulb ho bisogno di una lampadina nuova [o beezon-yo day]

lighter (cigarette) l'accendino m [achen-deeno]

lightning il fulmine [foolmeenay]

like (verb) piacere [p-yachairay]

I like it mi piace [mee pee-achay]

I like going for walks mi piace fare passeggiate

I like you mi piaci [pee-achee]

I don't like it non mi piace

do you like ...? ti/le piace...? [tee/lay]

I'd like a beer vorrei una birra [vor-ray]

I'd like to go swimming vorrei andare a fare una nuotata [andaray]

would you like a drink? vuoi/vuole qualcosa da bere? [vwoy/vwolay kwalkoza da bairay]

would you like to go for a walk? ti/le va di fare una passeggiata?

what's it like? com'è? [komay]

like this così [kozee]

I want one like this ne voglio uno/una come questo/questa [nay vol-yo – komay kwesto/kwesta]

lime il lime [la-eem]

line la linea [leen-ay-a]

could you give me an outside line? mi dà la linea, per favore?

lips le labbra

lip salve la pomata per le labbra [pair lay]

lipstick il rossetto

liqueur il liquore [leekworay]

listen ascoltare [askoltaray]

litre* il litro

a litre of white wine un litro di vino bianco

76

little piccolo

just a little, thanks solo un po', grazie

a little milk un po' di latte

a little bit more ancora un po'

live (verb) vivere [**vee**vairay]

we live together conviviamo [konveev-**ya**mo]

dialogue

where do you live? dove abita? [**do**vay]

I live in London abito a Londra

lively (person, town) pieno di vita [p-**yay**no dee **vee**ta]

liver il fegato [**fay**gato]

loaf la pagnotta [pan-**yot**-ta]

lobby (in hotel) l'atrio m

lobster l'aragosta f

local locale [lo**kal**ay]

can you recommend a local wine/restaurant? mi può consigliare un vino/un ristorante del posto? [mee pwo konseel-**ya**ray]

lock la serratura [sair-rat**oo**ra]

(verb) chiudere a chiave [k-**yoo**dairay a k-**ya**vay]

it's locked è chiuso a chiave [ay k-**yoo**zo]

lock in chiudere dentro

lock out chiudere fuori [fw**oo**ree]

I've locked myself out mi sono chiuso/chiusa fuori [k-**yoo**zo]

locker (for luggage etc) l'armadietto m [armad-**yet**-to]

lollipop il lecca-lecca

Lombardy la Lombardia

London Londra

long lungo [**loon**go]

how long will it take to fix it? quanto ci vuole per accomodarlo? [kwanto chee vw**o**lay pair]

how long does it take? quanto tempo ci vuole?

a long time tanto tempo

one day/two days longer ancora un giorno/due giorni

long-distance call l'inter-urbana f [een-tairoorb**a**na]

look: I'm just looking, thanks sto solo dando un'occhiata, grazie [ok-**ya**ta]

you don't look well hai/ha una brutta cera [a-ee/a **oo**na broot-ta **chai**ra]

look out! attenzione! [at-tentz-**yo**nay]

can I have a look? posso dare un'occhiata? [**da**ray]

look after badare a [ba**da**ray]

look at guardare [gw**ar**daray]

look for cercare [**chair**karay]

I'm looking for ... sto cercando... [**chair**kando]

look forward to non vedere l'ora di [ve**dai**ray]

I'm looking forward to it non vedo l'ora [**vay**do]

loose (handle etc) che si sta staccando [kay]

lorry il camion [**kam**-yon]

lose perdere [**pair**dairay]
I'm lost, I want to get to ...
mi sono perso/persa, voglio
andare a... [**pair**so – **vol**yo
an**dar**ay]
I've lost my bag ho perso la
borsa [o]
lost property (office) l'ufficio
oggetti smarriti m [oof-**fee**cho
oj-**jet**-tee zmar-**ree**tee]
lot: a lot, lots molto
not a lot non molto
a lot of Parmesan molto
parmigiano
a lot of sauce molta salsa
a lot of people molta gente
[**jen**tay]
a lot of boys molti ragazzi
a lot of drinks molte bevande
a lot bigger molto più
grande [p-yoo]
I like it a lot mi piace molto
[mee pee-**achay**]
lotion la lozione [lotz-**yon**ay]
loud forte [**for**tay]
lounge (in house, hotel) il salone
[sa**lon**ay]
(in airport) la sala d'attesa [at-
tayza]
love l'amore m [a**mor**ay]
(verb) amare [a**mar**ay]
I love Italy mi piace molto
l'Italia [mee p-**yachay**]
lovely bello
(meal) delizioso [deleetz-**yozo**]
low basso
luck la fortuna [for**toona**]
good luck! buona fortuna!
[**bwona**]

luggage i bagagli [ba**gal**-yee]
luggage trolley il carrello
lump (on body) il gonfiore [gonf-
yoray]
lunch il pranzo [**prantzo**]
lungs i polmoni
luxurious lussuoso [loos-soo-**ozo**]
luxury il lusso [**loos**-so]

M

machine la macchina [mak-
keena]
mad (insane) pazzo [**patzo**]
(angry) furioso [fooree-**ozo**]
magazine la rivista
maid (in hotel) la cameriera
[kamair-**yaira**]
maiden name il cognome da
nubile [kon-**yomay** da **noo**beelay]
mail la posta
see post
(verb) impostare [eempo**staray**]
is there any mail for me? c'è
posta per me? [chay – may]
mailbox la buca delle lettere
[**booka** del-lay let-**tairay**]
main principale
[preenchee**palay**]
main course la portata
principale
main post office l'ufficio
postale centrale m [oof-**fee**cho
po**stalay** chen**tralay**]
main road (in town) la strada
principale [preenchee**palay**]
(in country) la strada maestra
[**my**stra]

mains switch l'interruttore generale **m** [eentair-root-toray jenairalay]

make fare [faray]

(noun: brand name) la marca

I make it 50 euros secondo i miei calcoli sono cinquanta euro [cheenkwanta **ay-oo**ro]

what is it made of? di che cosa è fatto/fatta? [kay koza]

make-up il trucco [trook-ko]

man l'uomo **m** [womo]

manager il direttore [deeret-toray]

can I see the manager? posso parlare con il direttore? [parlaray]

manageress la direttrice [deeret-treechay]

manual (car with manual gears) la macchina con il cambio manuale [mak-keena kon eel kamb-yo manoo-alay]

many molti/molte [moltay]

not many non molti/molte

map (city plan) la pianta [p-yanta]

(road map, geographical) la cartina

March marzo [martzo]

margarine la margarina [margareena]

market il mercato [mairkato]

marmalade la marmellata d'arance [daranchay]

married: I'm married (said by a man/woman) sono sposato/ sposata

are you married? (said to a man/ woman) è sposato/sposata? [ay]

mascara il mascara

match (football etc) la partita

matches i fiammiferi [f-yam-meefairee]

material (fabric) la stoffa

matter: it doesn't matter non importa

what's the matter? che c'è? [kay chay]

mattress il materasso

May maggio [maj-jo]

may: may I have another bottle? potrei avere un'altra bottiglia? [potray avairay]

may I come in? posso entrare? [entraray]

may I see it? posso vederlo/ vederla? [vedairlo/vedairla]

may I sit here? posso sedere qui? [sedairay kwee]

maybe forse [forsay]

mayonnaise la maionese [ma-yonayzay]

me*: that's for me è per me [ay pair may]

send it to me mandalo/lo mandi a me

me too anch'io [ankee-o]

meal il pasto

dialogue

did you enjoy your meal? le è piaciuto? [lay ay p-yachooto]

it was excellent, thank you
era ottimo, grazie [aira]

mean (verb) significare [seen-yeefeekaray]
what do you mean? che cosa intendi/intende? [kay koza eentendee/eentenday]

dialogue

what does this word mean? cosa significa questa parola? [koza seen-yeefeeka kwesta]
it means ... in English in inglese significa... [eenglayzay]

measles il morbillo [morbeel-lo]
meat la carne [karnay]
mechanic il meccanico [mek-kaneeko]
medicine la medicina [medeecheena]
Mediterranean il Mediterraneo [medeetair-ranay-o]
medium (adj: size) medio [mayd-yo]
medium-dry semisecco
medium-rare non troppo cotto
medium-sized di taglia media [tal-ya mayd-ya]
meet (someone) incontrare [eenkontraray]
(each other) incontrarsi

nice to meet you piacere di conoscerla [pee-achairay dee konoshair-la]
where shall I meet you? dove ci incontriamo? [dovay chee]
meeting la riunione [r-yoon-yonay]
meeting place il luogo d'incontro [lwogo]
melon il melone [melonay]
men gli uomini [lyo-meenee]
mend riparare [reepararay]
could you mend this for me? me lo può riparare? [may – pwo]
menswear l'abbigliamento da uomo m [ab-beel-yamento da womo]
mention (verb) nominare [nomeenaray]
don't mention it prego [praygo]
menu il menù [menoo]
may I see the menu, please? mi dà il menù, per favore?
see page 204 for Menu Reader
message il messaggio [mes-saj-jo]
are there any messages for me? ci sono messaggi per me? [chee – pair may]
I want to leave a message for ... vorrei lasciare un messaggio per... [vor-ray lasharay]
metal il metallo
metre* il metro

microwave (oven) il forno a microonde [meekro-**o**nday]
midday mezzogiorno [met-zoj**o**rno]
at midday a mezzogiorno
middle: in the middle nel mezzo [m**e**tzo]
in the middle of the night in piena notte [p-y**ay**na]
the middle one quello/quella in mezzo [kwel-lo]
midnight mezzanotte [metzan**o**t-tay]
at midnight a mezzanotte
might: I might (not) go può darsi che io (non) ci vada [pwo – kay **ee**-o non chee]
I might want to stay another day forse dovrò fermarmi ancora un giorno [f**o**rsay]
migraine l'emicrania f [emeekr**a**n-ya]
Milan Milano [meel**a**no]
mild (taste) leggero [lej-j**ai**ro]
(weather) mite [m**ee**tay]
mile* il miglio [m**ee**l-yo]
milk il latte [l**a**t-tay]
milkshake il frappé [frap-p**ay**]
millimetre* il millimetro
minced meat la carne macinata [k**a**rnay mache**e**nata]
mind: never mind non fa niente [n-y**e**ntay]
I've changed my mind ho cambiato idea [o kamb-y**a**to eed**ay**-a]

dialogue

do you mind if I open the window? le dispiace se apro la finestra? [lay deespee-**a**chay say]
no, I don't mind no, faccia pure [f**a**cha p**oo**ray]

mine*: it's mine è mio/mia [**a**y]
mineral water l'acqua minerale f [**a**kwa meen-air**a**lay]
minibar il frigobar
mints le mentine [ment**ee**nay]
minute il minuto [meen**oo**to]
in a minute in un attimo
just a minute un attimo
mirror lo specchio [sp**e**k-yo]
Miss (la) signorina [seen-yor**ee**na]
miss: I missed the bus ho perso l'autobus [o p**ai**rso]
missing smarrito
one of my ... is missing non trovo uno/una dei miei/delle mie... [day mee-y**ay**/del-lay mee-**ay**]
there's a suitcase missing manca una valigia
mist la nebbiolina [neb-yol**ee**na]
mistake lo sbaglio [zb**a**l-yo]
I think there's a mistake credo ci sia un errore [kr**ay**do chee s**ee**-a oon air-r**o**ray]
sorry, I've made a mistake chiedo scusa, mi sono sbagliato/sbagliata [k-y**ay**do sk**oo**za mee – sbal-y**a**to]

misunderstanding l'equivoco
m [ekwee-voko]
mix-up: sorry, there's been
a mix-up mi dispiace,
è successa un po' di
confusione [mee deesp-yachay
ay sooches-sa – konfooz-yonay]
mobile phone il telefonino
[telayfoneeno]
modern moderno [modairno]
modern art gallery la galleria
d'arte moderna [gal-lairee-a
dartay]
moisturizer l'idratante m [ee-
dratantay]
moment: I won't be a moment
(won't be long) faccio in un
attimo [facho]
monastery il monastero
[monastairo]
Monday lunedì [loonedee]
money i soldi
month il mese [mayzay]
monument il monumento
[monoo-mento]
moon la luna [loona]
moped il motorino
more* più [p-yoo]
can I have some more water,
please? vorrei ancora acqua,
per favore [vor-ray]
more expensive/interesting
più caro/interessante
[p-yoo]
more than 50 più di
cinquanta
more than that di più
a lot more molto di più

dialogue

would you like some
more? ne vuole ancora?
[nay vwolay]
no, no more for me, thanks
no, basta per me, grazie
[pair may]
how about you? e lei?
[ay lay]
I don't want any more,
thanks non ne voglio più,
grazie [nay vol-yo p-yoo]

morning la mattina
this morning questa mattina
[kwesta]
in the morning di mattina
mosquito la zanzara [tzantzara]
mosquito repellent
l'insettifugo m [eenset-
teefoogo]
most: I like this one most of all
questo/questa mi piace più
di tutti/tutte [kwesto – mee
p-yachay p-yoo dee toot-tee/toot-
tay]
most of the time la maggior
parte del tempo [maj-jor
partay]
most tourists la maggior
parte dei turisti [day]
mostly per lo più [pair lo p-yoo]
mother la madre [madray]
motorbike la motocicletta
[moto-cheeklet-ta]
motorboat il motoscafo
motorway l'autostrada f
[owtostrada]

mountain la montagna
[montan-ya]

in the mountains in
montagna

mountaineering l'alpinismo m

mouse il topo

moustache i baffi

mouth la bocca

mouth ulcer la stomatite
[stomateetay]

move (verb) muovere
[mwovairay]

he's moved to another room
si è trasferito in un'altra
stanza [see ay trasfaireeto]

could you move your
car? potrebbe spostare
la macchina? [potreb-bay
spostaray]

could you move up a little? si
può spostare un po' più in
là? [see pwo – p-yoo]

where has it been moved to?
dove è stato trasferito? [dovay
ay]

movie il film [feelm]

movie theater il cinema
[cheenema]

Mr (il) signor [seen-yor]

Mrs (la) signora [seen-yora]

Ms (la) signora

much molto

much better/worse molto
meglio/peggio [mayl-yo/pej-jo]

much hotter molto più caldo
[p-yoo]

not much non molto

not very much non molto

I don't want very much non

voglio molto [vol-yo]

mud il fango

mug (for drinking) il bicchierone
[beek-yaironay]

I've been mugged sono stato
aggredito [ag-gredeeto]

mum la mamma

mumps gli orecchioni [orek-
yonee]

museum il museo [moozay-o]

mushrooms i funghi [foongee]

music la musica [moozeeka]

musician il/la musicista
[moozeecheesta]

Muslim (adj) musulmano

mussels le cozze [kotzay]

must*: I must devo [dayvo]

I mustn't drink alcohol non
devo bere alcol [bairay]

mustard la senape [saynapay]

my* il mio, la mia, i miei [mee-
yay], le mie [lay mee-ay]

myself: I'll do it myself lo farò
da me [may]

by myself da solo

N

nail (finger) l'unghia f [oong-ya]
(metal) il chiodo [k-yodo]

nail varnish lo smalto per le
unghie [pair lay oong-yay]

name il nome [nomay]

my name's John mi chiamo
John [k-yamo]

what's your name? come
si chiama? [komay see
k-yama]

what is the name of this street? come si chiama questa strada? [**kwes**ta]

napkin il tovagliolo [toval-**yo**lo]

Naples Napoli

nappy il pannolino

narrow (street) stretto

nasty (person) antipatico
(weather, accident) brutto [**broot**-to]

national nazionale [natz-yo**nalay**]

nationality la nazionalità [natz-yo**naleeta**]

natural naturale [natoo**ralay**]

nausea la nausea [**now**zay-a]

navy (blue) blu marino

Neapolitan (adj) napoletano

near vicino a [vee**chee**no]

is it near the city centre? è vicino al centro della città? [ay]

do you go near the Colosseum? passa vicino al Colosseo?

where is the nearest ...? dov'è il... più vicino? [**dov**ay eel ... p-yoo]

nearby vicino [vee**chee**no]

nearly quasi [**kwa**zee]

necessary necessario [neches-**sar**-yo]

neck il collo

necklace la collana

necktie la cravatta

need: I need ... ho bisogno di... [o beez**on**-yo dee]

do I need to pay? devo pagare? [**day**vo pa**gar**ay]

needle l'ago m

negative (film) la negativa

neither: neither (one) of them nessuno dei due [nays-**soo**no day doo-ay]

neither ... nor ... né... né... [nay]

nephew il nipote [nee**po**tay]

net (in sport) la rete [**ray**tay]

Netherlands i Paesi Bassi [pa-**ay**zee]

network map la piantina dei trasporti pubblici [**poob**-bleechee]

never mai [ma-ee]

dialogue

have you ever been to Rome? è mai stato a Roma? [eh]
no, never; I've never been there no, mai; non ci sono mai stato [chee]

new nuovo [**nwo**vo]

news (radio, TV etc) le notizie [no**teet**zee-ay]

newsagent's il giornalaio [jorna**la**-yo]

newspaper il giornale [jorna**lay**]

newspaper kiosk l'edicola f

New Year l'anno nuovo m [**nwo**vo]

Happy New Year! felice anno nuovo! [fe**lee**-chay]

New Year's Eve la notte di Capodanno, la notte di San Silvestro [**not**-tay dee]

New Zealand la Nuova
Zelanda [nwova tzaylanda]
New Zealander: I'm a New
Zealander sono neozelandese
[nay-otzelandayzay]
next prossimo
the next turning/street on the
left la prossima svolta/strada
a sinistra
at the next stop alla prossima
fermata
next week la settimana
prossima
next to vicino a [veecheeno]
nice (food) buono [bwono]
(looks, view etc) bello
(person) simpatico
niece la nipote [neepotay]
night la notte [not-tay]
at night di notte
good night buonanotte
[bwonanot-tay]

dialogue

do you have a single room
for one night? avete una
stanza singola per una
notte? [avaytay oona stantza]
yes, madam sì, signora
how much is it per night?
quanto si paga per notte?
[pair]
it's 75 euros for one night
settantacinque euro per
notte [set-tantacheenkway
ay-ooro]
thank you, I'll take it grazie,
la prendo [gratzee-ay]

nightclub il night
nightdress la camicia da notte
[kameecha da not-tay]
night porter il portiere di
notte [port-yairay dee]
no no
I've no change non ho
spiccioli [o speech-yolee]
there's no ... left non c'è
più... [cheh p-yoo]
no way! assolutamente no!
oh no! (upset) oh no!
nobody nessuno [nes-soono]
there's nobody there non c'è
nessuno [chay]
noise il rumore [roomoray]
noisy: it's too noisy c'è troppo
rumore
non-alcoholic analcolico
none nessuno [nes-soono]
nonsmoking compartment la
carrozza per non fumatori
[kar-rotza pair non foomatoree]
noon mezzogiorno
[medzojorno]
no-one nessuno [nes-soono]
nor: nor do I nemmeno io
[nem-mayno ee-o]
normal normale [normalay]
north il nord
in the north al nord
north of Rome a nord di
Roma
northern settentrionale [set-
tentr-yonalay]
Northern Ireland l'Irlanda del
Nord f [eerlanda]
Norway la Norvegia [norvayja]
nose il naso

nosebleed il sangue dal naso [sangway]

not* non

  no, I'm not hungry no, non ho fame [o famay]

  I don't want any, thank you non ne voglio, grazie [nay vol-yo]

  it's not necessary non è necessario [ay neches-sar-yo]

  I didn't know that non lo sapevo [sapayvo]

  not that one – this one non quello – questo [kwel-lo – kwesto]

note (banknote) la banconota

notebook il notes

notepaper (for letters) la carta da lettere [let-tairay]

nothing niente [n-yentay]

  nothing for me, thanks per me niente, grazie [pair may]

  nothing else nient'altro

novel il romanzo [romantzo]

November novembre [novembray]

now adesso

number il numero [noomairo]

  I've got the wrong number ho sbagliato numero [o zbal-yato]

  what is your phone number? qual è il suo numero di telefono? [kwal ay eel soo-o]

number plate la targa

nurse (man/woman) l'infermiere m [enfairm-yairay]/ l'infermiera f

nursery slope la pista per principianti [pair preencheep-yantay]

nut (for bolt) il dado

nuts le noci [nochee]

O

o'clock*: at 7 o'clock alle sette [al-lay]

occupied (toilet) occupato [ok-koopato]

October ottobre [ot-tobray]

odd (strange) strano

of* di [dee]

off (lights) spento

  it's just off corso Europa è una traversa di corso Europa [ay – travairsa]

  we're off tomorrow partiamo domani [part-yamo]

offensive offensivo

office (place of work) l'ufficio m [oof-feecho]

officer (said to policeman) agente [ajentay]

often spesso

  not often non spesso

  how often are the buses? ogni quanto passano gli autobus? [on-yee kwanto]

oil l'olio m [ol-yo]

ointment l'unguento m [oongwento]

OK d'accordo

  are you OK? tutto bene? [toot-to baynay]

  is that OK with you? ti/le va bene? [lay]

  is it OK to ...? si può...? [pwo]

that's OK thanks va bene così grazie [kozee]

I'm OK (nothing for me) io sono a posto [ee-o]

(I feel OK) sto bene

is this train OK for ...? questo treno va bene per...? [kwesto]

I said I'm sorry, OK ho chiesto scusa, va bene? [o k-yesto skooza]

old vecchio [vek-yo]

dialogue

how old are you? quanti anni ha? [kwantee an-nee a]

I'm twenty-five ho venticinque anni [o]

and you? e lei? [ay lay]

old-fashioned fuori moda [fworee]

old town (old part of town) la città vecchia [cheet-ta vek-ya]

in the old town nella città vecchia

olive oil l'olio di oliva m [ol-yo]

olives le olive [oleevay]

black/green olives le olive nere/verdi [nairay/vairday]

omelette la frittata

on* su [soo]

on the street/beach sulla strada/sulla spiaggia

is it on this road? è su questa strada? [ay soo kwesta]

on the plane sull'aereo

on Saturday sabato

on television alla televisione

I haven't got it on me non ce l'ho con me [non chay lo kon may]

this one's on me (drink) offro io da bere [ee-o da bairay]

the light wasn't on la luce non era accesa [loochay non aira achayza]

what's on tonight? cosa c'è da vedere stasera? [koza chay da vedairay stasaira]

once (one time) una volta

at once (immediately) immediatamente [eem-med-yatamentay]

one* uno [oono], una [oona]

the white one quello bianco, [kwel-lo], quella bianca

one-way ticket: a one-way ticket to ... un biglietto di sola andata per... [beel-yet-to – pair]

onions le cipolle [cheepol-lay]

only solo

only one solo uno

it's only 6 o'clock sono solo le sei

I've only just got here sono appena arrivato [ap-payna]

on/off switch l'interruttore m [eentair-root-toray]

open (adj) aperto [apairto]

(verb: door, of shop) aprire [apreeray]

when do you open? quando aprite? [kwando apreetay]

I can't get it open non riesco ad aprirlo/aprirla [r-yesko ad apreerlo/apreerla]

in the open air all'aria aperta
opening times l'orario di apertura m [orar-yo dee apairtoora]
open ticket il biglietto aperto [beel-yet-to apairto]
opera l'opera f [opaira]
operation (medical) l'operazione f [opairatz-yonay]
operator (telephone) il/la centralinista [chentraleeneesta]
opposite: the opposite direction la direzione opposta [deeretz-yonay]
the bar opposite il bar di fronte [frontay]
opposite my hotel di fronte al mio albergo
optician l'ottico m
or o
orange (fruit) l'arancia f [arancha]
(colour) arancione [aranchonay]
orange juice il succo d'arancia [sook-ko]
(freshly squeezed) la spremuta d'arancia [spremoota]
(fizzy) l'aranciata f [aranchata]
orchestra l'orchestra f
order: can we order now? (in restaurant) possiamo ordinare ora? [pos-yamo ordeenaray]
I've already ordered, thanks ho già ordinato, grazie [o ja]
I didn't order this non ho ordinato questo [kwesto]
out of order fuori servizio [fworee sairveetz-yo]
ordinary ordinario

other altro
the other one l'altro, l'altra
the other day l'altro giorno
I'm waiting for the others aspetto gli altri [aspet-to l-yee]
do you have any others? ne avete degli altri? [nay avaytay dayl-yee]
otherwise altrimenti
our* il nostro, la nostra, i nostri, le nostre
ours* il nostro, la nostra, i nostri, le nostre
out: he's out è fuori [ay fworee]
three kilometres out of town tre chilometri fuori città [keelometree fworee cheet-ta]
outdoors all'aperto [apairto]
outside fuori di [fworee dee]
can we sit outside? possiamo sedere fuori? [pos-yamo sedairay]
oven il forno
over: over here qui [kwee]
over there lì
over 500 più di cinquecento [p-yoo]
it's over è finito/finita [ay]
overcharge: you've overcharged me c'è un errore nel conto [chay oon air-roray]
overlook: I'd like a room overlooking the courtyard vorrei una stanza che dia sul cortile [vor-ray – kay dee-a sool korteelay]
overcoat il soprabito
overnight (travel) di notte [dee not-tay]

overtake sorpassare [sorpassaray]

owe: how much do I owe you? quanto le devo? [kwanto lay dayvo]

own: my own ... il mio...

are you on your own? è da solo/sola? [ay]

I'm on my own sono da solo/sola

owner (man/woman) il proprietario [propree-etar-yo], la proprietaria

P

pack (verb) fare le valigie [faray lay valeejay]

a pack of ... un pacco di...

package (small parcel) il pacco

package holiday la vacanza organizzata [vakantza organeetzata]

packed lunch il pranzo al sacco [prantzo]

packet: a packet of cigarettes un pacchetto di sigarette [pak-ket-to dee seegaret-tay]

padlock il lucchetto [look-ket-to]

Padua Padova [padova]

page (of book) la pagina [pajeena]

could you page Mr ...? può far chiamare il signor...? [pwo – k-yamaray]

pain il dolore [doloray]

I have a pain here mi fa male qui [mee fa malay kwee]

painful doloroso

painkillers gli analgesici [analjayzeechee]

paint la vernice [vairneechay]

painting il dipinto

pair: a pair of ... un paio di... [pa-yo]

Pakistani pachistano [pakeestano]

palace il palazzo [palatzo]

pale pallido

pale blue blu chiaro [k-yaro]

pan la pentola

panties le mutande [mootanday]

pants (underwear: men's/women's) le mutande

(US) i pantaloni

pantyhose il collant [kol-lan]

paper la carta

(newspaper) il giornale [jornalay]

a piece of paper un pezzo di carta [petzo]

paper handkerchiefs i fazzoletti di carta [fatzolet-tee]

parcel il pacco

pardon (me)? (didn't understand/hear) prego? [praygo]

parents i genitori [jeneetoree]

parents-in-law i suoceri [swochairee]

park il parco

(verb: the car) parcheggiare [parkej-jaray]

can I park here? posso parcheggiare qui? [kwee]

parking lot il parcheggio [parkej-jo]

part la parte [partay]
partner (boyfriend, girlfriend etc)
  il/la partner
party (group) il gruppo [groop-
  po]
  (celebration) la festa
pass (in mountains) il passo
passenger (man/woman) il
  passeggero [pas-sej-jairo], la
  passeggera
passport il passaporto
past: in the past in passato
  just past the information
  office appena dopo l'ufficio
  informazioni [ap-payna]
path il sentiero [sent-yairo]
pattern il motivo
pavement il marciapiede
  [marchap-yayday]
  on the pavement sul
  marciapiede
pavement café il caffé
  all'aperto [kaf-fay
  al-lapairto]
pay (verb) pagare [pagaray]
  can I pay, please? il conto,
  per favore
  it's already paid for è già
  pagato [ay ja]

dialogue

who's paying? chi paga?
  [kee]
I'll pay pago io [ee-o]
no, you paid last time,
I'll pay no, tu hai pagato
l'altra volta, pago io [a-ee]

pay phone il telefono
  pubblico
peaceful tranquillo
  [trankweelo]
peach la pesca
peanuts le arachidi [arakeedee]
pear la perla [pairla]
peas i piselli
peculiar strano
pedestrian crossing il
  passaggio pedonale [pas-saj-jo
  pedonalay]
pedestrian precinct la zona
  pedonale [tzona]
peg (for washing) la molletta
  (for tent) il picchetto [peek-ket-
  to]
pen la penna
pencil la matita
penfriend il/la corrispondente
  [kor-reespondentay]
penicillin la penicillina
  [peneecheel-leena]
penknife il temperino
  [tempaireeno]
pensioner (man/woman) il
  pensionato [pens-yonato], la
  pensionata
people la gente [jentay]
  the other people in the hotel
  le altre persone all'albergo
  [lay altray pairsonay]
  too many people troppa
  gente [trop-pa]
pepper (spice) il pepe [paypay]
  (vegetable) il peperone
  [peperonay]
peppermint (sweet) la
  caramella alla menta

per: per night a notte [not-tay]
how much per day? quanto
(costa) al giorno? [kwanto]
per cent per cento [pair
chento]
perfect perfetto [pairfet-to]
perfume il profumo [profoomo]
perhaps forse [forsay]
perhaps not forse no
period (of time) il periodo
[pairee-odo]
(menstruation) le mestruazioni
[mestroo-atz-yonee]
perm la permanente
[pairmanentay]
permit il permesso [pairmes-so]
person la persona [pairsona]
personal stereo il
walkman®
petrol la benzina [bentzeena]
petrol can la latta di benzina
[bentzeena]
petrol station la stazione
di servizio [statz-yonay dee
sairveetz-yo]
pharmacy la farmacia
[farmachee-a]
phone il telefono [telayfono]
(verb) telefonare [telefonaray]
phone book l'elenco
telefonico m
phone box la cabina telefonica
phonecard la scheda
telefonica [skayda], la carta
telefonica
phone number il numero
di telefono [noomairo dee
telayfono]
photo la fotografia [fotografee-a]

excuse me, could you take a
photo of us? scusi, può farci
una fotografia? [skoozee, pwo
farchee]
phrasebook il frasario [frazar-
yo]
piano il pianoforte
pickpocket (man/woman) il
borsaiolo [borsa-yolo], la
borsaiola
pick up: will you be there to
pick me up? vieni/viene a
prendermi lì? [vyaynee/vyaynay
a prendairmee]
picnic il picnic
picture (painting) il quadro
[kwadro]
(photo) la fotografia [fotografee-
a]
pie (meat) il pasticcio
[pasteecho]
(fruit) la torta
piece il pezzo [petzo]
a piece of ... un pezzo
di...
pill la pillola [pillola]
I'm on the pill prendo la
pillola
pillow il cuscino [koosheeno]
pillow case la federa
[faydaira]
pin lo spillo [speel-lo]
pineapple l'ananas m
pineapple juice il succo
d'ananas [sook-ko]
pink rosa
pipe (for smoking) la pipa
(for water) il tubo [toobo]
pipe cleaners gli scovolini

pity: it's a pity è un peccato [ay]

pizza la pizza

place il posto

is this place taken? è occupato questo posto? [ay ok-koopato kwesto]

at your place a casa tua/sua [too-a/soo-a]

at his place a casa sua

plain (not patterned) in tinta unita [ooneeta]

plane l'aereo m [a-airay-o]

by plane in aereo

plant la pianta [p-yanta]

plaster cast il gesso [jes-so]

plasters i cerotti [chairot-tee]

plastic la plastica

(credit card) la carta di credito [kraydeeto]

plastic bag il sacchetto di plastica [sak-ket-to]

plate il piatto [p-yat-to]

platform il marciapiede [marchapyayday]

which platform is it for Milan, please? su quale binario parte il treno per Milano, per favore? [soo kwalay beenar-yo partay eel trayno pair]

play (verb: game, sport) giocare [jokaray]

(instrument) suonare [swonaray]

(noun: in theatre) la commedia [kom-mayd-ya]

playground il parco giochi [jokee]

pleasant piacevole [p-yachayvolay]

please per favore [pair favoray]

yes please sì, grazie [see gratzee-ay]

could you please ...? potrebbe per favore...? [potrayb-bay]

please don't ... per favore non...

pleased to meet you piacere di conoscerla [p-yachairay dee konoshairla]

pleasure il piacere

my pleasure (not at all) non c'è di che [chay dee kay]

plenty: plenty of ... molto/molta/molti/molte...

there's plenty of time c'è (ancora) molto tempo [chay]

that's plenty, thanks basta così, grazie [kozee gratzee-ay]

pliers le pinze [peentzay]

plug (electrical) la spina

(for car) la candela [kandayla]

(in sink) il tappo

plumber l'idraulico m [eedrowleeko]

p.m.* del pomeriggio [pomaireej-jo](in the evening) di sera [saira]

poached egg l'uovo in camicia m [lwovo een kameecha]

pocket la tasca

point: two point five due virgola cinque

there's no point è inutile [ay eenooteelay]

points (in car) le puntine [poonteenay]

poisonous velenoso [velenozo]

police la polizia [poleetzee-a]
(military police) i carabinieri
[karabeen-yairee]
call the police! chiamate la
polizia! [k-yamatay]
policeman il poliziotto
[poleetz-yot-to]
police station il
commissariato
policewoman la donna
poliziotto [poleetz-yot-to]
polish il lucido [loocheedo]
polite educato [edookato]
polluted inquinato
[eenkweenato]
pony il pony
pool (for swimming) la piscina
[peesheena]
poor (not rich) povero [povairo]
(quality) scadente [skadentay]
Pope il Papa
pop music la musica pop
[moozeeka]
pop singer il/la cantante pop
[kantantay]
population la popolazione
[popolatz-yonay]
pork il maiale [ma-yalay]
port il porto
porter (in hotel) il portiere [port-
yairay]
portrait il ritratto
posh chic [sheek]
possible possibile [pos-
seebeelay]
is it possible to ...? è
possibile...? [ay]
as soon as possible al più
presto possibile [p-yoo]

post (mail) la posta
(verb) impostare [eempostaray]
could you post this for me?
potrebbe imbucare questa
per me? [potreb-bay eembookaray
kwesta pair may]
postbox la buca delle lettere
[booka del-lay let-tairay]
postcard la cartolina
postcode il codice postale
[kodeechay postalay]
poster il manifesto
post office l'ufficio postale **m**
[oof-feecho postalay]
poste restante il fermo posta
[fairmo]
potato la patata
potato chips le patatine
[patateenay]
pots and pans le pentole
[pentolay]
pottery la ceramica
[chairameeka]
pound (money) la sterlina
[stairleena]
(weight)* la libbra
power cut l'interruzione della
corrente **f** [eentair-rootz-yonay
del-la kor-rentay]
power point la presa di
corrente [prayza dee]
practise: **I want to practise
my Italian** voglio esercitarmi
a parlare italiano [vol-yo
esaircheetarmee a parlaray]
prawns i gamberetti
[gambairet-tee]
prefer: **I prefer ...** preferisco...
[prefaireesko]

pregnant incinta [eencheenta]

prescription (for medicine) la ricetta [reechet-ta]

present il regalo

president (of country) il/la presidente [prezeedentay]

pretty grazioso [gratz-yozo]

it's pretty expensive è piuttosto caro [ay p-yootosto karo]

price il prezzo [pretzo]

priest il sacerdote [sachairdotay]

prime minister il primo ministro

printed matter le stampe [stampay]

priority (in driving) la precedenza [prechedentza]

prison la prigione [preejonay]

private privato

private bathroom il bagno in camera [ban-yo een kamaira]

probably probabilmente [probabeelmentay]

problem il problema [problayma]

no problem! nessun problema

program(me) il programma

promise: I promise prometto

pronounce: how is this pronounced? come si pronuncia? [komay see pronooncha]

properly (repaired, locked etc) bene [baynay]

protection factor il fattore di protezione [fat-toray dee protetz-yonay]

Protestant protestante [-tantay]

public convenience i gabinetti pubblici [poob-bleechee]

public holiday la festa nazionale [natzyonalay]

pudding il dessert [des-sair]

pull tirare [teeraray]

pullover il pullover

puncture la foratura [foratoora]

purple viola [v-yola]

purse (for money) il portamonete [portamonaytay] (US) la borsetta

push spingere [speenjairay]

pushchair il passeggino [pas-sej-jeeno]

put mettere [met-tairay]

where can I put ...? dove posso mettere…? [dovay]

could you put us up for the night? ci può ospitare per una notte? [chee pwo ospeetaray pair]

pyjamas il pigiama [peejama]

Q

quality la qualità [kwaleeta]

quarantine la quarantena [kwarantayna]

quarter il quarto [kwarto]

quayside: on the quayside sulla banchina [sool-la bankeena]

question la domanda

queue la fila

quick veloce [velochay]

that was quick che velocità [kay velocheeta]

what's the quickest way
there? qual è il modo più
rapido per arrivarci? [kwal
ay eel modo p-yoo rapeedo pair
arreevarchee]
fancy a quick drink? ti/le va
di bere qualcosa
rapidamente? [lay – bairay
kwalkoza rapeedamentay]
quickly velocemente
[velochementay]
quiet (place, hotel) tranquillo
[trankweel-lo]
quiet! silenzio! [seelentz-yo]
quite (fairly) abbastanza [ab-
bastantza]
(very) molto
that's quite right è proprio
giusto [ay – joosto]
quite a lot moltissimo

R

rabbit il coniglio [coneel-yo]
race (for runners, cars) la corsa
racket (tennis, squash) la
racchetta [rak-ket-ta]
radiator il radiatore [rad-
yatoray]
radio la radio
on the radio alla radio
rail: by rail in treno [trayno]
railway la ferrovia [fair-
rovee-a]
rain la pioggia [p-yoj-ja]
in the rain sotto la pioggia
it's raining piove [p-yovay]
raincoat l'impermeabile m

[eempairmay-abeelay]
randy arrapato
rape lo stupro [stoopro]
rare (steak) al sangue [sangway]
rash (on skin) l'eruzione
cutanea f [erootz-yonay kootanay-
a]
raspberry il lampone
[lamponay]
rat il ratto
rate (for changing money) il
cambio [kamb-yo]
rather: it's rather good è
piuttosto buono [ay p-yoot-
tosto bwono]
I'd rather ... preferirei...
[prefaireeray]
razor il rasoio [raso-yo]
razor blades le lamette [lamet-
tay]
read (verb) leggere [lej-
jairay]
ready pronto
are you ready? sei/è pronto/
pronta? [say/ay]
I'm not ready yet non sono
ancora pronto/pronta

dialogue

when will it be ready?
quando sarà pronto?
[kwando]
it should be ready in a
couple of days dovrebbe
essere pronto tra un
paio di giorni [dovreb-bay
es-sairay – pa-yo dee
jornee]

real reale [ray-alay]
really veramente [vairamentay]
  I'm really sorry sono
  veramente spiacente [spee-
  achentay]
  that's really great è proprio
  magnifico
  really? davvero? [dav-vairo]
rearview mirror lo specchietto
  retrovisore [spek-yet-to
  retroveezoray]
reasonable (prices etc) moderato
receipt la ricevuta [reechevoota]
recently recentemente
  [rechentementay]
reception (in hotel) la reception
  (for guests) il ricevimento
  [reecheveemento]
  at reception alla reception
reception desk la reception
receptionist il/la receptionist
recognize riconoscere
  [reekonoshairay]
recommend: could you
  recommend ...? mi potrebbe
  consigliare...? [mee potreb-bay
  konseel-yaray]
record (music) il disco
red rosso
red wine il vino rosso
refund il rimborso
  can I have a refund? mi può
  rimborsare? [pwo reemborsaray]
region la regione [rejonay]
registered: by registered mail
  (per) raccomandata
registration number il numero
  di immatricolazione
  [noomairo dee eemmatreekolatz-

yonay]
relative il/la parente [parentay]
religion la religione [releejonay]
remember: I don't remember
  non ricordo
  I remember mi ricordo
  do you remember? ti ricordi/
  si ricorda?
rent (for apartment etc) l'affitto m
  (verb) noleggiare [nolej-jaray]
  to rent a nolo
rented car la macchina a
  noleggio [mak-keena a nolej-jo]
repair (verb) riparare
  [reepararay]
  can you repair it? lo/la può
  riparare? [pwo]
repeat ripetere [repetairay]
  could you repeat that? può
  ripetere? [pwo]
reservation la prenotazione
  [prenotatz-yonay]
  I'd like to make a reservation
  vorrei prenotare [vor-ray
  prenotaray]

dialogue

I have a reservation ho
prenotato [o]
yes sir, what name please?
sì, a che nome? [kay nomay]

reserve prenotare [prenotaray]

dialogue

can I reserve a table for
tonight? vorrei prenotare

un tavolo per stasera [vor-**ray** – pair stas**ai**ra]

yes madam, for how many people? sì, signora, per quante persone? [seen-**y**ora, pair kw**a**ntay pairs**o**nay]

for two per due

and for what time? per che ora? [pair kay]

for eight o'clock per le otto [lay]

and could I have your name please? il suo nome, per favore? [**soo**-o **no**may]

see **alphabet** for spelling

rest: I need a rest ho bisogno di riposarmi [o beez**o**n-yo]

the rest of the group il resto del gruppo

restaurant il ristorante [reestor**a**ntay]

restaurant car il vagone ristorante [va**go**nay reestor**a**ntay]

rest room la toilette [twal**et**] see **toilet**

retired: I'm retired sono in pensione [pens-y**o**nay]

return (ticket) il biglietto di andata e ritorno [beel-**yet**-to] see **ticket**

reverse charge call la telefonata a carico del destinatario

reverse gear la retromarcia [retrom**a**rcha]

revolting disgustoso [deezgoost**o**zo]

rib la costola

rice il riso [**ree**zo]

rich (person) ricco [**reek**-ko]

(food) sostanzioso [sostantz-**yo**zo]

ridiculous ridicolo

right (correct) giusto [**joo**sto]

(not left) destro

you were right avevi/aveva ragione [a**vay**vee/a**vay**va raj**o**nay]

that's right è giusto [ay]

this can't be right non è possibile [ay pos-**see**beelay]

right! d'accordo

is this the right road for ...? è la strada giusta per...? [ay – pair]

on the right a destra

turn right giri a destra [**jee**ree]

right-hand drive la guida a destra [**gwee**da]

ring (on finger) l'anello m

I'll ring you ti/le telefono [lay tel**ay**fono]

ring back ritelefonare [reetelefon**a**ray]

ripe (fruit) maturo [mat**oo**ro]

rip-off: it's a rip-off è un furto [ay oon **foo**rto]

rip-off prices i prezzi esorbitanti [**pret**zee]

risky rischioso [reesk-**yo**zo]

river il fiume [f-**yoo**may]

road la strada

is this the road for ...? è questa la strada per...? [ay **kwes**ta – pair]

down the road in fondo alla strada

road accident l'incidente

stradale m [eencheedentay stradalay]

road map la cartina stradale

roadsign il segnale stradale [sen-yalay]

rob: I've been robbed sono stato derubato/derubata! [dairoobato]

rock la roccia [rocha]
(music) il rock
on the rocks (with ice) con ghiaccio [g-yacho]

roll (bread) il panino

Roman (adj) romano
the Romans i Romani

Rome Roma

roof il tetto

roof rack il portapacchi [portapak-kee]

room la camera, la stanza [stantza]
in my room nella mia stanza [mee-a]

room service il servizio in camera [sairveetz-yo een]

rope la corda

rosé il rosé

roughly (approximately) grossomodo

round: it's my round tocca a me [may]

roundabout (for traffic) la rotatoria

round trip ticket il biglietto di andata e ritorno [beel-yet-to]
see ticket

route il tragitto [trajeet-to]
what's the best route? qual è il tragitto migliore? [kwalay

– meel-yoray]

rubber (material) la gomma
(eraser) la gomma (per cancellare) [pair kanchel-laray]

rubber band l'elastico m

rubbish (waste) i rifiuti [reef-yootee]
(poor quality goods) la porcheria [porkairee-a]

rubbish! (nonsense) sciocchezze! [shok-ketzay]

rucksack lo zaino [tza-eeno]

rude sgarbato [zgarbato]

ruins le rovine [roveenay]

rum il rum [room]
rum and coke la Coca-Cola® col rum

run (verb: person) correre [kor-rairay]
how often do the buses run? ogni quanto tempo passa l'autobus? [on-yee kwanto – lowtoboos]
I've run out of money sono rimasto senza soldi [sentza]

rush hour l'ora di punta f

S

sad triste [treestay]

saddle (for bike, horse) la sella

safe (not in danger) sicuro [seekooro]
(not dangerous) non pericoloso [paireekolozo]

safety pin la spilla di sicurezza [seekooretza]

sail la vela [vayla]

sailboard la tavola a vela
sailboarding il windsurf
salad l'insalata **f**
salad dressing il condimento per l'insalata [pair]
sale: for sale vendesi [vendesee]
salmon il salmone [sal-monay]
salt il sale [salay]
same: the same lo stesso
 the same as this come questo [komay kwesto]
 the same again, please un altro/un'altra, per favore
 it's all the same to me per me è lo stesso [pair may ay]
sand la sabbia
sandals i sandali
sandwich il panino imbottito
sanitary napkins gli assorbenti igienici [as-sorbentee eejayneechee]
sanitary towels gli assorbenti igienici
sardines le sardine [sardeenay]
Sardinia la Sardegna [sardayn-ya]
Saturday il sabato
sauce la salsa
saucepan la pentola
saucer il piattino [p-yat-teeno]
sauna la sauna [sowna]
sausage la salsiccia [salseecha]
say: how do you say ... in Italian? come si dice... in italiano? [komay see deechay ... een eetal-yano]
 what did he/she say? cos'ha detto? [koz a]

I said ... ho detto... [o]
he/she said ... ha detto... [a]
could you say that again? puoi/può ripetere, per favore? [pwoy/pwo reepetairay]
scarf (for neck) la sciarpa [sharpa]
 (for head) il foulard [foolar]
scenery il paesaggio [pa-ee-zaj-jo]
schedule (US) l'orario **m**
scheduled flight il volo di linea [leenay-a]
school la scuola [skwola]
scissors: a pair of scissors un paio di forbici [pa-yo dee forbeechee]
scooter lo scooter
Scotch lo scotch
Scotch tape® lo scotch
Scotland la Scozia [skotz-ya]
Scottish scozzese [skotzayzay]
 I'm Scottish sono scozzese
scrambled eggs le uova strapazzate [wova strapatzatay]
scratch il graffio [graf-fyo]
screw la vite [veetay]
screwdriver il cacciavite [kachaveetay]
scrubbing brush (for hands) lo spazzolino per le unghie [spatzoleeno pair lay oong-yay]
sea il mare [maray]
 by the sea sul mare [sool]
seafood i frutti di mare [froot-tee dee]
seafront il lungomare [loongomaray]
 on the seafront sul

lungomare [sool]

seagull il gabbiano [gab-yano]

search (verb) cercare
[chairkaray]

seashell la conchiglia [konkeel-ya]

seasick: I feel seasick ho mal
di mare [o – maray]
I get seasick soffro di mal di
mare

seaside: by the seaside sul
mare [sool]

seat il posto
is this anyone's seat? è libero
questo posto? [ay leebairo
kwesto]

seat belt la cintura di
sicurezza [cheentoora dee
seekooretza]

sea urchin il riccio di mare
[reecho dee maray]

seaweed le alghe marine
[algay mareenay]

secluded isolato

second (adj) secondo
(of time) il secondo
just a second! un attimo!

second class (travel) in seconda
classe [klassay]

second floor (UK) il secondo
piano (US) il primo piano

second-hand di seconda
mano

see vedere [vedairay]
can I see? posso vedere?
have you seen ...? hai/ha
visto... [a-ee/a]
I see (I understand) capisco
I saw him this morning l'ho

visto stamattina [lo]

self-catering apartment
l'appartamento (per le
vacanze) m [pair lay vakantzay]

self-service il self-service

sell vendere [vendairay]
do you sell ...? avete...?
[avaytay]

Sellotape® lo scotch

send mandare [mandaray]
I want to send this to England
voglio mandare questo in
Inghilterra [vol-yo – kwesto een
eengeeltair-ra]

senior citizen (man/woman) il
pensionato, la pensionata

separate separato

separated: I'm separated sono
separato/separata

separately (pay) a parte [partay]
(travel) separatamente
[separatamentay]

September settembre [set-tembray]

septic infetto

serious serio [sair-yo]

service charge (in restaurant) il
servizio [sairveetz-yo]

service station la stazione
di servizio [statz-yonay dee
sairveetz-yo]

serviette il tovagliolo [toval-yolo]

set menu il menù fisso
[menoo]

several diversi [deevairsee]

sew cucire [koocheeray]
**could you sew this back
on?** potrebbe riattaccarlo?

[potreb-bay r-yat-tak-karlo]

sex il sesso
  (sexual intercourse) il rapporto
  sessuale [ses-swalay]
sexy sexy
shade: in the shade all'ombra
shake: to shake hands
  stringersi la mano
  [streenjairsee]
shallow (water) poco profondo
shame: what a shame! che
  peccato! [kay]
shampoo lo shampoo
  shampoo and set shampoo e
  messa in piega [ay – p-yayga]
share (verb: room, table etc)
  dividere [deeveedairay]
sharp (knife) tagliente [tal-
  yentay]
  (taste) aspro
  (pain) acuto [akooto]
shattered (very tired) distrutto
  [deestroot-to]
shaver il rasoio [razo-yo]
shaving foam la schiuma da
  barba [sk-yooma]
shaving point la presa per il
  rasoio [prayza pair eel razo-yo]
she* lei [lay]
  is she here? è qui? [ay kwee]
sheet (for bed) il lenzuolo
  [lentz-wolo]
shelf lo scaffale [skaf-falay]
shellfish i frutti di mare [froot-
  tee dee maray]
sherry lo sherry
ship la nave [navay]
  by ship con la nave
shirt la camicia [kameecha]

shit! merda! [mairda]
shock lo shock
  **I got an electric shock from
  the ...** ho preso la scossa
  dal... [o prayzo]
shock-absorber
  l'ammortizzatore **m** [am-
  morteetzatoray]
shocking scandaloso
shoe la scarpa
  a pair of shoes un paio di
  scarpe [pa-yo dee skarpay]
shoelaces i lacci
shoe polish il lucido per
  le scarpe [loocheedo pair lay
  skarpay]
shoe repairer il calzolaio
  [kalzola-yo]
shop il negozio [negotz-yo]
shopping: I'm going shopping
  vado a far compere
  [kompairay]
shopping centre il centro
  commerciale [chentro kom-
  mairchalay]
shop window la vetrina
shore la riva
short (person) basso
  (time) poco
  (journey) corto
shortcut la scorciatoia
  [skorchato-ya]
shorts i calzoncini
  [kaltzoncheenee]
should: what should I do? cosa
  dovrei fare? [koza dovray faray]
  he shouldn't be long non ci
  dovrebbe mettere tanto [chee
  dovreb-bay met-tairay]

Sh

you should have told me
avresti dovuto dirmelo
[dovooto deermelo]

shoulder la spalla

shout (verb) gridare [greedaray]

show (in theatre) lo spettacolo

could you show me? mi
può far vedere? [mee pwo far
vedairay]

shower (in bathroom) la doccia
[docha]

with shower con doccia

shower gel il gel per la doccia
[pair]

shut (verb) chiudere
[k-yoodairay]

when do you shut? quando
chiudete? [kwando
k-yoodaytay]

when do they shut? quando
chiudono? [k-yoodono]

they're shut sono chiusi
[k-yoosee]

I've shut myself out mi sono
chiuso fuori [k-yoozo fworee]

shut up! stai zitto! [sty tzeet-
to]

shutter (on camera) l'otturatore
m [ot-tooratoray]

(on window) l'imposta f

shy timido

Sicily la Sicilia [seecheel-ya]

sick (US) malato

I'm going to be sick (vomit) sto
per vomitare [pair vomeetaray]
see ill

side il lato

the other side of town l'altra
parte della città [partay del-la

cheet-ta]

side lights le luci di posizione
[loochee dee poseetz-yonay]

side salad l'insalata f

side street la stradina
[stradeena]

sidewalk il marciapiede
[marchap-yayday]
see pavement

sight: the sights of ... le
attrazioni turistiche di... [at-
tratz-yonee tooreesteekay]

sightseeing: we're going
sightseeing andiamo a fare
un giro turistico [and-yamo a
faray oon jeero]

sightseeing tour il giro
turistico

sign (roadsign etc) il segnale
[sen-yalay]

signal: he didn't give a signal
non ha segnalato [a sen-yalato]

signature la firma

signpost il cartello stradale
[stradalay]

silence il silenzio [seelentz-yo]

silk la seta [sayta]

silly sciocco [shok-ko]

silver l'argento m [arjento]

silver foil la stagnola [stan-yola]

similar simile [seemeelay]

simple (easy) semplice
[sempleechay]

since: since yesterday da ieri
[yairee]

since I got here da quando
sono arrivato/arrivata
[kwando]

sing cantare [kantaray]

singer il/la cantante [kantantay]
single: a single to ... un
  biglietto di sola andata per...
  [beel-yet-to – pair]
 I'm single (man/woman) sono
  celibe/nubile [chaylee-bay/
  noobeelay]
single bed il letto a una piazza
  [p-yatza]
single room la camera singola
sink (in kitchen) l'acquaio m
  [akwa-yo]
sister la sorella
sister-in-law la cognata [kon-
  yata]
sit: can I sit here? posso sedere
  qui? [sedairay kwee]
 is anyone sitting here? è
  libero questo posto? [ay
  leebairo kwesto]
sit down sedersi [sedairsee]
size la taglia [tal-ya]
ski lo sci [shee]
 (verb) sciare [shee-aray]
 a pair of skis un paio di sci
  [pa-yo dee]
ski boots gli scarponi da sci
skiing lo sci
 we're going skiing andiamo a
  sciare [and-yamo a shee-aray]
ski instructor (man/woman) il
  maestro di sci [mystro dee
  shee]/la maestra di sci
ski-lift lo ski-lift
skin la pelle [pel-lay]
skin-diving l'immersione
  senza attrezzature f [eem-
  mairs-yonay sentza at-trez-
  zatooray]

skinny mingherlino
  [meengairleeno]
ski-pants i calzoni da sci
  [kaltzonee da shee]
ski-pass lo ski-pass
ski pole la racchetta da sci
  [rak-ket-ta da shee]
skirt la gonna
ski run la pista da sci [shee]
ski slope il campo da sci
ski wax la sciolina [shee-oleena]
sky il cielo [chaylo]
sleep (verb) dormire
  [dormeeray]
 did you sleep well? hai/ha
  dormito bene? [a-ee/a
  – baynay]
 I need a good sleep ho
  bisogno di fare una buona
  dormita [o beezon-yo dee faray
  oona bwona]
sleeper (on train) il vagone
  letto [vagonay]
sleeping bag il sacco a pelo
  [paylo]
sleeping car il vagone letto
  [vagonay]
sleeping pill il sonnifero [son-
  neefairo]
sleepy: I'm feeling sleepy ho
  sonno [o]
sleeve la manica
slide (photographic) la
  diapositiva
slip (under dress) la sottoveste
  [sot-to-vestay]
slippery scivoloso [sheevolozo]
Slovenia la Slovenia [slo-
  vayn-ya]

slow lento
  slow down! (driving) rallenta!
  (speaking) parla/parli più
  lentamente! [p-yoo lentamentay]
slowly lentamente
  could you say it slowly?
  puoi/può dirlo più
  lentamente? [pwoy/pwo deerlo
  p-yoo]
  very slowly molto lentamente
small piccolo
smell: it smells (smells bad)
  puzza [pootza]
smile (verb) sorridere [sor-
  reedairay]
smoke il fumo [foomo]
  do you mind if I smoke? le/ti
  dispiace se fumo? [lay/tee
  deespeeachay say]
  I don't smoke non fumo
  do you smoke? fuma/fumi?
snack: I'd just like a snack
  vorrei fare uno spuntino [vor-
  ray faray oono spoon-teeno]
sneeze lo sternuto [stairnooto]
snorkel il respiratore
  [respeeratoray]
snow la neve [nayvay]
  it's snowing nevica [nayveeka]
so: it's so expensive è così
  caro [ay]
  it's so good è proprio buono
  [bwono]
  not so fast più piano [p-yoo]
  so am I anch'io [ankee-o]
  so do I anch'io
  so-so così così
soaking solution (for
  contact lenses) la soluzione

conservante e disinfettante
per le lenti a contatto [solootz-
yonay konsairvantay ay deeseenfet-
tantay pair lay]
soap il sapone [saponay]
soap powder il detersivo
  (in polvere) [detairseevo een
  polvairay]
sober sobrio
sock il calzino [kaltzeeno]
socket (electrical) la presa
  [praysa]
soda (water) il seltz
sofa il divano
soft (material etc) morbido
soft-boiled egg l'uovo alla
  coque [wovo al-la kok]
soft drink la bibita (analcolica)
soft lenses le lenti morbide
  [morbeeday]
sole la suola [swola]
  could you put new soles on
  these? può risuolare queste
  scarpe? [pwo reeswolaray kwestay
  skarpay]
some: can I have some
  water/rolls? potrei avere
  dell'acqua/dei panini? [potray
  avairay – day]
  can I have some? posso
  averne un po'? [avairnay]
somebody, someone
  qualcuno [kwal-koono]
something qualcosa [kwalkoza]
  something to drink qualcosa
  da bere [bairay]
sometimes qualche volta
  [kwalkay]
somewhere da qualche parte

[partay]

son il figlio [feel-yo]

song la canzone [kantzonay]

son-in-law il genero [jaynairo]

soon presto

I'll be back soon torno fra poco

as soon as possible al più presto possibile [p-yoo – posseebeelay]

sore: it's sore mi fa male [malay]

sore throat il mal di gola

sorry: (I'm) sorry scusa/mi scusi [skooza/mee skoozee]

sorry? (didn't understand) prego? [praygo]

sort: what sort of ...? che tipo di...? [kay]

soup la minestra, la zuppa [tzoop-pa]

sour (taste) aspro

south il sud [sood]

in the south al sud

South Africa il Sudafrica [soodafreeka]

South African (adj) sudafricano [soodafree-kano]

I'm South African (man/woman) sono sudafricano/sudafricana

southeast il sud-est [soodest]

southwest il sud-ovest [soodovest]

souvenir il souvenir

spanner la chiave inglese [k-yavay eenglayzay]

spare part il pezzo di ricambio [petzo dee reekamb-yo]

spare tyre la gomma di scorta

spark plug la candela [kandayla]

speak: do you speak English? parla inglese? [eenglayzay]

I don't speak ... non parlo...

dialogue

can I speak to Roberto? posso parlare con Roberto? [parlaray]

who's calling? chi parla? [kee]

it's Patricia sono Patricia

I'm sorry, he's not in, can I take a message? mi dispiace, non c'è; vuole lasciare un messaggio? [mee deesp-yachay, non chay; vwolay lasharay oon mes-saj-jo]

no thanks, I'll call back later no, grazie, richiamo più tardi [reek-yamo p-yoo]

please tell him I called gli dica che ho chiamato, per favore [l-yee – kay o k-yamato]

spectacles gli occhiali [ok-yalee]

speed la velocità [velocheeta]

speed limit il limite di velocità [leemee-tay dee]

speedometer il tachimetro [takeemetro]

spell: how do you spell it? come si scrive? [komay see skreevay]

see alphabet

spend spendere [spendairay]

spider il ragno [ran-yo]

spin-dryer la centrifuga [chentreefooga]

splinter la scheggia [skej-ja]

spoke (in wheel) il raggio [raj-jo]

spoon il cucchiaio [kook-ya-yo]

sport lo sport

sprain: I've sprained my ... mi sono slogato... [zlogato]

spring (season) la primavera [preema-vaira]

(of car, seat) la molla

square (in town) la piazza [p-yatza]

stairs le scale [skalay]

stale (bread) raffermo [raffairmo]

(taste) sa di vecchio [vek-yo]

stall: the engine keeps stalling il motore si spegne in continuazione [motoray see spen-yay een konteenoo-atz-yonay]

stamp il francobollo

dialogue

a stamp for England, please un francobollo per l'Inghilterra, per favore [pair]

what are you sending? per che cosa? [kay koza]

this postcard per questa cartolina [kwesta]

standby (flight) il volo stand-by

star la stella

start l'inizio m [eeneetz-yo]

(verb) cominciare [komeencharay]

when does it start? quando comincia? [kwando komeencha]

the car won't start la macchina non parte [makkeena]

starter (of car) lo starter

(food) l'antipasto m

starving: I'm starving sto morendo di fame [famay]

state (in country) lo stato

the States (USA) gli Stati Uniti [l-yee – ooneetee]

station la stazione [statz-yonay]

statue la statua [statoo-a]

stay: where are you staying? dove'è alloggiato/ alloggiata? [dovay ay al-loj-jato]

I'm staying at ... sono (alloggiato/alloggiata) a...

I'd like to stay another two nights vorrei fermarmi ancora due notti [vor-ray fairmarmee]

steak la bistecca

steal rubare [roobaray]

my bag has been stolen mi hanno rubato la borsa [mee an-no roobato]

steep (hill) ripido

steering lo sterzo [stairtzo]

step: on the steps sui gradini

stereo lo stereo [stairay-o]

sterling la sterlina [stairleena]

steward (on plane) lo steward

stewardess la hostess

sticking plaster il cerotto [chairot-to]

still ancora

I'm still waiting sto ancora aspettando

is he still there? è ancora lì? [ay]

keep still! sta' fermo/ferma! [fairmo]

sting: I've been stung sono stato punto [poonto]

stockings le calze [kaltzay]

stomach lo stomaco

stomach ache il mal di stomaco

stone (rock) la pietra [p-yetra]

stop (verb) fermare [fairmaray]

please, stop here (to taxi driver etc) fermi qui, per favore [fairmee kwee]

do you stop near ...? ferma vicino a...? [veecheeno]

stop doing that! smettila! [zmet-teela]

stopover la sosta

storm la tempesta

straight: straight ahead avanti diritto

a straight whisky un whisky liscio [leesho]

straightaway immediatamente [eem-med-yatamentay]

strange (odd) strano

stranger (man/woman) lo straniero [stran-yairo]/la straniera

I'm a stranger here non sono di qui [kwee]

strap (on watch) il cinturino [cheentooreeno]

(on dress) la spallina

(on suitcase) la cinghia [cheeng-ya]

strawberry la fragola

stream il ruscello [rooshel-lo]

street la strada

on the street sulla strada [sool-la]

streetmap la piantina della città [p-yanteena del-la cheet-ta]

string lo spago

strong forte [fortay]

stuck bloccato

the key's stuck la chiave si è bloccata [k-yavay see ay]

student (man/woman) lo studente/la studentessa [stoodentay/stoodentes-sa]

stupid stupido [stoopeedo]

suburb la periferia

subway (US) la metropolitana

suddenly improvvisamente [eemprov-veezamentay]

suede la pelle scamosciata [pel-lay skamo-shata]

sugar lo zucchero [tzook-kairo]

suit il completo [komplayto]

it doesn't suit me (jacket etc) non mi sta bene [baynay]

it suits you ti sta bene

suitcase la valigia [valeeja]

summer l'estate f [estatay]

in the summer d'estate

sun il sole [solay]

in the sun al sole

out of the sun all'ombra

sunbathe prendere il sole [prendairay eel solay]

sunblock (cream) la crema a

protezione totale [krayma a protetz-yonay totalay]

sunburn la scottatura [skottatoora]

sunburnt scottato

Sunday la domenica [domayneeka]

sunglasses gli occhiali da sole [ok-yalee da solay]

sun lounger (chair) il lettino

sunny assolato
it's sunny c'è il sole [chay eel solay]

sun roof (in car) il tetto apribile [apree-beelay]

sunset il tramonto

sunshade il parasole [parasolay]

sunshine la luce del sole [loochay del solay]

sunstroke il colpo di sole

suntan l'abbronzatura f [abbrontzatoora]

suntan lotion la lozione solare [lotz-yonay solaray]

suntanned abbronzato [abbrontzato]

suntan oil l'olio solare m [ol-yo solaray]

super fantastico

supermarket il supermercato [soopair-mairkato]

supper la cena [chayna]

supplement (extra charge) il supplemento [soop-plemento]

sure sicuro [seekooro]
are you sure? sei/è sicuro/sicura? [say/ay]
sure! certo! [chairto]

surname il cognome [kon-

yomay]

swearword la parolaccia [parolacha]

sweater il maglione [mal-yonay]

sweatshirt la felpa

Sweden la Svezia [zvetzee-a]

Swedish (adj) svedese [zvedayzay]

sweet (taste) dolce [dolchay]
(noun: dessert) il dolce

sweets le caramelle [karamel-lay]

swelling il gonfiore [gonf-yoray]

swim (verb) nuotare [nwotaray]
I'm going for a swim vado a fare una nuotata [faray oona nwotata]
let's go for a swim andiamo a fare una nuotata [and-yamo]

swimming costume il costume da bagno [kostoomay da ban-yo]

swimming pool la piscina [pee-sheena]

swimming trunks il costume da bagno [kostoomay da ban-yo]

Swiss svizzero [zveetzairo]

switch l'interruttore m [eentair-root-toray]

switch off (engine, TV, lights) spegnere [spen-yairay]

switch on (engine, TV, lights) accendere [achendairay]

Switzerland la Svizzera [sveetzaira]

swollen gonfio [gonf-yo]

T

table il tavolo
 a table for two un tavolo per
 due [pair]
table cloth la tovaglia [toval-ya]
table tennis il ping-pong
table wine il vino da tavola
tailback (of traffic) la coda
tailor il sarto
take (pick up, catch) prendere
 [prendairay]
 (accept) accettare [achetaray]
 can you take me to the
 airport? può portarmi
 all'aeroporto?
 do you take credit cards?
 accettate carte di credito?
 [achet-tatay kartay dee kraydeeto]
 fine, I'll take it va bene, lo/la
 prendo [baynay]
 can I take this? (leaflet etc)
 posso prenderlo/prenderla?
 how long does it take?
 quanto ci vuole? [kwanto chee
 vwolay]
 it takes three hours ci
 vogliono tre ore [chee vol-
 yono]
 is this seat taken? è occupato
 questo posto? [ay ok-koopato
 kwesto]
 pizza to take away una pizza
 da portare via [portaray vee-a]
 can you take a little off here?
 (to hairdresser) può tagliare un
 po' qui? [pwo tal-yaray oon po
 kwee]

talcum powder il talco
talk (verb) parlare [parlaray]
tall alto
tampons i tamponi
tan l'abbronzatura f [ab-
 brontzatoora]
 to get a tan abbronzarsi [ab-
 brontzarsee]
tank (of car) il serbatoio
 [sairbato-yo]
tap il rubinetto [roobeenet-to]
tape (cassette) la cassetta
 (sticky) il nastro adesivo
 [adezeevo]
tape measure il metro a
 nastro
tape recorder il registratore
 [rejeestratoray]
taste il gusto [goosto]
 can I taste it? posso
 assaggiarlo/assaggiarla? [as-
 saj-jarlo]
taxi il taxi
 will you get me a taxi? mi
 può chiamare un taxi? [pwo
 k-yamaray]
 where can I find a taxi? dove
 posso prendere un taxi?
 [dovay – prendairay]

dialogue

to the airport/to
Hotel Centrale please
all'aeroporto/all'albergo
Centrale, per favore
how much will it be?
quanto verrà a costare?
[kwanto – kostaray]

30 euros trenta euro [ay-ooro]
that's fine, right here, thanks va bene qui, grazie [baynay kwee]

taxi-driver il tassista
taxi rank il posteggio dei taxi [postej-jo day]
tea (drink) il tè [tay]
tea for one/two, please un/due tè, per favore
teabags le bustine di tè [boosteenay dee tay]
teach: could you teach me? mi puoi/può insegnare? [mee pwoy/pwo eensen-yaray]
teacher l'insegnante m/f [eensen-yantay]
team la squadra [skwadra]
teaspoon il cucchiaino da tè [kook-kee-a-eeno da tay]
tea towel lo strofinaccio [strofeenacho]
teenager l'adolescente m/f [adoleshentay]
telegram il telegramma
telephone
see phone and speak
television la televisione [televeez-yonay]
tell: could you tell him ...? potresti/potrebbe dirgli...? [potreb-bay deerl-yee]
temperature (weather) la temperatura [tempairatoora] (fever) la febbre [feb-bray]
temple (building) il tempio
tennis il tennis

tennis ball la palla da tennis
tennis court il campo da tennis
tennis racket la racchetta da tennis [rak-ket-ta]
tent la tenda
term (at university, school) il trimestre [treemestray]
terminus (rail) il capolinea [kapoleenay-a]
terrible terribile [tair-reebeelay]
terrific fantastico
than* di [dee]
smaller than più piccolo di [p-yoo]
thanks, thank you grazie [gratzee-ay]
thank you very much grazie mille [meel-lay]
thanks for the lift grazie del passaggio
no thanks no grazie

dialogue

thanks grazie [gratzee-ay]
that's OK, don't mention it prego [praygo]

that: that man quell'uomo [kwel womo]
that woman quella donna [kwel-la]
that one quello/quella lì [kwel-lo]
I hope that ... spero che... [spairo kay]
that's nice (food) è buono/buona [bwono]

is that ...? (quello/quella)
è...?

that's it (that's right)
esattamente [ezat-tamentay]

the* il, lo, la [eel] ; i, gli, le
[l]-yee, lay]

theatre il teatro [tay-atro]

their(s)* il loro, la loro, i loro,
le loro

them*: for them per loro
with them con loro
I gave it to them l'ho dato a
loro [lo]
who? – them chi? – loro [kee]

then (at that time) allora
(after that) poi [poy]

there là
over there laggiù [laj-joo]
up there lassù [las-soo]
is there ...? c'è...? [chay]
are there ...? ci sono...? [chee]
there is ... c'è...
there are ... ci sono...
there you are (giving something)
ecco qua [kwa]

thermometer il termometro
[tairmometro]

thermos flask il thermos
[tairmos]

these: these men questi
uomini [kwestee]
these women queste donne
[kwestay]
can I have these? vorrei
questi/queste [vor-ray]

they* loro

thick spesso
(stupid) ottuso [ot-toozo]

thief il ladro

thigh la coscia [kosha]

thin sottile [sot-teelay]
(person) magro

thing la cosa [koza]
my things le mie cose [lay
mee-ay kozay]

think pensare [pensaray]
I think so penso di sì
I don't think so non credo
[kraydo]
I'll think about it ci penserò
[chee pensairo]

third party insurance l'R.C.A.
[air-ray chee a]

thirsty: I'm thirsty ho sete [o
saytay]

this questo/questa [kwesto]
this man quest'uomo
this woman questa donna
this one questo/questa (qui)
[kwee]
this is my wife questa è mia
moglie [mol-yay]
is this ...? (questo/questa)
è...?

those quelli/quelle [kwel-lee/
kwel-lay]
those men quegli uomini
[kwayl-yee]
those women quelle donne
those children quei bambini
[kway]
which ones? – those quali?
– quelli/quelle [kwalee]

thread il filo

throat la gola

throat pastilles le pastiglie per
la gola [pasteel-yay pair]

through attraverso [at-travairso]

does it go through ...? (train, bus) passa per...? [pair]
throw (verb) gettare [jet-taray]
throw away (verb) buttare via [boot-taray]
thumb il pollice [pol-leechay]
thunderstorm il temporale [temporal-ay]
Thursday il giovedì [jovedee]
ticket il biglietto [beel-yet-to]

dialogue

a return to Rome un biglietto di andata e ritorno per Roma [pair]
coming back when? il ritorno per quando? [kwando]
today/next Tuesday oggi/ martedì prossimo [oj-jee]
that will be 15 euros quindici euro [kween-deechee ay-ooro]

ticket office la biglietteria [beel-yet-tairee-a]
tide la marea [maray-a]
tie (necktie) la cravatta
tight (clothes etc) attillato
it's too tight è troppo stretto [ay]
tights il collant [kol-lan]
till la cassa
time* il tempo
what's the time? che ore sono? [kay oray]
this time questa volta [kwesta]

last time l'ultima volta [loolteema]
next time la prossima volta
four times quattro volte [kwat-tro voltay]
timetable l'orario **m**
tin (can) il barattolo
tinfoil la carta stagnola [stan-yola]
tin opener l'apriscatole **m** [apree-skatolay]
tiny piccolo
tip (to waiter etc) la mancia [mancha]
tired stanco
I'm tired sono stanco/stanca
tissues i fazzolettini di carta [fatzolet-teenee]
to: to Naples/London a Napoli/Londra
to Italy/England in Italia/ Inghilterra [een eetal-ya/ eenghil-tair-ra]
to the post office all'ufficio postale [oof-feecho postalay]
toast (bread) il pane tostato [panay]
today oggi [oj-jee]
toe il dito del piede [p-yayday]
together insieme [eens-yaymay]
we're together (in shop etc) siamo insieme [s-yamo]
can we pay together? possiamo pagare insieme? [pos-yamo pagaray]
toilet la toilette [twalet]
where is the toilet? dov'è la toilette? [dovay]

I have to go to the toilet devo andare alla toilette [**day**vo anda**ray**]

toilet paper la carta igienica [eej**ay**neeka]

token (for phone, shower) il gettone [jet-to**nay**]

tomato il pomodoro

tomato juice il succo di pomodoro [**sook**-ko]

tomato ketchup il ketchup

tomorrow domani

tomorrow morning domani mattina

the day after tomorrow dopodomani

toner (cosmetic) il tonico

tongue la lingua [**leen**gwa]

tonic (water) l'acqua tonica f [**ak**wa]

tonight (before 10 p.m.) stasera (after 10 p.m.) stanotte [sta**not**-tay]

tonsillitis la tonsillite [tonseel-**lee**tay]

too (excessively) troppo (also) anche [**an**kay]

too hot troppo caldo

too much troppo

me too anch'io [an**kee**-o]

tooth il dente [**den**tay]

toothache il mal di denti

toothbrush lo spazzolino da denti [spatzo**lee**no]

toothpaste il dentifricio [dentee**free**cho]

top: on top of ... su... [soo]

at the top in cima [**chee**ma]

top floor l'ultimo piano

[**ool**teemo]

topless in topless

torch la torcia elettrica [**tor**cha]

total il totale [to**ta**lay]

tour (noun) il giro [**jee**ro]

is there a tour of ...? ci sono visite guidate di...? [chee – **vee**zeetay gwee**da**tay]

tour guide la guida [**gwee**da]

tourist il/la turista [too**ree**sta]

tourist information office l'ufficio informazioni m [oof-**fee**cho eenformatz-**yo**nay]

tour operator l'operatore turistico m [opaira**to**ray too**ree**steeko]

towards verso [**vair**so]

towel l'asciugamano m [ashooga**ma**no]

tower la torre [**tor**-ray]

town la città [chee**ta**]

in town in città

just out of town appena fuori città [ap-**pay**na fwo**ree**]

town centre il centro (della città) [**chen**tro **del**-la **chee**ta]

town hall il municipio [moonee**chee**p-yo]

toy il giocattolo [jo**kat**-tolo]

track (US) il marciapiede [marchap**yay**day]

see platform

tracksuit la tuta da ginnastica [**too**ta da jeen**na**steeka]

traditional tradizionale [tradeetz-**yo**na-lay]

traffic il traffico

traffic jam l'ingorgo m

traffic lights il semaforo

trailer (for carrying tent etc) il
  rimorchio [reemork-yo]
  (US) la roulotte [roolot]
trailer park il campeggio per
  roulotte [kampej-jo pair]
train il treno [trayno]
  by train in treno

dialogue

> is this train for ...? questo
> treno va a...? [kwesto]
> sure sì
> no, you want that platform
> there no, deve andare a
> quel binario [dayvay andaray
> a kwel beenar-yo]

trainers (shoes) le scarpe
  da ginnastica [skarpay da
  jeennasteeka]
train station la stazione
  ferroviaria [statz-yonay fair-rov-
  yar-ya]
tram il tram
translate tradurre [tradoor-ray]
  could you translate that?
  puoi/può tradurlo? [pwoy/pwo]
translation la traduzione
  [tradootz-yonay]
translator (man/woman) il
  traduttore [tradoot-toray], la
  traduttrice [tradoot-treechay]
trashcan la pattumiera [pat-
  toom-yaira]
travel viaggiare [v-yaj-jaray]
  we're travelling around
  stiamo visitando la regione
  [st-yamo – rejonay]

travel agent's l'agenzia di
  viaggi f [ajentz-ya dee vee-aj-jee]
traveller's cheque il traveller's
  cheque
tray il vassoio [vas-so-yo]
tree l'albero m [albairo]
tremendous fantastico
trendy alla moda
trim: just a trim please (to
  hairdresser) solo una spuntatina
  per favore [spoontateena]
trip (excursion) la gita [jeeta]
  I'd like to go on a trip to ...
  vorrei fare una gita a... [vor-
  ray faray]
trolley il carrello
trouble i problemi
  [problaymee]
  I'm having trouble with ... ho
  difficoltà con... [o]
  sorry to trouble you scusi
  il disturbo [skoozee eel
  deestoorbo]
trousers i pantaloni
true vero [vairo]
  that's not true non è vero [ay]
trunk il bagagliaio [bagal-ya-yo]
trunks (swimming) il costume
  da bagno [kostoomay da ban-yo]
try (verb) provare [provaray]
  can I have a try? posso
  provare?
try on provare
  can I try it on? posso
  provarlo/provarla?
T-shirt la maglietta [mal-yet-ta]
Tuesday il martedì [martedee]
tuna il tonno

114

tunnel il tunnel [toon-nel]

Turin Torino [toreeno]

turn: turn left/right giri a sinistra/destra [jeeree]

turn off: where do I turn off? dove devo girare? [dovay dayvo jeeraray]

can you turn the heating off? può spegnere il riscaldamento? [pwo spen-yairay]

turn on: can you turn the heating on? può accendere il riscaldamento? [achendairay]

turning (in road) la svolta

Tuscany la Toscana [toskana]

TV la TV [tee voo]

tweezers le pinzette [peentzet-tay]

twice due volte [doo-ay voltay]

twice as much il doppio [dop-yo]

twin beds i letti gemelli [jemel-lee]

twin room la camera a due letti [doo-ay]

twist: I've twisted my ankle mi sono slogato la caviglia [mee sono zlogato la kaveel-ya]

type il tipo

a different type of ... un tipo diverso di... [deevairso]

typical tipico

tyre lo pneumatico [p-nay-oomateeko]

Tyrrhenian Sea il Mar Tirreno [teer-rayno]

ugly brutto [brootto]

ulcer l'ulcera f [oolchaira]

umbrella l'ombrello m

uncle lo zio [tzee-o]

unconscious privo di sensi

under (in position) sotto
(less than) meno di [mayno]

underdone (meat) al sangue [sangway]

underground (railway) la metropolitana

underpants le mutande [mootanday]

understand capire [kapeeray]
I understand capisco
I don't understand non capisco
do you understand? capisci/capisce? [kapeeshee/kapeeshay]

unemployed disoccupato [deezok-koopato]

United States gli Stati Uniti [statee ooneetee]

university l'università f [ooneevairseeta]

unleaded petrol la benzina senza piombo [bentzeena senza p-yombo]

unlimited mileage il chilometraggio illimitato [keelometraj-jo]

unlock aprire [apreeray]

unpack disfare le valigie [deesfaray lay valeejay]

until finché [feenkay]

unusual insolito

up su [soo]
  up there lassù [las-soo]
  he's not up yet (not out of bed)
  non si è ancora alzato [non see
  ay – altzato]
  what's up? che c'è? [kay chay]
upmarket chic [sheek]
upset stomach il disturbo di
  stomaco
upside down sottosopra
upstairs al piano superiore
  [soopair-yoray]
urgent urgente [oorjentay]
us* noi [noy], ci [chee]
  with us con noi
  for us per noi [pair]
USA gli USA [oo-sa]
use (verb) usare [oozaray]
  may I use ...? posso usare...?
useful utile [ooteelay]
usual solito
  the usual (drink etc) il solito

V

vacancy: do you have any
  vacancies? (hotel) avete
  camere libere? [avaytay
  kamairay leebairay]
vacation la vacanza [vakantza]
  see holiday
  (from university) le vacanze
  [vakantzay]
vaccination il vaccino
  [vacheeno]
vacuum cleaner
  l'aspirapolvere m
  [aspeerapolvairay]

valid (ticket etc) valido
  how long is it valid for? per
  quanto tempo è valido? [pair
  kwanto – ay]
valley la valle [val-lay]
valuable (adj) di valore [valoray]
  can I leave my valuables
  here? posso lasciare qui
  i miei oggetti di valore
  [lasharay kwee ee mee-yay oj-jet-
  tee dee]
value il valore [valoray]
van il furgone [foorgonay]
vanilla la vaniglia [vaneel-ya]
  a vanilla ice cream un gelato
  alla vaniglia [jelato]
vary: it varies dipende
  [deependay]
vase il vaso [vazo]
Vatican City la Città del
  Vaticano [cheetta del vateekano]
veal il vitello
vegetables la verdura
  [vairdoora]
vegetarian (man/woman) il
  vegetariano [vejetar-yano], la
  vegetariana
vending machine il
  distributore automatico
  [deestreebootoray owtomateeko]
Venetian (adj) veneziano
  [venetz-yano]
Venice Venezia [venaytz-ya]
very molto
  very little for me per me
  molto poco [pair may]
  I like it very much mi piace
  moltissimo [mee pee-achay]
vest (under shirt) la canottiera

Up

[kanot-tyaira]

via la via [vee-a]

video (film) la videocassetta
(recorder) il videoregistratore
[veeday-o-rejeestratoray]

view la vista

villa la villa

village il paese [pa-ayzay]

vinegar l'aceto m [acheto]

vineyard la vigna [veen-ya]

visa il visto

visit (verb) visitare [veezeetaray]

I'd like to visit ... mi
piacerebbe visitare... [mee
pee-achaireb-bay]

vital: it's vital that ... è di vitale
importanza che... [ay dee
veetalay eemportantza kay]

vodka la vodka

voice la voce [vochay]

volcano il vulcano

voltage il voltaggio [voltaj-jo]

vomit vomitare [vomeetaray]

W

waist la vita

waistcoat il gilet [jeelay]

wait (verb) aspettare [aspet-
taray]

wait for me aspettami/mi
aspetti

don't wait for me non
aspettarmi/mi aspetti

can I wait until my wife/
partner gets here? posso
aspettare fino a quando
arriva mia moglie/la mia

partner? [kwando]

can you do it while I wait?
può farlo adesso? [pwo]

could you wait here for me?
mi può aspettare qui?
[kwee]

waiter il cameriere [kamair-
yairay]

waiter! cameriere!

waitress la cameriera [kamair-
yaira]

waitress! cameriera!

wake: can you wake me up at
5.30? mi può dare la sveglia
alle cinque e mezza? [pwo
daray la svayl-ya]

wake-up call la sveglia
[svayl-ya]

Wales il Galles [gal-les]

walk: is it a long walk? ci si
mette molto a piedi? [chee see
met-tay – p-yayday]

it's only a short walk è a
due passi da qui [ay a doo-ay
– kwee]

I'll walk vado a piedi

I'm going for a walk vado a
fare una passeggiata [faray
oona pas-sej-jata]

Walkman® il walkman

wall il muro [mooro]

wallet il portafoglio [porta-
fol-yo]

wander: I like just wandering
around mi piace andarmene
in giro [mee pee-achay
andarmenay een jeero]

want: I want a ... voglio un/
uno/una... [vol-yo]

I don't want any ... non voglio nessun/nessuno/nessuna... [nes-soon]

I want to go home voglio andare a casa [andaray]

I don't want to non voglio

he wants to ... vuole... [vwolay]

what do you want? cosa vuole?

ward (in hospital) la corsia [korsee-a]

warm caldo

I'm so warm sento molto caldo

was*: he/she/it was ... era... [aira]

wash (verb) lavare [lavaray]

can you wash these? può lavare questi/queste? [pwo – kwestee/kwestay]

washer (for bolt etc) la rondella

washhand basin il lavabo

washing (clothes) il bucato

washing machine la lavatrice [lavatreechay]

washing powder il detersivo per bucato [detairseevo pair]

washing-up liquid il detersivo liquido per i piatti [leekweedo pair ee p-yat-tee]

wasp la vespa

watch (wristwatch) l'orologio m [orolojo]

will you watch my things for me? può dare un'occhiata alla mia roba? [pwo daray oon ok-yata alla mee-a]

watch out! attenzione! [at-tentz-yonay]

watch strap il cinturino (dell'orologio) [cheentooreeno del orolojo]

water l'acqua f [akwa]

may I have some water? vorrei un po' d'acqua [vor-ray]

water bus (in Venice) il vaporetto

waterproof (adj) impermeabile [eempairmay-abeelay]

waterskiing lo sci acquatico [shee akwa-teeko]

wave (in sea) l'onda f

way: could you tell me the way to ...? mi può indicare come si arriva a...? [mee pwo eendeekaray komay]

it's this way da questa parte [kwesta partay]

it's that way da quella parte [kwel-la]

is it a long way to ...?... è molto lontano/lontana? [ay]

no way! assolutamente no! [as-solootamentay]

dialogue

could you tell me the way to ...? come si fa per andare a...? [komay – pair andaray]

go straight on until you reach the traffic lights vada dritto fino al semaforo

turn left giri a sinistra [jeeree]

take the first on the right
prenda la prima a destra
see where

we* noi [noy]
weak (person, drink) debole
[daybolay]
weather il tempo

dialogue

what's the weather
forecast? come sono le
previsioni del tempo?
[komay – lay preveez-yonee]
it's going to be fine farà
bel tempo
it's going to rain pioverà
[p-yovaira]
it'll brighten up later si
rasserenerà più tardi
[p-yoo]

wedding il matrimonio
wedding ring la vera [vaira]
Wednesday il mercoledì
[mairkoledee]
week la settimana
a week (from) today oggi a
otto [oj-jee]
a week (from) tomorrow
domani a otto
weekend il fine settimana
[feenay]
at the weekend durante il
fine settimana
weight il peso [payzo]
weird strano
weirdo il tipo strano

welcome: welcome to ...
benvenuto a... [benvenooto]
you're welcome (don't mention
it) prego [praygo]
well: I don't feel well non mi
sento bene [baynay]
she's not well non sta bene
you speak English very well
parla inglese molto bene
[eenglay-zay]
well done! bravo!
this one as well anche
questo/questa [ankay kwesto]
well well! (surprise) guarda,
guarda! [gwarda]

dialogue

how are you? come va?
[komay]
very well, thanks
benissimo, grazie
– and you? – è lei? [ay lay]

well-done (meat) ben cotto
Welsh gallese [gal-layzay]
I'm Welsh sono gallese
were*: we were eravamo
west l'ovest m
in the west ad ovest
West Indian (adj) delle Indie
occidentali [del-lay eendee-ay
ocheedentalay]
wet umido [oomeedo], bagnato
[ban-yato]
what? cosa?
what's that? cos'è? [kozay]
what should I do? cosa
dovrei fare? [dovray faray]

Wh

119

what a view! che vista! [kay]
what bus is it? che autobus è?
[kay – ay]
wheel la ruota [rwota]
wheelchair la sedia a rotelle
[sayd-ya a rotel-lay]
when? quando? [kwando]
when we get back quando
torniamo
when's the train/ferry? a
che ora parte il treno/il
traghetto? [kay – partay]
where? dove? [dovay]
I don't know where it is non
so dov'è [dovay]

dialogue

where is the cathedral?
dov'è il duomo? [dovay]
it's over there è laggiù [ay
laj-joo]
could you show me where
it is on the map? puoi/può
farmi vedere dov'è sulla
cartina? [pwoy/pwo – vedairay
dovay]
it's just here è proprio qui
[kwee]
see way

which: which bus? quale
autobus? [kwalay owtoboos]

dialogue

which one? quale? [kwalay]
that one quello/quella
[kwel-lo/kwel-la]

this one? questo/questa?
[kwesto]
no, that one no, quello/
quella

while: while I'm here mentre
sono qui [mentray – kwee]
whisky il whisky
white bianco [b-yanko]
white wine il vino bianco
who? chi? [kee]
who is it? chi è? [ay]
the man who ... l'uomo che...
[lwomo kay]
whole: the whole week tutta la
settimana [toot-ta]
the whole lot tutto
whose: whose is this? di chi
è questo/questa? [dee kee ay
kwesto]
why? perché? [pairkay]
why not? perché no?
wide largo
wife la moglie [mol-yay]
will*: will you do it for me? lo
farà per me? [pair may]
wind il vento
window (of house) la finestra
(of shop) la vetrina
near the window vicino alla
finestra [veecheeno]
in the window (of shop) in
vetrina
window seat il posto vicino al
finestrino [veecheeno]
windscreen il parabrezza
[parabretza]
windscreen wipers i
tergicristalli [tairjeekreestal-lee]

windsurfing il windsurf

windy: it's windy c'è vento [chay]

wine il vino

can we have some more wine? ancora vino, per favore

wine list la lista dei vini [day]

winter l'inverno **m** [eenvairno]

in the winter d'inverno

winter holiday le vacanze invernali [va-kantzay eenvairnalee]

wire il filo di ferro [fair-ro] (electric) il filo (elettrico)

wish: best wishes tanti auguri [owgooree]

with con

I'm staying with ... sono ospite di... [ospeetay]

without senza [sentza]

witness il/la testimone [testeemonay]

will you be a witness for me? può farmi da testimone? [pwo]

woman la donna

wonderful meraviglioso [mairaveel-yozo]

won't*: it won't start non parte [partay]

wood (material) il legno [len-yo] (forest) il bosco

wool la lana

word la parola

work il lavoro

it's not working non funziona [foontz-yona]

I work in ... lavoro a/in...

world il mondo

worry: I'm worried sono preoccupato/preoccupata [pray-ok-koopato]

worse: it's worse è peggio [ay pej-jo]

worst il peggio [pej-jo]

worth: is it worth a visit? vale la pena di visitarlo/visitarla? [valay la payna]

would: would you give this to ...? può dare questo/ questa a...? [pwo daray kwesto]

wrap: could you wrap it up? può incartarlo? [pwo]

wrapping paper la carta da pacchi [pak-kee]

wrist il polso

write scrivere [skreevairay]

could you write it down? può scrivermelo? [pwo skreevairmelo]

how do you write it? come si scrive? [komay see skreevay]

writing paper la carta da lettere [let-tairay]

wrong: it's the wrong key è la chiave sbagliata [ay la k-yavay zbal-yata]

this is the wrong train questo è il treno sbagliato [kwesto]

the bill's wrong c'è un errore nel conto [chay oon air-roray]

sorry, wrong number mi scusi, ho sbagliato numero [mee skoozee o noomairo]

sorry, wrong room mi scusi, ho sbagliato camera

there's something wrong with ... c'è qualcosa che non

va nel/nello/nella... [chay kwalkoza kay]
what's wrong? cosa c'è che non va? [koza chay kay]

X

X-ray i raggi X [raj-jee eeks]

Y

yacht lo yacht
yard* lo yard
(backyard etc) il cortile [korteelay]
year l'anno m
yellow giallo [jal-lo]
yes sì
yesterday ieri [yairee]
  yesterday morning ieri mattina
  the day before yesterday l'altro ieri
yet ancora

dialogue

is it here yet? è (già) arrivato? [ay ja]
no, not yet no, non ancora
you'll have to wait a little longer yet devi/deve aspettare ancora un po' [dayvay aspet-taray]

yoghurt lo yogurt [yogoort]
you* (singular, polite) lei [lay]

(singular, familiar) tu
(plural) voi [voy]
this is for you questo/questa è per te/lei [kwesto – ay pair tay/lay]
with you con te/lei
young giovane [jovanay]
your(s)* (singular, polite) (il) suo [soo-o], (la) sua, (i) suoi [swoy], (le) sue [soo-ay]
(singular, familiar) (il) tuo [too-o], (la) tua, (i) tuoi [twoy], le tue [too-ay]
(plural) (il) vostro, (la) vostra, (i) vostri, (le) vostre [vostray]
youth hostel l'ostello della gioventù m [joventoo]

Z

zero lo zero [tzairo]
zip la cerniera lampo [chairn-yaira]
  could you put a new zip on? potrebbe cambiare la cerniera lampo? [potreb-bay kamb-yaray]
zip code il codice postale [kodeechay postalay]
zoo lo zoo [tzo-o]

Italian

→

English

A

a* at; in; to; per
 a persona per person
abbaglianti full beam
abbassare [ab-bas-saray] to
 lower, to pull down
abbastanza [ab-bastantza]
 enough; quite, rather
abbiamo* we have
abbigliamento da bambino m
 [ab-beel-yamento] children's
 wear
abbigliamento da donna
 ladies' wear
abbigliamento da uomo
 menswear
abbigliamento per signora
 ladies' clothing
abbonamento m [ab-bonamento]
 season ticket
abbonamento mensile
 [menseelay] monthly ticket
abbronzante m [ab-brontzantay]
 suntan lotion
abbronzarsi [ab-brontzarsee] to
 get a tan
abbronzato [ab-brontzato]
 tanned
abbronzatura f [ab-brontzatoora]
 suntan
abile [abeelay] skilful
abitante m/f [abeetantay]
 inhabitant
abitare [abeetaray] to live
abiti mpl [abeetee] clothes
abito m [abito] dress; suit
abitudine f [abeetoodeenay]

habit
a.C. (avanti Cristo) B.C.
accanto beside
acceleratore m [achelairatoray]
 accelerator
accendere [achendairay] to
 switch on; to light
 mi fa accendere? have you
 got a light?
accendere i fari switch on
 headlights
accendino m [achendeeno]
 lighter
accensione f [achens-yonay]
 ignition
accento m [achento] accent
accessori moda mpl fashion
 accessories
accesso riservato ai
 viaggiatori muniti di biglietto
 access only for passengers in
 possession of tickets
accettare [achet-taray] to
 accept
accettazione f [achet-tatz-yonay]
 check-in
acciaio m [acha-yo] steel
accidenti! [acheedentee] damn!
accomodati come in; take
 a seat
accomodi: si accomodi [ak-
 komodee] come in; take a seat
accompagnare [ak-kompan-
 yaray] to accompany
accompagnatore m [ak-kompan-
 yatoray], accompagnatrice f
 [ak-kompan-yatreechay] tour
 leader
acconciatore m ladies'

hairdresser

accordo m agreement

d'accordo all right, OK

essere d'accordo (con) [es-sairay] to agree (with)

accreditare [ak-kraydeetaray] to credit

acetone m [achetonay] nail polish remover

A.C.I. (Automobile Club d'Italia) m [achee] Italian Automobile Association

acqua f [akwa] water

acqua di Colonia [dee kolon-ya] eau de Cologne

acquaio m [akwa-yo] sink

acqua potabile [potabeelay] drinking water

addormentarsi to fall asleep

addormentato [ad-dormentato] asleep

adesso now

adolescente m/f [adoleshentay] teenager

adulto m adult

aereo (m) [a-airay-o] plane; air (adj)

andare in aereo to fly

aerobica f [a-airobeeka] aerobics

aeromobile m [a-airomobeelay] aeroplane

aeroplano m [a-airoplano] aeroplane

aeroporto m [a-airoporto] airport

aerostazione f [a-airostatz-yonay] air terminal

affamato starving

affari mpl business

affermare [af-fermaray] to maintain

afferrare [af-fer-raray] to catch

affettare [af-fet-taray] to slice

affittare [af-feet-taray] to rent

affittasi to let, to rent

affitto m rent

dare in affitto to let

prendere in affitto to hire, to rent

affollato crowded

affondare [af-fondaray] to sink

affrancare [af-frankaray] to stamp; to frank

affrancatura f postage

affrancatura per l'estero postage abroad

affrettarsi to hurry

agenda f [ajenda] diary

agenzia f [ajentzee-a] agency

agenzia di viaggi(o) [dee vee-aj-jee-o] travel agency

agenzia immobiliare [eem-mobeel-yaray] estate agent

agenzia turistica travel agency

aggiungere [aj-joonjairay] to add

aggiustare [aj-joostaray] to mend

aggressivo aggressive

agitare prima dell'uso shake before use

agitato [ajeetato] agitated

agli* [al-yee] at the; to the; with

ago m [ago] needle

agosto m August

agricoltore m [agreekoltoray]

farmer

ai* [a-ee] at the; to the; with

ai binari to the platforms/tracks

ai treni to the trains

aiutare [a-yootaray] to help

aiuto m [a-yooto] help

al* at the; to the

ala f wing

alba f sunrise

albergo m [albairgo] hotel

albergo a 5/4/3/2 stelle 5/4/3/2-star hotel

albergo di categoria lusso [kataygoree-a] luxury hotel

albero m [albairo] tree

albero a gomiti m crankshaft

alghe marine fpl [algay mareenay] seaweed

alimentari mpl groceries

alla* at the; to the; with

allacciare le cinture fasten your seat belts

allarme m [al-larmay] alarm

allattare [al-lat-taray] to breastfeed

alle* [al-lay] at the; to the; with

allegria f [al-legree-a] cheerfulness

allegro cheerful

allenarsi to train

allievo m, allieva f [al-l-yevo] pupil

allo* at the; to the

alloggiare [al-loj-jaray] to stay

alloggio m [al-loj-jo] accommodation

allora then

e allora? so what?

allungare [al-loongaray] to stretch; to extend

almeno [al-mayno] at least

Alpi fpl [alpee] Alps

al... piano on/to ... floor

alpinismo m [alpeeneezmo] mountaineering

alpinista m/f mountaineer

al portatore to the bearer

alt stop, halt

alternatore m [al-tairnatoray] alternator

altitudine f [alteetoodeenay] altitude

alto high, tall

altopiano m plateau

altra, altri, altre [altray] other

altrimenti [altreementee] otherwise

altro other

un altro another

alunno m, alunna f pupil

alzare [altzaray] to lift, to raise

alzarsi [altzarsee] to get up, to stand up

amare [amaray] to love

amaro bitter

ambasciata f [ambashata] embassy

ambiente m [amb-yentay] environment

ambulanza f [amboolantza] ambulance

ambulatorio m [amboolator-yo] out-patients' department; surgery

americano (m), americana (f) American

amico m, **amica** f friend

ammalato ill, (US) sick

ammettere [am-met-tairay] to admit

ammobiliato [am-mobeel-yato] furnished

ammortizzatore m [am-morteedzatoray] shock absorber

amore m [amoray] love

fare l'amore [faray] to make love

ampere: da 15 ampere [ampairay] 15-amp

anabbaglianti mpl dipped headlights

analgesico m [analjayzeeko] painkiller

A.N.A.S. f (Azienda Nazionale Autonoma delle Strade) national road maintenance authority

anche [ankay] also; even

anche a te/lei [a tay/lay] the same to you

ancora f [ankora] anchor

ancora [ankora] still

ancora più... [p-yoo] even more ...

ancora un/uno/una... another/one more ...

ancora (una volta) (once) again

non ancora not yet

andare* [andaray] to go

andarsene [andarsenay] to go away

andarsene in fretta to rush away

andar via to go away

andate* [andatay] you go

andato* gone

andiamo* we go

anello m ring

angolo m corner; angle

animale m [aneemalay] animal

annegare [an-negaray] to drown

anniversario di matrimonio m wedding anniversary

anno m year

annoiarsi [an-noyarsee] to be bored

anno nuovo m [nwovo] New Year

annullare [an-nool-laray] to cancel

annullato cancelled

antenato m ancestor

antenna f aerial

antibiotico m antibiotic

anticamera f waiting room

Antica Roma f Ancient Rome

antichità fpl [anteekeeta] antiques

anticipo: in anticipo [een anteecheepo] in advance; early

antico ancient

antidolorifico m painkiller

antigelo m [anteejelo] antifreeze

antiquariato m [anteekwar-yato] antique; antiques shop

antisettico m antiseptic

antistaminico m antihistamine

aperto* open

apparecchio m [ap-parek-yo] phone

apparecchio m **acustico** [akoosteeko] hearing aid

apparire [ap-par**ee**ray] to appear

appartamento m flat, apartment

appartamento ammobiliato furnished flat/apartment

appassionato (di) very keen (on)

appena [ap-**pay**na] just; hardly, scarcely

appeso [ap-**pay**so] hanging

appetito m [ap-pet**ee**to] appetite

appoggiato [ap-poj-**ja**to] leaning

approvare [ap-pro**va**ray] to approve

appuntamento m [ap-poon-ta**men**to] appointment

apre alle... opens at ...

apribottiglie m [apreebot-**teel**-yay] bottle opener

aprile m [ap**ree**lay] April

aprire* [ap**ree**ray] to open

apriscatole m [apree**ska**tolay] tin opener

AR (andata e ritorno) return (ticket), round trip ticket

AR (avviso di ricevimento) receipt for registered letters which you return to sender

arancione [aran**cho**nay] orange

arbitro m referee

arco m arch

area di servizio f [ser**veetz**-yo] service area

argento m [ar**jen**to] silver

argomento m topic, subject

aria f [ar-ya] air

avere l'aria... to look ...

aria condizionata f [konditz-yon**a**ta] air-conditioning

armadietto m [armad-**yet**-to] locker; cupboard

armadio m [ar**mad**-yo] cupboard; wardrobe

arrabbiarsi [ar-rab-**yar**see] to get angry

arrabbiato angry

arrestare [ar-re**sta**ray] to arrest

arrivare [ar-ree**va**ray] to arrive

arrivederci [ar-reeve**dair**chee] goodbye

arrivo m arrival

arrivo previsto per le ore... expected time of arrival ...

arrogante [ar-ro**gan**tay] arrogant

arroganza f [ar-ro**gan**tza] arrogance

arrostire [ar-ro**stee**ray] to roast

arte f [**ar**tay] art

articoli da regalo mpl gifts

articoli per la casa household goods

articoli per la cucina kitchen articles

articoli sportivi sports gear

artificiale [arteefee**cha**lay] artificial

artigianato m [arteejan**a**to] crafts

artista m/f artist

ascensore f [ashen**so**ray] lift, elevator

asciugacapelli m [ashoogakapel-lee] hair dryer

asciugamano m [ashooga**ma**no] towel

asciugamano da bagno bath towel

asciugamano piccolo hand towel

asciugare [ashoogaray] to dry

asciugarsi [ashoogarsee] to dry oneself

asciugarsi le mani to dry one's hands

asciugatrice f [ashoogatreechay] tumble dryer

asciugatura con fon f [ashoogatoora] blow-dry

asciutto [ashoot-to] dry

ascoltare [askoltaray] to listen

asilo m [azeelo] nursery school

asilo nido crèche

asino m donkey

asma f [azma] asthma

aspettare [aspet-taray] to wait (for)

aspirapolvere m [aspeerapolvairay] vacuum cleaner

passare l'aspirapolvere to vacuum

aspirina f [aspeereena] aspirin

aspro sour

assaggiare [as-saj-jaray] to taste

asse da stiro m [as-say da steero] ironing board

assegno m [as-sen-yo] cheque, (US) check

pagare con un assegno to pay by cheque

assente [as-sentay] absent

assicurata f [as-seekoorata] registered letter

assicurazione f [as-seekooratz-yonay] insurance

assicurazione di viaggio [vee-aj-jo] travel insurance

assistenza auto repairs

associazione f [as-sochatz-yonay] society, association

assolato sunny

assolutamente [as-soloot-amentay] absolutely

assorbente igienico m [as-sorbentay eejeneeko] sanitary towel, sanitary napkin

atlante (geografico) f [atlantay jay-ografeeko] atlas

atlante stradale [stradalay] road atlas

atleta m/f [atlayta] athlete

atletica f [atlayteeka] athletics

attaccapanni m coat rack

attaccato stuck

attenda wait

attenti al cane beware of the dog

attento careful, attentive

attenzione f [at-tentz-yonay] care, attention

attenzione! look out!; caution!

attenzione: per l'uso leggere attentamente le istruzioni interne warning: before use read instructions inside carefully

atterraggio m [at-tair-raj-jo] landing

atterraggio di fortuna emergency landing

atterrare [at-tair-raray] to land

attillato tight

attimo: un attimo just a

minute

attraente [at-tra-**en**tay]
attractive

attraversare [at-travairs**a**ray] to
go through; to cross

attraverso [at-trav**air**so]
through

attrezzatura f [at-tretzat**oo**ra]
equipment

auguri: tanti auguri [tant**ee**
owg**oo**ree] best wishes

aula f [**ow**la] classroom

aumentare [owment**a**ray] to
increase

australiano (m) [owstral-**y**ano],
australiana (f) Australian

austriaco (m) [owstr**ee**-ako],
austriaca (f) Austrian

autentico [owt**en**teeko] genuine

autista m/f [owt**ee**sta] driver

auto f [**ow**to] car

autoambulanza f
[owtoambul**an**tza] ambulance

autobus m [**ow**toboos] bus

autofficina f garage (for repairs)

autogrill m [owtogr**ee**l]
motorway/highway
restaurant

autolavaggio m [owtolav**aj**-jo]
car wash

automobilista m/f
[owtomobeel**ee**sta] car driver

autonoleggio m car rental

autorimessa f [owtoreem**es**-sa]
garage

autostop: fare l'autostop to
hitchhike

autostrada f motorway,
freeway, highway

autunno m [owt**oon**-no]
autumn, Fall

avanti come in; cross now
  avanti diritto straight ahead
  più avanti further on

avere m [av**ai**ray] credit

avere* to have

avete* [av**ay**tay] you have

avuto* had

Avv. (avvocato) lawyer

avventura f [av-vent**oo**ra]
adventure

avviarsi [av-vee-**ar**see] to set off

avvicinarsi [av-veecheen**ar**see] to
approach

avviso m [av-v**ee**zo] notice

avvocato m lawyer

azioni fpl [atz-y**o**nee] shares,
stocks

azzurro [adz**oor**-ro] sky-blue

B

bacio m [**ba**cho] kiss

baffi mpl moustache

bagagli mpl [bag**al**-yee]
luggage, baggage

bagagliaio m [bagal-**y**a-yo]
boot, trunk; left luggage,
baggage check

bagaglio a mano m [bag**al**-yo]
hand luggage/baggage

bagaglio in eccesso [ech**es**-so]
excess baggage

bagnato [ban-**y**ato] wet

bagnato fradicio [frad**ee**cho]
soaked

bagnino m [ban-**yee**no], **bagnina**
f lifeguard

bagno m [ban-yo] bath; bathroom

andare in bagno to go to the bathroom/toilet/rest room

fare il bagno to have a bath; to have a swim

bagnoschiuma m [ban-yosk-yooma] bubble bath

baia f [ba-ya] bay

balconata f balcony, dress-circle

balcone m [balkonay] balcony

ballare [bal-laray] to dance

balletto m ballet

ballo m dancing; dance

balsamo m conditioner

bambino m, **bambina** f child

bambola f doll

banca f bank

banchina f [bankeena] platform, (US) track; quayside

banchina non transitabile soft verge

banco m desk

banco informazioni [eenformatz-yonee] information desk

bancomat® m cash dispenser, automatic teller

banconota f banknote, (US) bill

bandiera f [band-yaira] flag

barare [bararay] to cheat

barattolo m tin

barba f beard

farsi la barba to shave

barbiere m [barb-yairay] barber's

barca (a motore) f [motoray] (motor) boat

barca a remi [raymee] rowing boat

barca a vela [vayla] sailing boat

basket m basketball

basso low

basta (così)! [kozee] that's enough!

bastare [bastaray] to be enough

battello m passenger ferry; steamer

battere [bat-tairay] to beat

batteria f [bat-tairee-a] battery; drums

beauty-case m toilet bag(s)

bebè m/f [bebay] baby

belga (m/f) Belgian

Belgio m [beljo] Belgium

bello beautiful

bene [baynay] good; fine; well

bene, grazie [gratzee-ay] fine, thanks

ti sta bene! it serves you right!

va bene! that's fine!, it's OK!; that's right

benissimo! excellent!

benvenuto! [benvaynooto] welcome!

benzina f [bendzeena] petrol, (US) gas

benzina normale [normalay] two- or three-star petrol, regular gas

benzina senza piombo [sentza p-yombo] unleaded petrol/gas

benzina super four-star

petrol, premium

benzina verde [**vai**rday]
unleaded petrol/gas

bere* [**bai**ray] to drink

berretto m [bair-ret-to] cap

beve* [**ba**yvay] he/she/it
drinks; you drink

bevete* [bev**ay**tay] you drink

bevi* [**bay**vee] you drink

beviamo* we drink

bevo* [**bay**vo] I drink

bevono* they drink

bevuto* drank

biancheria da bambino f
[b-yanka**ree**-a] children's
underwear

biancheria da donna ladies'
lingerie

biancheria da letto bed linen

biancheria da uomo men's
underwear

biancheria intima underwear

biancheria per la casa
household linen

bianco [b-**yan**ko] white
bianco e nero [ay n**ai**ro] black
and white

bibita f [**bee**beeta] soft drink

biblioteca f [beebl-yot**e**ka]
library

bicchiere m [beek-y**ai**ray] glass

bicicletta f [beecheek**le**t-ta]
bicycle
andare in bicicletta to cycle

bidello m [beed**el**-lo], **bidella** f
caretaker

bigiotteria f [bijot-tair**ee**-a]
costume jewellery

bigliettaio m [beel-yet-**ta**-yo]

conductor

biglietteria f [beel-yet-tair-**ee**-a]
ticket office; box-office

biglietteria automatica
[owtom**a**teeka] ticket vending
machine

biglietto m [beel-y**et**-to] ticket;
banknote, (US) bill

biglietto chilometrico
[keelom**e**treeko] ticket allowing
travel up to a maximum
specified distance

biglietto d'accesso ai treni
[dach**es**-so a-**e**e tr**ay**nee]
platform ticket

biglietto da visita business
card

biglietto di andata e ritorno
[reet**or**no] return (ticket),
round trip ticket

biglietto di auguri [owg**oo**ree]
(greetings/birthday) card

biglietto di sola andata single
(ticket), one-way ticket

biglietto per viaggi in comitiva
[vee-**a**j-jee] group/party ticket

biglietto ridotto [reed**ot**-to]
reduced rate ticket

biglietto valido per più corse
[val**ee**do pair p-yoo k**or**say] multi-
journey ticket

bilancia (pesapersone) f
[beelanch**ee**-a payzapairs**o**nay]
(bathroom) scales

bilanciatura gomme f
[beelanchat**oo**ra g**o**m-may]
wheel-balancing

binario m [been**ar**-yo] platform,
(US) track

biondo [b-**yo**ndo] blond

birreria f [beer-rair**ee**-a] bar specializing in beer

bisogno: ho bisogno di [o beez**on**-yo] I need

bivio m [**beev**-yo] junction

bloccato blocked; stuck

blocchetto di biglietti m [blok-**ket**-to dee beel-**yet**-tee] book of tickets

boa f [**bo**-a] buoy

bocca f mouth

bollire [bol-**lee**ray] to boil; to be boiling

bomba f bomb; type of ice cream; doughnut

bonifico bancario m [bon**ee**feeko bank**ar**-yo] credit transfer

bordo: a bordo on board

borgo medioevale m [med-yo-ayv**a**lay] medieval village

borsa f bag

borsa dell'acqua calda [del-lakwa] hot-water bottle

borsaiolo m [borsa-**yo**lo], **borsaiola** f pickpocket

borsellino m purse

borsetta f handbag, (US) purse

bosco m wood, forest

bottiglia f [bot-**teel**-ya] bottle

bottone m [bot-**to**nay] button

braccialetto m [brachal**et**-to] bracelet

braccio m [**bra**cho] arm

branda f campbed

bravo good; skilful

bravo! well done!

bravura f skilfulness

breve [**bray**vay] short, brief

brillante [breel-l**an**tay] brilliant

britannico British

brocca f jug

bruciare [brooch**a**ray] to burn

brutto [br**oot**-to] ugly

buca delle lettere f [del-lay let-tairay] letter box, mailbox

bucato f laundry

fare il bucato to do the washing

buco m hole

buffet m snack bar(s); sideboard(s)

buffo [b**oof**-fo] funny

buio (m) [b**oo**-yo] dark

buona fortuna! [bw**o**na fort**oo**na] good luck!

buonanotte [bwonan**o**t-tay] good night

buon appetito! [bwon ap-pet**ee**to] enjoy your meal!

buonasera [bwonas**ai**ra] good evening

buon compleanno! [komplay-**an**-no] happy birthday!

buongiorno [bwonj**o**rno] good morning

buono [bw**o**no] good

buon viaggio! [vee-**aj**-jo] have a good trip!

bussola f [b**oos**-sola] compass

busta f [b**oos**ta] envelope

busta imbottita [eembot-t**ee**ta] padded envelope

butano m [boot**a**no] camping gas

buttare via [boot-t**a**ray v**ee**-a] to throw away

C

C (caldo) hot
C (Celsius) C
cabina f cabin; beach hut
cabina telefonica [telefoneeka] phone box
caccia f [kacha] hunting
 andare a caccia to go hunting
cacciavite m [kachaveetay] screwdriver
cadere [kadairay] to fall
 far cadere to drop
caduta massi falling rocks
caffè m [kaffay] coffee(s); café(s)
caffetteria f [kaf-fet-tairee-a] coffee bar, coffee house
caffettiera f [kaf-fet-yaira] coffeepot; coffee maker
C.A.I. m (Club Alpino Italiano) Italian Alpine Club
calciatore m [kalchatoray], calciatrice f [kalchatreechay] football player
calcio m [kalcho] football; kick
 giocare a calcio [jokaray] to play football
calcolare [kalkolaray] to calculate
calcolatore m [kalkolatoray] calculator
caldo (m) heat; warm; hot
 avere caldo to be warm
 fa caldo it's warm/hot
calendario m [kalendar-yo] calendar

calmarsi to calm down
calvo bald
calzature fpl [kaltzatooray] footwear
calze fpl [kaltzay] socks; stockings
calzini mpl [kaltzeenee] socks
calzolaio m [kaltzola-yo] shoe repairer's
calzoleria f [kaltzolairee-a] shoe repairer's
calzoncini mpl [kaltzoncheenee] shorts
calzoni mpl [kaltzonee] trousers, (US) pants
cambiare [kamb-yaray] to change
cambiarsi [kamb-yarsee] to change
cambiavalute m [kamb-yavalootay] bureau de change
cambio m [kamb-yo] change; bureau de change; gears
camera f [kamaira] room
camera da letto bedroom
camera d'aria [dar-ya] inner tube
camera doppia [dop-ya] double room
camera doppia con bagno/servizi [ban-yo/sairveetzee] double room with bathroom
camera doppia senza bagno [sentza] double room without bathroom
camera singola [seengola] single room
cameriera f [kamair-yaira] maid; waitress

cameriere m [kamair-yairay] waiter

camiceria f [kameechairee-a] shirt shop

camicetta f [kamichet-ta] blouse

camicia f [kameecha] shirt

camicia da notte [not-tay] nightdress

caminetto m fireplace

camino m chimney

camion m [kam-yon] lorry

camminare [kam-meenaray] to walk

campagna f [kampan-ya] countryside; campaign

campana f bell (church)

campanello m bell; doorbell

campeggio m [kampej-jo] camping; campsite

campeggio per roulotte [roolot] caravan site, trailer park

campionato m [kamp-yonato] championship

campione senza valore sample, no commercial value

campo m course; court; field

campo da golf golf course

campo da hockey hockey field

campo da tennis tennis court

campo di calcio [kalcho] football pitch

campo sportivo [sporteevo] sports ground

canadese (m/f) [kanadayzay] Canadian

canale m [kanalay] canal; channel

cancellato [kanchel-lato] cancelled

cancello m [kanchel-lo] gate

candela f [kandayla] candle; spark plug

candeliere m [kandel-yairay] candlestick

cane m [kanay] dog

canna da pesca f fishing rod

cannuccia f [kan-noocha] straw

canoa f [kano-a] canoe; canoeing

canottaggio m [kanot-taj-jo] rowing; canoeing

canotto m (rubber) dinghy

cantare [kantaray] to sing

cantina f cellar

canto m singing

canzone f [kantzonay] song

C.A.P. (Codice di Avviamento Postale) m postcode, zip code

cap. (capitolo) chapter

caparra f deposit

capelli mpl hair

capire [kapeeray] to understand

capisco: non capisco [kapeesko] I don't understand

capitale f [kapeetalay] capital city

capitano m captain

capo m boss

capolavoro m masterpiece

capolinea m [kapoleenay-a] terminus

cappella f chapel

cappello m hat

cappotto m coat

capra f goat

carabinieri mpl [karabeen-yairee]
military police force

carattere m [karat-tairay]
character

carburatore m [karbooratoray]
carburettor

carcere m [karchairay] prison

carino nice, pleasant

carnevale m [karnevalay]
carnival

caro dear, expensive

carreggiata f [kar-rej-jata]
roadway

carrello m (luggage/baggage)
trolley

carrozza f [kar-rotza] coach,
carriage, car

carrozza cuccette [koochet-tay]
sleeping car

carrozza letti [let-tee] sleeping
car

carrozza ristorante
[reestorantay] restaurant car

carrozzeria f [kar-rotzairee-a] car
body shop

carrozzina f [kar-rotzeena] pram

carta f card; paper

carta assegni [as-sen-yee]
cheque/check card

carta da disegno [deesen-yo]
drawing paper

carta da lettere [let-tairay]
writing paper

carta da pacchi [pak-kee]
brown paper

carta d'argento [darjento]
senior citizens' railcard for
reduced fares

carta di credito [kraydeeto]
credit card

carta d'identità identity card

carta d'imbarco boarding pass

carta geografica [jay-ografeeka]
map

carta igienica [eejeneeka] toilet
paper

carta verde [vairday] under-26
reduced fare railcard

carte fpl [kartay] cards

cartella f school-bag;
briefcase

cartina f map

cartoleria f [kartolairee-a]
stationer's

cartolibreria f [kartoleebrairee-a]
stationery and book shop

cartolina f postcard

cartone m [kartonay] cardboard

casa f [kaza] house

casalinga f [kazaleenga]
housewife

casalinghi mpl household
goods

cascata f waterfall

caseggiato m [kasej-jato] block
(of apartments)

casella postale f [postalay]
P.O. Box

casello autostradale m [kazel-lo
owtostradalay] motorway/
highway toll booth

caserma dei carabinieri f
[kasairma day karabeen-yairee]
military police station

caserma dei vigili del fuoco
[veejeelee del fwoko] fire station

caso: per caso [pair kazo] by
chance

in caso di emergenza
rompere il vetro in case of
emergency break the glass
in caso di sosta in galleria
accendere i fari e spegnere il
motore if stopping in tunnel,
switch on headlights and
switch off engine

cassa f [kas-sa] till, cashdesk,
cashier

cassa automatica
[owtomateeka] cash dispenser,
automatic teller

cassa continua [konteenwa]
cash dispenser, automatic
teller

cassetta f box; cassette

cassetta delle lettere [del-lay
let-tairay] postbox, mailbox

cassetta di sicurezza
[seekooretza] safe-deposit box

cassetto m drawer

cassettone m [kas-set-tonay]
chest of drawers

cassiere m [kas-syairay],
cassiera f cashier, teller

castello m castle

catena f [katayna] chain

catenaccio m [katenacho] bolt

catino m basin

cattedrale f [kat-taydralay]
cathedral

cattiveria f [kat-teevair-ya]
nastiness; naughtiness

cattivo [kat-teevo] bad

cattolico Catholic

causa f [kowza] cause

cavallo m horse
andare a cavallo to go horse
riding

cavatappi m corkscrew

caviglia f [kaveel-ya] ankle

cazzo m prick

CC (Carabinieri) military
police force

c/c (conto corrente) m [kor-
rentay] current account

CE f [chay] EC

c'è [chay] there is
non c'è he/she/it is not here
non c'è... there is no ...

celeste [chelestay] light blue

celibe [chayleebay] single (man)

cena f [chayna] dinner (evening
meal); supper

cenare [chenaray] to have
dinner

cenno m [chen-no] sign

centinaia fpl [chenteena-ya]
hundreds

cento [chento] hundred

centralino m [chentraleeno] local
exchange, operator

centrifuga f [chentreefooga]
spin-dryer

centro m [chentro] centre

centro città [cheet-ta] city
centre

centro commerciale [kom-
merchalay] shopping centre

centro culturale [kooltooralay]
arts centre

centro della città [cheet-ta] city
centre

centro (di) informazioni
turistiche [eenformatz-
yonee tooreestekay] tourist
information office

centro sportivo sports centre

centro storico old town

ceramica f [cherameeka] pottery

cera per auto f [chaira pair **ow**to] car wax

cercare [chairkaray] to look for

cerchio m [cha**i**rk-yo] circle

cerniera lampo f [chairn-y**ai**ra] zip

cerotto m [cher**ot**-to] sticking plaster, Bandaid®

certamente [chairtamentay] certainly

cestino m [chest**ee**no] basket; wastepaper basket

cfr. (confronta) cf.

charter: il volo charter m charter flight

che [kay] that, which; than

che? what?

check-in: fare il check-in to check in

chi [kee] who?

chiacchierare [k-yak-yair**a**ray] to chat

chiacchierone (m) [k-yak-yair**o**nay], chiacchierona (f) chatterbox; talkative

chiamare [k-yam**a**ray] to call

come si chiama? [**k**omay see k-yama] what's your name?

come ti chiami? what's your name?

chiamata f [k-yam**a**ta] call

chiamata a carico del destinatario [kar**ee**ko del desteenatar-yo] reverse charge call

chiamata in teleselezione [teleseletz-y**o**nay] direct dialling

chiamata interurbana [eentairoorbana] long-distance call

chiamata urbana [oorbana] local call

chiaro [k-yaro] clear; light

chiave f [k-ya**v**ay] key; spanner

chiave inglese [eengl**a**yzay] wrench

chiedere [k-y**a**ydairay] to ask

chiesa f [k-y**a**yza] church

chilo m [keelo] kilo

chilometro m [keel**o**metro] kilometre

chimica f [k**ee**meeka] chemistry

chiodo m [k-y**o**do] nail (metal)

chirurgia f [keeroorjee-a] surgery

chirurgo m [keer**oo**rgo] surgeon

chitarra f [keetar-ra] guitar

chiude alle... closes at ...

chiudere [k-y**oo**dairay] to close

chiudere a chiave [k-yavay] to lock

chiudere bene dopo l'uso close tightly after use

chiudi il becco! [k-y**oo**dee eel bek-ko] shut up!

chiuso* (dalle... alle...) [k-y**oo**zo] closed (from ... to ...)

chiuso per ferie closed for holidays/vacation

chiuso per turno closing day

chiusura settimanale... closed on ...

ci* [chee] here; there; us; each other; to us; ourselves

ci sono there are

ciao! [chow] hello!; cheerio!, goodbye!

ciascuno [chaskoono], ciascuna each

cibo m [cheebo] food

ciclismo m [cheekleesmo] cycling

ciclista m/f [cheekleesta] cyclist

cieco [chee-ayko] blind

cielo m [chaylo] sky

ciglia fpl [cheel-ya] eyelashes

cima: in cima (a) [cheema] at the top (of)

cimitero m [cheemeetairo] cemetery

cinghia della ventola f [cheeng-ya] fan belt

cinquanta [cheenkwanta] fifty

cinque [cheenkway] five

cintura f [cheentoora] belt

cintura di sicurezza [dee seekooretza] seat belt

ciò [cho] this; that

circa [cheerka] about

circonvallazione f [cheerkonvallatz-yonay] ring road

C.I.T. (Compagnia Italiana Turismo) m [cheet] Italian tourist organization

città f [cheet-ta] town(s); city, cities

per la città local mail only

cittadina f [cheet-tadeena] citizen; city dweller; town

cittadino m citizen; city dweller

clacson m horn

classe f [klas-say] class; classroom

classe economica economy class

clienti: i clienti sono pregati di lasciare libere le camere entro le ore 12 del giorno di partenza on day of departure, guests are requested to vacate rooms before midday

clima m climate

clinica f clinic

coda f tail; queue

coda del treno [trayno] rear of the train

code traffic queues ahead

codice della strada m [kodeechay] highway code

codice di avviamento postale [av-yamento postalay] postcode, zip code

cofano m bonnet, (US) hood

cognata f [kon-yata] sister-in-law

cognato m brother-in-law

cognome m [kon-yomay] surname

coi [koy] with the

coiffeur m hair stylist

coincidenza f [ko-eencheedentza] connection (travelling)

col with the

colazione f [kolatz-yonay] breakfast

colla f glue

collana f necklace

collant m [kol-lan] tights, pantyhose
collasso m collapse
collasso cardiaco heart failure
colle m [kol-lay] hill
collegamenti internazionali international connections
collegio m [kol-layjo] boarding school
colletto m collar
collezionare [kol-letz-yonaray] to collect
collezione f [kol-letz-yonay] collection (stamps etc)
collina f hill
collo m neck
colloquio m [kol-lokw-yo] interview; conversation
colonna f column
colore m [koloray] colour
colorificio m [koloreefeecho] paint and dyes shop
colpa: è colpa mia it's my fault
colpi di sole mpl [solay] highlights
colpire [kolpeeray] to hit; to knock
colpo di sole m [solay] sunstroke
coltello m knife
coltello da cucina [koocheena] kitchen knife
coltello da pane [panay] bread knife
comandante m/f [komandantay] pilot
comando dei vigili del fuoco m [day veejeelee del fwoko] fire

department headquarters
comando dei vigili urbani [oorbanee] municipal headquarters of traffic police
come [komay] like; as
come? how?; what?; sorry?, pardon me?, what did you say?
come, scusi? [skoozee] pardon?, pardon me?
come stai/sta/state? [sta-ee/sta/statay] how are you?
come va? how are things?
comico (m) [komeeko] comic; comedy; comedian
cominciare [komeencharay] to start
comitiva f group
commedia f [kom-mayd-ya] play; comedy
commesso m, commessa f shop assistant
commissariato (di polizia) m [kom-mees-sar-yato dee poleetzee-a] police station
comodo comfortable
compact (disc) m compact disc
compagna f [kompan-ya] schoolfriend; partner
compagnia aerea f [kompan-yee-a a-airay-a] airline
compagno m [kompan-yo] schoolfriend; partner
comperare [kompararay] to buy
compere: andare a fare le compere [kompairay] to go shopping
competizione f [kompeteetz-

Co

141

yonay] competition; race

compilare [kompeelaray] to fill in

compleanno m [komplay-an-no] birthday

completamente [kompletamentay] completely, entirely

completo m [komplayto] suit; outfit

completo full; no vacancies

complicato complicated

complimento m compliment

comporre [kompor-ray] to dial

comportamento m behaviour

comportarsi to behave

composizione [kompozeetz-yonay] medicinal composition

comprare [kompraray] to buy

compreso [komprayzo] included

compressa f tablet

comune m [komoonay] town hall; municipal district

comunicazione f [komooneekatz-yonay] phone call

comunque [komoonkway] however

con with

concerto m [konchairto] concert

concessionario m [konches-yonar-yo] agent, dealer

conchiglia f [konkeel-ya] shell

condoglianze fpl [kondol-yantzay] condolences

condotta f behaviour

conducente m/f [kondoochentay] driver

conferenza f [konfairentza]

lecture; conference

conferma: dare conferma to confirm

confermare [konfairmaray] to confirm

confetto m sugar-coated pill; sugar-coated almond

confezione f [konfetz-yonay] pack; packaging

confine m [konfeenay] border

confusione f [konfooz-yonay] confusion; mess

congelatore m [konjelatoray] freezer

congratulazioni! [kongratoolatz-yonee] congratulations!

congresso m conference

conoscere [konoshairay] to know

consegnare [konsen-yaray] to deliver

conservare in frigo keep refrigerated

conservare in luogo asciutto keep in a dry place

consigliare [konseel-yaray] to recommend

consolato m consulate

consumarsi: da consumarsi preferibilmente entro... best before ...

contagioso [kontajozo] infectious

contanti mpl cash

pagare in contanti to pay cash

contare [kontaray] to count

contascatti m [kontaskat-tee] time-unit counter(s)

contatto: mettersi in contatto con to contact

contenere [kontenairay] to contain

contento happy; pleased

contenuto m [kontenooto] contents

continuare [konteenwaray] to continue, to go on

continui [konteenwee] keep going

continuo [konteenwo] continuous

conto m bill, (US) check

conto corrente [kor-rentay] current account

conto in banca bank account

contraccettivo m [kontrachet-teevo] contraceptive

contraccezione f [kontra-chetz-yonay] contraception

contraddire [kontrad-deeray] to contradict

contrario a [kontrar-yo] opposed to

contrassegno IVA [kontras-sen-yo eeva] proof that VAT has been paid

contro against

controllare [kontrol-laray] to check

controllo automatico della velocità m automatic speed check

controllo bagagli [bagal-yee] baggage control

controllo biglietti ticket inspection

controllo passaporti passport control

controllo radar della velocità radar speed check

controllore m [kontrol-loray] ticket inspector; bus conductor

conversare [konvairsaray] to converse

conversazione f [konvairsatz-yonay] conversation

convincente [konveenchentay] convincing

convincere [konveenchairay] to convince, to persuade

convinto convinced

coperchio m [kopairk-yo] lid

coperta f [kopairta] blanket

coperto m cover charge
al coperto indoors

coppa f cup

copriletto m bedspread

coraggioso [koraj-jozo] brave

corda f rope

cordiale [kord-yalay] friendly

cornice f [korneechay] frame

coro m choir

corpo m body

corrente (f) [kor-rentay] current; draught

correnti pericolose fpl dangerous currents

correre [kor-rairay] to run

corridoio m [kor-reedo-yo] corridor; aisle

corridore m [kor-reedoray] runner

corriera f [kor-yaira] coach, long-distance bus

corrispondente m/f [kor-reespondentay] penfriend

corrispondenza f [kor-reespondentza] mail; correspondence

corruzione f [kor-rootz-yonay] corruption

corsa f race; running

corsa semplice [sempleechay] one way (ticket)

corsia di emergenza f [emairjentza] emergency lane

corso m course; main street

corso di lingua [leengwa] language course

cortile m [korteelay] courtyard

corto short

cosa f [koza] thing

cosa? what?

cosa hai/ha detto? what did you say?

coscia f [kosha] thigh

così [kozee] like this; so

così grande [granday] so big

così così so-so

costa f coast

costare [kostaray] to cost

costola f rib

costruire [kostroo-eeray] to build

costume m [kostoomay] custom

costume da bagno [kostoomay da ban-yo] swimsuit; swimming trunks

cotone m [kotonay] cotton

cotone idrofilo [eedrofeelo] cotton wool

cotto: ben cotto well done

poco cotto underdone

troppo cotto overdone

C.P. (Casella Postale) f P.O. Box

cravatta f tie, necktie

credenza f [kredentza] dresser; cupboard

credere [kraydairay] to believe, to think

non posso crederci! [kredairchee] I can't believe it!

credito m [kraydeeto] credit

crema f [krayma] (for face etc) cream; custard

crema detergente [detairjentay] cleansing cream

crema idratante [eedratantay] moisturizer

crema solare [solaray] suntan lotion

cremeria f [kremairee-a] dairy shop, also selling ice cream and cakes

cretino (m) idiot, fool; stupid

C.R.I. (Croce Rossa Italiana) f Italian Red Cross

cric m jack

criminalità f crime(s)

crisi f [kreezee] crisis, crises

critica f criticism

criticare [kreeteekaray] to criticize

crociera f [krochaira] cruise

crudele [kroodaylay] cruel

cruscotto m [krooskot-to] dashboard

cuccetta f [koochet-ta] couchette

cucchiaino m [kook-ya-eeno] teaspoon; coffeespoon

cucchiaio m [kook-ya-yo] spoon

un cucchiaio (di) a spoonful (of)

cucina f [koocheena] kitchen; cooker; cooking, cookery

cucinare [koocheenaray] to cook

cucire [koocheeray] to sew

cuffia da bagno f [ban-yo] bathing cap

cugino m [koojeeno], **cugina** f cousin

cultura f [kooltoora] culture

cunetta o dosso dips or blind summits

cuoca f [kwoka] cook

cuocere [kwochairay] to cook; to bake

cuoco m [kwoko] cook

cuoio m [kwo-yo] leather

cuore m [kworay] heart

cupola m dome, cupola

curioso [koor-yozo] curious

curva f [koorva] bend

curva pericolosa dangerous bend

cuscino m [koosheeno] pillow; cushion

CV (cavallo vapore) h.p.

D

da* from; by; at; to

dà* he/she it gives; you give

da consumarsi entro... use by ...

dado m nut (for bolt); dice

dagli* [dal-yee] from the; by the

dai* [da-ee] from the; by the; you give

dallo, dal, dalla, dalle* [dal-lay] from the; by the

dama f draughts

danese (m/f) [danayzay] Danish; Dane

Danimarca f Denmark

danneggiare [dan-nej-jaray] to damage

danno* (m) they give; damage

dappertutto [dap-pairtoot-to] everywhere

dare* (m) [daray] to give; debit

data f date

data di nascita [nasheeta] date of birth

date* [datay] you give

davanti m [davantee] front (part)

davanti a in front of

passare davanti (a) to pass, to go past

da vendersi dietro presentazione di ricetta medica to be sold on prescription only

da vendersi entro... sell by ...

davvero [dav-vairo] really?

ah, davvero? is it?; do they? etc

d.C. (dopo Cristo) A.D.

debito m [daybeeto] debt

debole [daybolay] weak

decidere [decheedairay] to decide

decimo (m) [daycheemo] tenth

decollare [dekol-laray] to take off

decollo m take-off

degente m/f [dejentay] inpatient

del, dei [**day**], **degli*** [**day**l-yee] some; of the

delfino m dolphin

delicato frail, delicate

delizioso [deleetz-y**o**zo] lovely, delicious; charming

dello, della, delle* [**del**-lay] some; of the

deltaplano m hang-gliding

deludere [del**oo**dairay] to disappoint

deluso [del**oo**zo] disappointed

denaro m money

dente m [**den**tay] tooth

dentiera f [dent-y**ai**ra] dentures

dentifricio m [denteefr**ee**cho] toothpaste

dentista m/f dentist

dentro inside

dépliant m [**day**plee-ant] brochure(s); leaflet(s)

deposito m [dep**o**zeeto] deposit

deposito bagagli [bag**a**l-yee] left luggage, baggage check

deposito bancario [bankar-yo] deposit account

depresso depressed

deputato m, **deputata** f MP

descrivere [deskr**ee**vairay] to describe

desidera? [dezeedaira] what would you like?; can I help you?

destinatario m [desteenatar-yo] addressee

destinazione f [desteenatz-yonay] destination

destra f right

a destra on/to the right

detersivo liquido per i piatti m [detairs**ee**vo leekweedo pair ee p-yat-ti] washing-up liquid

detersivo per bucato [book**a**to] washing powder

detestare [detestaray] to hate

deve* [**day**vay] he/she/it must; you must

devi* [**day**vee] you must

deviazione f [dev-yatz-y**o**nay] diversion

devo* [**day**vo] I must

devono* they must

di* of; than

diabetico [dee-ab**ay**teeko] diabetic

dialetto m dialect

diamante m [dee-am**a**ntay] diamond

diamo* we give

diapositiva f [dee-apozeet**ee**va] slide

diario m [dee-**a**r-yo] diary

diarrea f [dee-ar-r**ay**-a] diarrhoea

dibattito m debate

dica? yes?

dice* [**dee**chay] he/she/it says; you say

dicembre m [deech**e**mbray] December

dichiarare [deek-yararay] to declare

dichiarazione f [deek-yaratz-y**o**nay] statement

dici* [**dee**chee] you say

diciamo* [deech-y**a**mo] we say

diciannove [deechan-no-vay]

nineteen

diciassette [deechas-**set**-tay] seventeen

diciotto [deech**ot**-to] eighteen

dico* I say

dicono* they say

dieci [dee-**ay**chee] ten

dieta f [d-**yay**ta] diet
  essere a dieta to be on a diet

dietro m [d-**yay**tro] back, rear; at the back
  dietro (a) behind

difendere [deef**en**dairay] to defend

difettoso [deefet-**to**zo] faulty

difficile [deef-**fee**cheelay] difficult

diligente [deeleej**en**tay] hard-working

dimenticare [deementeek**a**ray] to forget

dimenticarsi to forget

diminuire [deemeenw**ee**ray] to lessen

dimostrazione f [deemostratz-**yo**ne] demonstration

dintorni **mpl** environs
  nei dintorni di in the vicinity of

Dio m [**dee**-o] God
  Dio mio! my God!

dipendere: dipende [deep**en**day] it depends

dipingere [deep**ee**njairay] to paint

dipinto m painting

dire* [**dee**ray] to say; to tell

diretto (m) direct; through train

direttore m [deeret-**to**ray] manager; headmaster

direttrice f [deeret-**tree**chay] manageress; headmistress

direzione f [deeretz-**yo**nay] direction

disaccordo m [deezak-**ko**rdo] disagreement

disastro m [deez**a**stro] disaster

discesa f [deesh**ay**sa] descent; slope; exit

disco m record

discorso m speech

discoteca f disco

discreto [deeskr**ay**to] discreet

discutere (di) [deesk**oo**tairay] to discuss; to argue

disegnare [deesen-**ya**ray] to draw

disegno m [dees**en**-yo] drawing

disfare: disfare le valigie [deesf**a**ray lay val**ee**jay] to unpack

disinfettante m [deezeenfet-**tan**tay] disinfectant, antiseptic

disoccupato [deezok-koo**pa**to] unemployed

disoccupazione f [deezok-koopatz-**yo**nay] unemployment

disordinato [deezordeen**a**to] untidy

dispiacere: le dispiace se...? [lay deesp-y**a**chay say] do you mind if I ...?
  mi dispiace (tanto)! I'm (so) sorry!

dispiaciuto [deesp-yach**oo**to] sorry

disporsi su due file get into

two lanes

dispositivo m [deespozeeteevo] device

dispositivo di emergenza emergency button/handle

distante [deestantay] far away

distanza f [deestantza] distance

disteso [deestayzo] lying down

distinta di versamento f [deesteenta dee vairsamento] paying-in slip

distratto absent-minded; inattentive

distribuire [deestreebweeray] to distribute

distribuito da... [deestreebweeto] distributed by ...

distributore m [deestreebootoray] distributor, dispenser; petrol station, gas station

distributore (automatico) di biglietti [owtomateeko dee beelyet-tee] ticket machine

disturbare [deestoorbaray] to disturb

disuguale [deezoogwalay] unequal

ditale m [deetalay] thimble

dite* [deetay] you say

dito m finger

dito del piede [p-yayday] toe

ditta f [deet-ta] firm, company

divano m [deevano] sofa

diversi [deevairsee], diverse [deevairsay] several

diverso different

divertente [deevairtentay] amusing

divertirsi [deevairteersee] to enjoy oneself

dividere [deeveedairay] to divide

divieto di accesso no entry

divieto di accesso ai non addetti ai lavori no access – works only

divieto di accesso – escluso residenti/bus/taxi residents/ buses/taxis only

divieto di affissione stick no bills

divieto di balneazione no bathing

divieto di fermata no stopping

divieto di pesca no fishing

divieto di sosta no parking

divieto di transito no thoroughfare

divorziato [deevortz-yato] divorced

dizionario m [deetz-yonar-yo] dictionary

do* I give

dobbiamo* we must

docce fpl [dochay] showers

doccia f [docha] shower
 fare la doccia to have a shower

dodici [doh-deechee] twelve

Dogana f Customs

Dogana merci Customs for freight

Dogana passeggeri passenger Customs

dolce (m) [dolchay] sweet; cake

dolci mpl [dolchay] confectionery; cakes

dollaro m dollar

dolore m [doloray] pain

doloroso [dolorozo] painful

domanda f question

domandare [domandaray] to ask

domani [domanee] tomorrow

 a domani see you tomorrow

domenica f [domayneeka] Sunday

 la domenica on Sundays

 la domenica e i giorni festivi Sundays and public holidays

donna f woman

donne ladies (toilet), ladies rest room

dopo after; afterwards

dopobarba m aftershave

doposciampo m [doposhampo] conditioner

doppio [dop-yo] double

dormire [dormeeray] to sleep

 andare a dormire to go to bed

dottore (Dott.) m [dot-toray] doctor

dottoressa (Dott.ssa) f doctor

dove? [dovay] where?

 dove si trova...? where is ...?

dovere* (m) [dovairay] to have to, must; to owe; duty

dovete* [dovaytay] you must

dovuto* had to

dozzina f [dodzeena] dozen

 (una) dozzina (di) a dozen (of)

drammatico dramatic

dritto straight on

droga f drug(s)

drogheria f [drogairee-a] grocer's

dubitare [doobeetaray] to doubt

due [doo-ay] two

due pezzi mpl [petzee] bikini

dune fpl [doonay] sand dunes

dunque [doonkway] therefore, so; well (then)

duomo m [dwomo] cathedral

durante [doorantay] during

 durante la marcia reggersi agli appositi sostegni please hold on while vehicle is in motion

duro [dooro] hard

E

e [ay] and

è* [ay] he/she/it is; you are

ebreo [ebray-o] Jewish

ecc. (eccetera) etc

eccetto [echet-to] except

ecco [ek-ko] here is/are; here you are; that's it

 ecco qua! [kwa] here you are!

edicola f newsagent's

edificio m [edeefeecho] building

educato [edookato] polite

effettua: si effettua dal... al... this service is available from ... until ...

Egr.Sig. (egregio signore) Mr (in letters)

elastico (m) rubber band; elastic

elenco telefonico m [telayfoneeko] telephone directory

elettrauto m [elet-trowto]

workshop for car electrical repairs

elettricista m [elet-treech**eesta**] electrician

elettricità f [elet-treech**eeta**] electricity

elettrico [elet-tr**eeko**] electric

elettrodomestici mpl [elet-trodom**esteechee**] electrical appliances

elicottero m helicopter

emergenza f [emairj**entza**] emergency; emergency lane

emissione del biglietto take your ticket here

emozionante [emotz-yon**antay**] exciting

E.N.I.T. (Ente Nazionale Italiano per il Turismo) m [en**eet**] Italian national tourist board

enorme [en**ormay**] enormous

enoteca f [enot**ayka**] wine-tasting shop

entrare [entr**aray**] to go in; to come in

entrata f entrance

entrata con abbonamento o biglietto già convalidato entry for those with season tickets or with validated tickets

entrata libera admission free

entusiasmante [entooz-yazm**antay**] fascinating; exciting

E.P.T. (Ente Provinciale per il Turismo) m Italian local tourist board

equipaggio m [ekeepaj-jo] crew

equitazione f [ekweetatz-y**onay**] horse riding

equivoco m [ekw**eevoko**] misunderstanding

erba f [**air**ba] grass

errore m [er-r**oray**] mistake

esagerare [esajair**aray**] to exaggerate

esame m [es**amay**] examination

esattamente [esat-tam**entay**] exactly

esatto [es**at**-to] correct

esaurito sold out

esausto [es**ow**sto] exhausted

escluso frontisti residents only

escluso sabato e festivi except Saturdays and Sundays/holidays

escursione f [eskoors-y**onay**] excursion, outing; hike

esempio m [es**emp**-yo] example **per esempio** for example

esente da tasse [es**ent**ay da tas-say] duty-free

esercizio m [ezairch**eetz**-yo] exercise; shop

espresso m strong black coffee; express letter; express train

esprimere [espr**eemairay**] to express

essere* [**es**-sairay] to be

esso [**es**-so] it

est m east

estate f [est**atay**] summer

estero: all'estero [al-l**estairo**] abroad

estetista f beautician
estintore m [esteentoray] fire
  extinguisher
età f [ayta] age
etichetta f [eeteeket-ta] label
etto(grammo) m hundred
  grams
Eurocity m international fast
  train
europeo [ay-ooropay-o]
  European
evitare [eeveetaray] to avoid

F

fa* he/she/it does; you do;
  ago
fabbrica f factory
facchino m [fak-keeno] porter
faccia f [facha] face
facciamo* [fachamo] we do
faccio* [facho] I do
facile [facheelay] easy
fai* [fa-ee] you do
fai da te m [da tay] DIY
falso false
fame: avere fame [avairay
  famay] to be hungry
famiglia f [fameel-ya] family
famoso famous
fanno* they do
fantastico (m) terrific; fantasy
  film/movie
fa' pure! [pooray] do as you
  please!; please, do!
fare* [faray] to make; to do
farfalla f butterfly
fari mpl headlights

fari posteriori [postair-yoree]
  rear lights
farmacia f [farmachee-a]
  chemist's, pharmacy
farmacia di turno duty
  chemist's, late-night
  pharmacy
faro m light; lighthouse
fasciatura f [fashatoora]
  bandage
fastidio m [fasteed-yo] nuisance
fate* [fatay] you do
fatica f [fateeka] hard work;
  strain
fatto a mano handmade
fattoria f farm
fattura f [fat-toora] invoice
favore m [favoray] favour
  per favore please
favorevole a [favorayvolay] in
  favour of
fazzolettini di carta mpl
  [fatzolet-teenee] tissues,
  Kleenex®
fazzoletto m [fatzolet-to]
  handkerchief
febbraio m [feb-bra-yo]
  February
febbre f [feb-bray] temperature
febbre da fieno f [f-yayno] hay
  fever
federa f [faydaira] pillowcase
fegato m [faygato] liver
felice [feleechay] happy
feriale: giorno feriale [jorno fair-
  yalay] working day
feriali mpl working days
ferita f wound
ferito injured

fermare [fairmaray] to stop

fermarsi to stop

fermata (dell'autobus) f [fairmata del-lowtoboos] (bus) stop

fermata a richiesta [reek-yesta] request stop

fermata facoltativa [fakoltateeva] request stop

fermata obbligatoria [ob-bleegator-ya] compulsory stop

fermata prenotata bus or tram stopping

fermo! [fairmo] don't move!

fermo per manutenzione closed for repairs

fermo posta m poste restante

ferragosto m August 15th (public holiday)

ferramenta f hardware store(s)

ferro m [fair-ro] iron; knitting needle

ferro da stiro [steero] iron (for ironing)

ferrovia f [fair-rovee-a] railway

Ferrovie dello Stato fpl [fair-rovee-ay] Italian State Railways

festa f party; holiday, vacation

festivi mpl public holidays

fetta f slice

FFSS (Ferrovie dello Stato) fpl Italian state railways

fiala f [f-yala] phial

fiammifero m [f-yam-meefairo] match (light)

fianco m [f-yanko] side; hip

fidanzata f [feedantzata] fiancée

fidanzato (m) fiancé; engaged

fidarsi to trust

fido m credit

fiera f [f-yaira] funfair; trade fair

fiero proud

figlia f [feel-ya] daughter

figlio m son

figlio di puttana! [dee] son of a bitch!

fila f queue
  fare la fila to queue

film m film, movie

filo m thread

filo di ferro wire

filtro m filter

finale f [feenalay] final

finalmente [feenalmentay] at last

finché [feenkay] until

fine (f) [feenay] end; thin; fine (blade, pen etc); refined

fine del tratto autostradale end of motorway/highway

fine settimana [set-teemana] weekend

finestra f window

finestrino m window (on plane, train)

finire [feeneeray] to finish

fino thin; fine (blade, pen etc); even
  fino a until

finocchio m [feenok-yo] fennel; poof

fioraio m [f-yora-yo] florist

fiore m [f-yoray] flower

fiorentino [f-yorenteeno] Florentine

Firenze f [feerentzay] Florence

firma f signature
firmare [**feer**maray] to sign
fischio m [**feesk**-yo] whistle
fisica f [**feez**eeka] physics
fiume m [f-**yoo**may] river
flacone m [fla**ko**nay] medicine
  bottle
foglia f [**fol**-ya] leaf
folla f crowd
fon m hair dryer
fondo m bottom
  in fondo a at the end/bottom
  of
fondotinta m [fondo**teen**ta]
  foundation cream
fontana f fountain
footing m jogging
foratura f [fora**too**ra] puncture
forbici mpl [**for**beechee] scissors
forchetta f [for**ket**-ta] fork
foresta f forest
forfora f dandruff
forma f form
  in forma fit
formica f [for**mee**ka] ant
fornaio m [**for**na-yo] baker's
fornello m cooker; hob
fornire [for**nee**ray] to supply
forniture per ufficio fpl office
  supplies
forno m oven
forno a microonde [meekro-
  onday] microwave (oven)
forse [**for**say] maybe, perhaps
forte [**for**tay] strong; loud
fortuna f [for**too**na] luck
fortunatamente
  [fortoonata**men**tay] fortunately
foruncolo m spot

fotografare [fotografa**ray**] to
  photograph
fotografia f [fotografee-a]
  photograph; photography
  fare fotografie [fotografee-ay]
  to take photographs
fotografo m photographer
fotoottica f camera shop and
  optician
foulard m [**foo**lar] headscarf
fra between; in; through
  fra l'altro besides
fragile [**fraj**eelay] frail
francamente [franka**men**tay]
  frankly
francese (m/f) [fran**chay**zay]
  French; Frenchman;
  Frenchwoman
Francia f [**fran**cha] France
franco m franc
francobollo m [franko**bol**-lo]
  stamp
frasario m [**fraz**ar-yo]
  phrasebook
frase f [**fraz**ay] sentence
fratello m brother
frattura f [frat-**too**ra] fracture
frazione f [fratz-**yo**nay] fraction;
  administrative division of a
  municipality
freccia f [**frec**ha] indicator;
  arrow
freddo (m) cold
  fa freddo it's cold
  avere freddo to be cold
freno m [**frayn**o] brake
  freno a mano handbrake
fresco fresh; cool (weather)
friggere [**freej**-jairay] to fry

Fr

friggitrice f [freej-jeetreechay]
deep-fat fryer

frigo m fridge

frigobar m minibar

frigorifero m [freegoreefairo]
fridge

frizione f [freetz-yonay] clutch;
friction

fronte f [frontay] forehead

di fronte a opposite; in front
of

frontiera f [front-yaira] border

frullatore m [frool-latoray] mixer

frusta f whisk

fruttivendolo m [froot-teevendolo]
greengrocer's

FS (Ferrovie dello Stato) fpl
Italian state railways

f.to (firmato) signed

fucile m [foocheelay] gun; rifle

fumare [foomaray] to smoke

fumatori smokers

fumetto m comic; strip
cartoon

fumo m [foomo] smoke

fune f [foonay] rope

funivia f [fooneevee-a] cable car

funzionare [foontz-yonaray] to
work

fuochi d'artificio mpl [fwokee
darteefeecho] fireworks

fuoco m [fwoko] fire

fuori [fworee] outside

fuori servizio out of order

furgone m [foorgonay] van

furioso [foor-yozo] furious

fusibile m [foozeebeelay] fuse

G

gabinetto m [gabeenet-to] toilet,
rest room

andare al gabinetto to go to
the toilet/rest room

galleria f [gal-lair-ee-a] tunnel;
balcony; circle

galleria d'arte [dartay] art
gallery

Galles m [gal-les] Wales

gallese (m/f) [gal-layzay] Welsh;
Welshman; Welshwoman

gamba f leg

gara f sporting event; race;
competition

garanzia f [garantzee-a]
guarantee

gasolio m [gazol-yo] diesel oil

gasolio invernale [eenvairnalay]
diesel containing anti-freeze

gatto m cat

gelateria f [jelatairee-a] ice
cream parlour

gelato (m) [jelato] frozen; ice
cream

gelo m [jaylo] frost

gelosia f [jelozee-a] jealousy

geloso [jelozo] jealous

gemelli mpl [jemel-lee] twins

generalmente [jenairalmentay]
generally

genere m [jaynairay] type

in genere mostly, generally

genero m [jaynairo] son-in-law

genitori mpl [jeneetoree] parents

gennaio m [jen-na-yo] January

Genova f [jenova] Genoa

gente f [jentay] people

gentile [jenteelay] kind

gentilezza f [jenteeletza]

kindness

Germania f [jerman-ya]
Germany

gesto m [jesto] gesture

gettare [jet-taray] to throw

gettare via to throw away

gettoni mpl [jet-tonee]
telephone tokens

ghiacciaio m [g-yacha-o] glacier

ghiaccio m [g-yacho] ice

già [ja] already

giacca f [jak-ka] jacket

giacca a vento anorak

giallo (m) [jal-lo] yellow;
thriller

giardini pubblici mpl [poob-bleechee] public gardens

giardino m [jardeeno] garden

ginecologo m [jeenaykologo]
gynaecologist

Ginevra f [jeenevra] Geneva

ginnastica f [jeen-nasteeka]
gymnastics; PE

ginocchio m [jeenok-yo] knee

giocare [jokaray] to play

giocatore m [jokatoray] player

giocatrice f [jokatreechay]
player

giocattolo m [jokat-tolo] toy

giochi per il computer mpl
[j-yokee] computer games

gioco m [joko] game

gioco di società [dee societa]
board game

gioielleria f [jo-yel-lairee-a]
jeweller's

gioielli mpl [jo-yel-lee] jewellery

gioielliere m [jo-yel-yairay]
jeweller

giornalaio m [jornala-yo]
newsagent's

giornale m [jornalay] newspaper

giornata f [jornata] day

giorni feriali mpl weekdays

giorni festivi public holidays

giorno m [jorno] day

giorno di chiusura [k-yoozoora]
closing day

giovane (m/f) [jovanay] young;
young person

giovedì m [jovaydee] Thursday

giradischi m [jeeradeeskee]
record player

girare [jeeraray] to turn

girarsi to turn

giri a destra [jeeree] turn right

giri a sinistra [seeneestra] turn
left

giro m [jeero] turn; walk,
stroll; tour

a giro di posta by return mail

andare a far un giro to go for
a stroll/drive

fare un giro in bicicletta
[beecheeklet-ta] to go for a
cycle ride

giro a piedi [p-yaydee] walk,
stroll

giro in barca boat trip

giro in macchina [mak-keena]
drive

gita f [jeeta] excursion,
outing; hike

gita in pullman coach trip

gita organizzata [organeedzata]
package tour

gita scolastica [skolasteeka]
school trip

giù [joo] down

giubbotti salvagente sotto la poltrona lifejackets are under the seat

giugno m [joon-yo] June

giusto [joosto] right, correct; fair

gli* [l-yee] the; to him; to them

goccia f [gocha] drop

gola f throat

golf m golf; jumper

gomito m elbow

gomma f rubber; tyre

gomma a terra flat tyre

gomma di scorta spare tyre

gommista m/f tyre repair specialist

gommone m [gom-monay] (rubber) dinghy

gonfio [gonf-yo] swollen

gonna f skirt

gorgo m whirlpool

governativo governmental; state

governo m government

gradino m step

grado m degree, level

grammatica f grammar

grammo m gramme

Gran Bretagna f [bretan-ya] Great Britain

granchio m [grank-yo] crab

grande [granday] big

grande magazzino m [magadzeeno] department store

grandine f [grandeenay] hail

grasso fat

gratis free

grato grateful

grattacielo m [grat-tachaylo] skyscraper

grattugiare [grat-toojaray] to grate

gratuito [gratoo-eeto] free

grazie [gratzee-ay] thank you

grazie a Dio! thank God!

grazie, anche a te/lei [ankay a tay/lay] thank you, the same to you

grazie mille [meel-lay] thank you very much

grazioso [gratz-yozo] pretty

Grecia f [grecha] Greece

greco (m) Greek

gridare [greedaray] to shout

grigio [greejo] grey

grosso big, large; thick

grotta f cave

gruccia f [groocha] coathanger

gruppo m group

gruppo sanguigno [sangween-yo] blood group

guancia f [gwancha] cheek

guanti mpl [gwantee] gloves

guanto di spugna m [dee spoon-ya] flannel

guardare [gwardaray] to look (at)

guardare in su [een soo] to look up

guardaroba m [gwardaroba] wardrobe; cloakroom

guasto (m) [gwasto] breakdown; broken, out of order; rotten

guerra f [gwair-ra] war

guida f [gweeda] guide; guidebook

guidare [gweedaray] to lead; to drive

guidare a passo d'uomo [dwomo] drive at walking speed

guida telefonica f [gweeda] telephone directory

guscio m [goosho] shell

gusto m taste

H

ha* [a] he/she it has; you have

hai* [a-ee] you have

hanno* [an-no] they have

ho* [o] I have

I

i* [ee] the

idea f [eeday-a] idea

idiota m/f [eed-yota] idiot

idraulico m [eedrowleeko] plumber

ieri [yairee] yesterday

il* [eel] the

imbarazzante [eembaratzantay] embarrassing

imbarazzato [eembaratzato] embarrassed

imbarazzo m [eembaratzo] embarrassment

imbarcarsi [eembarkarsee] to board, to embark

imbarco m [eembarko] boarding

imbarco immediato now boarding

imbrogliare [eembrol-yaray] to cheat

imbucare [eembookaray] to post, to mail

immediatamente [eem-med-yata-mentay] immediately

immersione f [eem-mers-yonay] skin-diving

immigrato m [eem-meegrato], immigrata f immigrant

imparare [eempararay] to learn

impaziente [eempatz-yentay] impatient

impermeabile (m) [eempairmay-abeelay] raincoat; waterproof

importante [eemportantay] important; significant; sizeable

importare: non importa [eemporta] it doesn't matter

imposta f tax

impostare [eempostaray] to post, to mail

imposte fpl [eempostay] shutters

improvvisamente [eemprovveezamentay] suddenly

in in; into; to

in macchina [mak-keena] by car

incartare [eencartaray] to wrap

incassare [eenkas-saray] to cash

incidente m [eencheedentay] accident

incinta [eencheenta] pregnant

incontro m meeting

incrocio m [eenkrocho] junction; crossroads, intersection

incrocio pericoloso dangerous junction

indicare [eendeekaray] to indicate; to point at; to show

indietro [eend-yaytro] behind; back

faccia marcia indietro [facha marcha] reverse

indirizzo m [eendeereeetzo] address

indubbiamente [eendoob-yamentay] undoubtedly

infarto m heart attack

infelice [eenfeleechay] unhappy

infermeria f [eenfairmairee-a] infirmary

infermiere m [eenfairm-yairay], **infermiera f** nurse

infezione f [eenfetz-yonay] infection

influenzare [eenfloo-entzaray] to influence

informare [eenformaray] to inform

informarsi (su) to get information (about)

informazioni fpl [eenformatz-yonee] (tourist) information

informazioni elenco abbonati directory enquiries

Ing. (ingegnere) engineer

ingannare [eengan-naray] to deceive

ingegnere m [eenjen-yairay] engineer

ingenuo [eenjaynwo] naïve

Inghilterra f [eengheeltair-ra] England

inglese (m/f) [eenglayzay] English; Englishman; Englishwoman

ingoiare [eengo-yaray] to swallow

ingorgo m traffic jam

ingrandimento m enlargement

ingrassaggio m [eengras-saj-jo] oiling, lubrication

ingresso m entrance (hall)

ingresso gratuito/libero admission free

iniezione f [eenyetz-yonay] injection

inizio m [eeneetz-yo] beginning

innumerevole [een-noomairayvolay] innumerable

inoltrare [eenoltraray] to forward

inquilino m [eenkweeleeno], **inquilina f** tenant

inquinato [eenkweenato] polluted

insegnante m/f [eensen-yantay] teacher

insegnare [eensen-yaray] to teach

inserire le monete insert coins

insettifugo m [eenset-teefoogo] insect repellent

insetto m [eenset-to] insect

insieme [eens-yaymay] together

insistere [eenseestairay] to insist

insonnia f [eenson-ya] insomnia

interessante [eentaires-santay] interesting

interessarsi di/a [eentaires-sarsee dee] to be interested in

internazionale [eentairnatz-

yonalay] international
interno internal; inside
  all'interno inside
intero whole
interruttore m [eentair-root-toray]
  switch
interruzione della corrente f
  [eentair-rootz-yonay del-la kor-
  rentay] power cut
intervallo m [eentairval-lo]
  interval; break; half-time
intervista f [eentairveesta]
  interview
intorno (a) around
intossicazione alimentare
  f [eentos-seekatz-yonay
  aleementaray] food poisoning
introdurre un biglietto alla
  volta insert only one ticket
  at a time
invalido disabled
  per invalidi for disabled
  people
inverno m winter
investire [eenvesteeray] to
  invest; to knock over
inviare [eenv-yaray] to send; to
  post, to mail
invidioso [eenveed-yozo]
  envious
invitare [eenveetaray] to invite
invito m invitation
io* [ee-o] I
Irlanda f [eerlanda] Ireland
Irlanda del Nord Northern
  Ireland
irlandese (m/f) [eerlandayzay]
  Irish; Irishman; Irishwoman
isola f [eezola] island

istituto m institute; secondary
  school; department
istruttore di nuoto m [eestroot-
  toray dee nwoto] swimming
  instructor
istruttrice di nuoto f [eestroot-
  treechay] swimming
  instructor
istruzioni per l'uso
  instructions for use
Italia f [eetal-ya] Italy
italiano (m) [eetal-yano]**, italiana**
  (f) Italian
itinerario m [eeteenairar-yo]
  route, itinerary
I.V.A. (Imposta sul Valore
  Aggiunto) f [eeva] VAT
I.V.A. compresa [komprayza]
  inclusive of VAT

K
K-way® m cagoule

L
L pound, £; lira
l (litro) litre
la* the; her; it; you
là there
  di là [dee] over there; that
  way; in the other room;
  from there
labbro m [lab-bro] lip
lacca per capelli f [kapel-lee]
  hair spray
lacci per le scarpe mpl [lachee
  pair lay skarpay] shoe laces
ladro m thief

laggiù [laj-**joo**] over there

lago m lake

laguna f lagoon

lamentarsi to complain

lametta f razor blade

lampada f lamp

lampada da comodino bedside lamp

lampadina f light bulb

lampione m [lamp-**yo**nay] street lamp

lana f wool

lanciare [lanch**aray**] to throw

largo wide

lasciare [lash**aray**] to leave; to let, to allow

lassativo m laxative

lato m side

latte detergente m [**lat**-tay detair**jentay**] skin cleanser

latteria f [lat-tair**ee**-a] dairy shop

lattina f can

laurea f [**low**ray-a] degree

lavabo m washbasin

lavanderia (automatica) f [lavandair**ee**-a owtom**a**teeka] launderette

lavandino m sink

lavare [lav**aray**] to wash

lavare a mano wash by hand

lavare a secco dry-clean only

lavare i panni to do the washing

lavare i piatti [p-yat-**tee**] to do the washing up

lavare la biancheria [b-yan-kair**ee**-a] to do the washing

lavare separatamente wash

separately

lavarsi [lav**arsee**] to wash, to have a wash

lavarsi i denti to brush one's teeth

lavasecco m dry-cleaner's

lavastoviglie f [lavastov**eel**-yay] dishwasher

lavatrice f [lavatr**ee**chay] washing machine

lavorare [lavor**aray**] to work

lavori in corso mpl roadworks

lavori stradali roadworks

lavoro m work

le*** [lay] the; to her; to you

legare [leg**aray**] to tie

legge f [**lej**-jay] law

leggere [**lej**-jairay] to read

leggero [lej-**jai**ro] light

legno m [**len**-yo] wood

lei*** [lay] she; her; you

lentamente [lent**a**mentay] slowly

lenti a contatto fpl contact lenses

lenti morbide fpl [**mor**beeday] soft lenses

lenti rigide fpl [**ree**jeeday] hard lenses

lenti semi-rigide fpl [**say**mee] gas permeable lenses

lento slow

lenzuolo m [lentz**wo**lo] sheet

lettera f [**let**-taira] letter

lettera tassata excess postage to be paid

letti a castello mpl bunk beds

lettino m cot; sun lounger

lettino pieghevole [p-yayg**ay**-

volay] lounger; campbed

letto m bed

andare a letto to go to bed

(ri)fare il letto to make the bed

letto a due piazze [doo-ay p-yatzay] double bed

letto a una piazza [p-yatza] single bed

leva del cambio f [layva del kamb-yo] gear lever

levare [layvaray] to remove

levata f [layvata] collection

lezione f [letz-yonay] lesson; class

li [lee] them

lì there

libbra f pound

libero vacant, free

libertà f freedom

libreria f [leebrairee-a] bookshop, bookstore; bookcase

libretto degli assegni m [daylyee as-sen-yee] cheque book, checkbook

libro m book

liceo m [leechay-o] secondary school

lima f [leema] file

lima per le unghie [oong-yay] nailfile

limite delle acque sicure m end of safe bathing area

limite di velocità speed limit

linea f [leenay-a] line

linea aerea [a-airay-a] airline

linea ferroviaria railway line

lingua f [leengwa] tongue; language

liquido tergicristallo m [leekweedo tairjeekreestal-lo] screen wash

liquori mpl [leekworee] spirits

lira sterlina f [stairleena] pound sterling

liscio [leesho] smooth; neat

lista f list; menu

listino dei cambi m exchange rates

L(it). (lire italiane) Italian lire

lite f [leetay] fight

litigare [leeteegaray] to argue, to quarrel

litigio m [leeteejo] argument, quarrel

litro m litre

livido m bruise

lo* the; him; it

località f locality

locanda f guesthouse, hotel

loggione m [loj-jonay] gallery, the gods

londinese (m/f) [londeenayzay] London (adj); Londoner

Londra f London

lontano far away

loro* they; them; you

il/la loro their(s); your(s)

lozione idratante f [lotz-yonay eedratantay] moisturizer

lozione solare [solaray] suntan lotion

L.st. (lira sterlina) pound

luce f [loochay] light

lucidare [loocheedaray] to polish

luci di posizione mpl [loochee dee pozeetz-yonay] sidelights

lucido per le scarpe m [loocheedo pair lay skarpay] shoe polish
luglio m [lool-yo] July
lui* [loo-ee] he; him
luna f [loona] moon
luna di miele [m-yelay] honeymoon
luna park m funfair
lunedì m [loonaydee] Monday
lunghezza f [loongetza] length
lungo long; along
lungomare m [loongomaray] esplanade, promenade
luogo di nascita m [lwogo dee nasheeta] place of birth

M

M (Metropolitana) underground, (US) subway
m (metro) metre
ma but
macchia f [mak-ya] stain
macchina f [mak-keena] car; machine
macchina da scrivere [skreevairay] typewriter
macchina del caffè [kaf-fay] coffee-maker
macchina fotografica camera
macchina obliteratrice [obleetairatreechay] ticket-stamping machine
macelleria f [machel-lairee-a] butcher's
macinacaffè m [macheena-kaf-fay] coffee grinder
madre f [madray] mother

maestra f [ma-aystra] primary school teacher; instructor
maestra di sci [shee] ski instructor
maestro m [ma-aystro] primary school teacher; instructor
maestro di sci [shee] ski instructor
maggio m [maj-jo] May
maggior: la maggior parte (di) [maj-jor partay] most (of)
maggiore [maj-joray] bigger
maglia f [mal-ya] sweater, pullover
lavoro a maglia m knitting
maglietta f [mal-yet-ta] T-shirt
maglione m [mal-yonay] sweater, jumper
mai [ma-ee] never
malato ill
malattia f disease
malattia venerea [vaynairay-a] VD
maldestro clumsy
mal di denti m [dentee] toothache
mal di gola sore throat
mal di mare [maray] seasickness
mal di testa headache
male m [malay] pain, ache
male badly
far male to hurt
maledetto damned, cursed
maledizione! [maledeetz-yonay] damn!
maleducato rude
malgrado despite
malinteso m [maleentayzo]

misunderstanding

malizia f [maleetz-ya] mischief; malice

malizioso [maleetz-yozo] mischievous

mancia f [mancha] tip (in restaurant etc)

mancino [mancheeno] left-handed

mandare [mandaray] to send

mangiacassette m [manjakas-set-tay] portable cassette player

mangianastri m [manja-nastree] cassette player

mangiare [manjaray] to eat

manica f sleeve

manifesto m poster

maniglia f [maneel-ya] handle; door knob

mano f hand

di seconda mano second-hand

mansarda f attic room

Mantova f Mantua

manuale di conversazione m [manwalay dee konvairsatz-yonay] phrasebook

maratona f marathon

Marche fpl [markay] Marches

marcia a senso unico alternato temporary one way system in operation

marcia normale normal speed lane

marciapiede m [marchap-yayday] pavement, sidewalk; platform, (US) track

marco m mark

mare m [maray] sea

sul mare at the seaside

marea f [maray-a] tide

alta/bassa marea high/low tide

mar Ionio m [ee-on-yo] Ionian Sea

marito m husband

mar Mediterraneo m [medeetair-ranay-o] Mediterranean

marmo m marble

marrone [mar-ronay] brown

martedì m Tuesday

martello m hammer

mar Tirreno m [teer-rayno] Tyrrhenian Sea

marzo m [martzo] March

mascella f [mashel-la] jaw

maschera f [maskaira] mask

maschilista m [maskeeleesta] male chauvinist

massa: una massa (di gente) f a crowd (of people)

massimo: al massimo at the most

materassino (gonfiabile) m [gonfee-abeelay] air mattress, Lilo®

materasso m mattress

materia f [matair-ya] subject

matita f pencil

matrimonio m wedding

mattina f morning

la/alla mattina in the morning

ogni mattina [on-yee] every morning

mattino m morning

il/al mattino in the morning

maturo [ma**too**ro] ripe

ma va? really?

ma va! I don't believe it!

mazza f [ma**tza**] club; bat

me* [may] me

meccanico m [mek-**ka**neeko] mechanic

medaglia f [me**dal**-ya] medal

media f [**mayd**-ya] average

medicina f [medee**chee**na] medicine

medico (di turno) m [**may**deeko dee **toor**no] doctor (on duty)

medio [**mayd**-yo] average; medium

Medioevo m [med-yo-**ayv**o] Middle Ages

Mediterraneo m [medeetair-ra**nay**-o] Mediterranean

medusa f [me**doo**za] jellyfish

meglio [**mayl**-yo] better

meglio così [ko**zee**] so much the better

meno (di) [**may**no dee] less (than)

mento m chin

mentre [**men**tray] while

menzionare [mentz-yo**nar**ay] to mention

meraviglioso [meraveel-**yo**zo] wonderful

mercato m [mair**ka**to] market

a buon mercato [bwon] cheap, inexpensive

merce f [**mair**chay] goods

la merce venduta non si cambia senza lo scontrino goods are not exchanged without a receipt

merceria f [mairchai**ree**-a] haberdashery

mercoledì m [mairkole**dee**] Wednesday

merda! [**mair**da] shit!

merenda f afternoon snack

far merenda to have an afternoon snack

mese m [**may**zay] month

messa f mass

messaggio m [mes-**saj**-jo] message

messa in piega f [p-**yayg**a] set

messa in piega con il fon blow-dry

mestiere m [mest-**yair**ay] job

mestruazioni fpl [mestrwatz-**yo**nee] period (menstruation)

metà f half

metà prezzo [**pretz**o] half price

metallo m metal

metro m metre

metrò m underground, (US) subway

metropolitana f underground, (US) subway

mettere m [**met**-tairay] to put

mettersi in viaggio [met-tairsee een v-**yaj**-jo] to set off on a journey

mezza: mezza dozzina (di) [**medz**a dod**zee**na dee] half a dozen (of)

mezzanotte f [medza**not**-tay] midnight

mezza pensione f [**medz**a pens-**yo**nay] half board

mezzo (m) [**medz**o] half;

middle
in mezzo a in the middle of
mezzogiorno m [medzo**jo**rno] midday
mezz'ora f [medz**o**ra] half an hour
mi* [mee] me; myself; to me
mia* [mee-a] my; mine
mi dica [mee **dee**ka] yes?; what would you like?
mie* [mee-ay] my; mine
miei* [m-**yay**-ee] my; mine
migliaia fpl [meel-ya-ya] thousands
migliorare [meel-yor**a**ray] to improve
migliori [meel-**yo**ree], **migliore** [meel-**yo**ray] best; better
milanese (m/f) [meelan**ay**zay] Milanese; person from Milan
milione [meel-**yo**nay] million
mille [**mee**lay] thousand
mingherlino [meengairl**ee**no] skinny
minimo least, slightest
come minimo [**ko**may] at least
ministero m ministry; board; office
minuto m minute
mio* [mee-o] my; mine
mirino m viewfinder
mi scusi [sk**oo**zee] excuse me; sorry
mi spiace [spee-**a**chay] I'm sorry
misto lana [**mee**sto] wool mixture
misurare [meezoor**a**ray] to measure

mitt. (mittente) sender
mittente m [meet-**ten**tay] sender
mobili mpl [m**o**beelee] furniture
moda f fashion
di moda fashionable
modulo m form
moglie f [m**o**l-yay] wife
molla f spring (mechanical)
molletta (da bucato) f clothes peg
molo m quay; pier; jetty
molta a lot, much; very
molti, molte [m**o**ltay] a lot; much; very; many, lots of
molto a lot; much; very
molto bene, grazie [**bay**nay] very well, thank you
momento: un momento, prego [**pray**go] one moment, please
mondo m world
moneta f [mon**ay**ta] coin; small change
monolocale m [monolok**a**lay] studio flat/apartment
montagna f [montan-ya] mountain
monumento ai caduti war memorial
moquette f [mok**et**] (fitted) carpet
morbido soft
morbillo m measles
morire [mor**ee**ray] to die
morso m bite
morte f [m**o**r-tay] death
morto dead
mosca f fly
moschea f [mosk**ay**-a] mosque

moscone m [moskonay] twin-hulled rowing boat

mostra f exhibition; show

mostrare [mostraray] to show

moto f motorbike

motore m [motoray] engine

motorino m moped

motoscafo m motorboat

movimenti mpl transactions

movimento m movement

mucca m cow

multa f fine

municipio m [mooneecheep-yo] town hall

munitevi di un carrello/cestino please take a trolley/basket

muovere [mwovairay] to move

muoversi [mwovairsee] to move

muoviti! [mwoveetee] hurry up!

muro m wall

muscolo m muscle

museo m [moozay-o] museum

musica f [moozeeka] music

mutande fpl [mootanday] underpants; pants, panties

mutuo m [mootwo] mortgage; bank loan

N

nafta f diesel oil

napoletano Neapolitan

Napoli f Naples

nascita f [nasheeta] birth

nascondere [naskondairay] to hide

nascondersi to hide

naso m [nazo] nose

nastro m tape; ribbon

nastro adesivo adhesive tape

nastro trasportatore [trasportatoray] conveyor belt

Natale m [natalay] Christmas
Buon Natale! [bwon] Merry Christmas!

natale native

nato born

natura f nature

naturale: al naturale [natooralay] (food) plain; natural

naturalmente [natooralmentay] naturally, of course

naturista m/f naturist, nudist

nausea: avere la nausea [avairay nowzay-a] to feel sick/queasy

nave f [navay] ship

nave di linea [leen-ya] liner

nave passeggeri [pas-sej-jairee] passenger ship

navigare [naveegaray] to sail

nazionale [natz-yonalay] national; domestic

nazionalità f [natz-yonaleeta] nationality

nazione f [natz-yonay] nation

ne* [nay] of him/her/them/it; about him/her/them/it
non ne ho [o] I don't have any
prendine [prendeenay] take some

né: né... né... [nay] neither ... nor ...

neanche [nay-ankay] not even

nebbia f fog

nebbioso [neb-yozo] foggy

necessario [neches-sar-yo]

necessary

negare [negaray] to deny

negli* [nayl-yee] in the

negoziante m/f [negotz-yantay] shopkeeper

negozio m [negotz-yo] shop

nello, nel, nella, nei [nay], nelle* [nel-lay] in the

nemmeno [nem-mayno] not even

neozelandese (m/f) [nay-o-dzaylandayzay] New Zealand (adj); New Zealander

neppure [nep-pooray] not even

nero (m) [nairo] black; (hair) dark

nervoso [nairvozo] nervous

nessun no; not any

nessun dubbio [doob-yo] no doubt

nessuno, nessuna no; none; nobody; not any

da nessuna parte [partay] nowhere

netto clean

peso netto net weight

neve f [nayvay] snow

nevica [nayveeka] it is snowing

nevicata f snowfall

nevischio m [neveesk-yo] sleet

niente [n-yentay] nothing

di niente don't mention it

nient'altro? [n-yentaltro] anything else?

niente pesce oggi no fish today

non fa niente it doesn't matter

night m night club

nipote m/f [neepotay] nephew/niece; grandson/ granddaughter

no no; not

nocivo [nocheevo] harmful

nodo m knot

noi* [noy] we; us

noioso [noy-ozo] boring

noleggiare [nolej-jaray] to rent; to hire out

noleggio barche [nolej-jo barkay] boat hire

noleggio biciclette [beecheeklet-tay] cycle hire

noleggio sci [shee] ski hire

nolo: a nolo for hire, to rent

nome m [nomay] name

nome da ragazza [ragatza] maiden name

nome da sposata married name

nome di battesimo [bat-tayzeemo] Christian name

non not

non... affatto not ... at all

non bucare [bookaray] do not pierce

non capisco [kapeesko] I don't understand

non esporre ai raggi solari do not expose to direct sunlight

non ferma a... does not stop at ...

non fumare no smoking

non fumatori nonsmokers

non lo so I don't know

non... mai [ma-ee] never, not ever

non... mica [meeka] not ...

at all

nonna f grandmother

non... neanche [nay-**an**kay] not even

non... nemmeno [nem-**may**no] not even

non... né... né [nay] neither ... nor ...

non... neppure [nep-**poo**ray] not even

non... nessuno [nays-**soo**no] no one; not anybody; nobody; not ... any; no

non... niente [n-**yen**tay] nothing; not anything

nonno m grandfather

non... nulla nothing; not anything

nono (m) ninth

non oltrepassare no trespassing

non oltrepassare la dose prescritta do not exceed the stated dose

nonostante [nonos**tan**tay] despite

non parlare al conducente do not speak to the driver

non... per niente [pair n-**yen**tay] not ... at all

non... più [p-yoo] no more, no longer, not ... any more

non toccare do not touch

nord m north

nord-est m north-east

norma: a norma di legge in accordance with the law

normale [nor**ma**lay] normal; (petrol/gas) 2- or 3-star,

regular gas

norvegese (m/f) [norvay**jay**zay] Norwegian

Norvegia f [nor**ve**ja] Norway

nostro, nostra, nostri, nostre* [**nos**tray] our(s)

nota f note

notare [no**ta**ray] to note

notificare [noteefee**ka**ray] to notify

notizie fpl [no**teetz**-yay] news

noto well-known

notte f [**not**-tay] night

la/di notte at night

novanta ninety

nove [**no**-vay] nine

novellino m, novellina f beginner

novello new

novembre m [no**vem**bray] November

nozze fpl [**notz**-zay] wedding

ns. (nostro) our(s)

nubile [**noo**beelay] (woman) unmarried

nudista m/f nudist

nudo naked

nulla nothing; anything

numeri di emergenza emergency phone numbers

numeri utili useful numbers

numero m [**noo**mairo] number

numero di telefono phone number

numero di volo flight number

numeroso [noomair**o**zo] numerous

nuocere [**nwo**cheray] to harm

nuora f [**nwo**ra] daughter-in-law

nuotare [nwotaray] to swim

nuoto m [nwoto] swimming

Nuova Zelanda f [nwova dzaylanda] New Zealand

nuovo new

di nuovo again

nuvola f cloud

nuvoloso [noovolozo] cloudy

O

O (ovest) West

o or

o... o... either ... or ...

obbligare [ob-bleegaray] to oblige; to force

obbligatorio [ob-bleegator-yo] obligatory

obiettare [ob-yet-taray] to object

obiettivo m lens; objective

obiezione f [ob-yetz-yonay] objection

occasione f [ok-kas-yonay] chance; bargain

d'occasione secondhand; bargain (price)

occhiali mpl [ok-yalee] glasses, eyeglasses; goggles

occhiali da sole [solay] sunglasses

occhiata f [ok-yata] glance

occhio m [ok-yo] eye

occhio! watch out!

occidentale [ocheedentalay] western

occorrere [ok-kor-rairay] to be needed

occupare [ok-kooparay] to occupy

occuparsi di [dee] to take care of

occupato [ok-koopato] engaged, occupied; taken; busy

occupazione f [ok-koopatz-yonay] occupation

oculista m/f oculist

odiare [od-yaray] to hate

odierno [od-yairno] today's; present

odorare [odoraray] to smell

odore m [odoray] smell

offendere [of-fendairay] to offend

offensivo offensive

offerta f [of-fairta] offer

offesa f [of-fayza] offence; insult

officina (meccanica) f [of-feecheena] garage (for car repairs)

offrire [of-freeray] to offer

oggetti smarriti lost property, lost and found

oggetto m [oj-jet-to] object; thing

oggi [oj-jee] today

ogni [on-yee] each, every; all

ogni abuso sarà punito penalty for misuse

ognuno [on-yoono], ognuna everyone

oliera f [ol-yaira] oil and vinegar cruet

olio m [ol-yo] oil

olio solare [solaray] suntan oil

oltre [oltray] beyond

oltre a in addition to

oltremare [oltray-maray] overseas

oltrepassare [oltray-passaray] to cross; to go beyond; to go past

ombra **f** shade

ombrello **m** umbrella

ombrellone **m** [ombrel-lonay] sunshade

ombretto **m** eye shadow

ombroso [ombrozo] shady

omosessuale (**m/f**) [omoses-swalay] homosexual

omosessualità **f** [omoses-swaleeta] homosexuality

On. (onorevole) MP

onda **f** wave

ondulato wavy

onestà **f** honesty

onesto honest

ONU **f** UN

opale **m** [opalay] opal

opera d'arte **f** [dartay] work of art

operare [opairaray] to carry out; to operate; to act; to work

operatore **m** [opairatoray] operator

operatrice **f** [opairatreechay] operator

operoso [opairozo] hardworking

opposto opposite

oppure [op-pooray] or

opuscolo **m** brochure

opzionale [optz-yonalay] optional

ora (**f**) hour; now; in a

moment

che ore sono? [kay **o**ray] what time is it?

ora di punta rush hour

ora locale [lokalay] local time

orario **m** [orar-yo] timetable, (US) schedule

orario degli spettacoli [dayl-yee] times of performances

orario di apertura opening hours

orario di visita [veezeeta] visiting hours

orario di volo flight time

orario estivo summer timetable/schedule

orario ferroviario railway timetable/schedule

orario invernale [eenvairnalay] winter timetable/ schedule

ordinare [ordeenaray] to order

ordinario [ordeenar-yo] ordinary, usual

ordinato tidy

ordine **m** [ordeenay] order

mettere in ordine [met-tairay een] to tidy up; to put away

orecchini **mpl** [orek-keenee] earrings

orecchio **m** [orek-yo] ear

organizzare [organeetzaray] to organize

orgoglioso [orgol-yozo] proud

oriente **m** [or-yentay] east

orlo **m** edge

ormai [orma-ee] by now

oro **m** gold

orologeria **f** [orolojairee-ya]

watchmaker

orologio m [oroloj-yo] clock; watch

orribile [or-reebeelay] horrible; awful

ortografia f spelling

ortolano m greengrocer

osare [ozaray] to dare

ospedale m [ospaydalay] hospital

ospitalità f hospitality

ospitare [ospeetaray] to put up (in accommodation)

ospite m/f [ospeetay] guest; host

osso m bone

ostello della gioventù m [joventoo] youth hostel

osteria f [ostairee-a] inn

otorinolaringoiatra m/f [otoreenolareengo-yatra] ear, nose and throat specialist

ottanta eighty

ottavo (m) eighth

ottenere [ot-tenairay] to obtain, to get

ottica f optician's

ottico m optician

ottimo excellent

otto eight

ottobre m [ot-tobray] October

otturatore m [ot-tooratoray] shutter (in camera)

otturazione f [ot-tooratz-yonay] filling (in tooth)

ovest m west

ovvio [ov-yo] obvious

ozioso [otz-yozo] lazy

P

pacchetto m [pak-ket-to] package, small parcel; packet (of cigarettes etc)

pacchi postali mpl parcels, packages

pacco m parcel, package

pace f [pachay] peace

padella f frying pan

padre m [padray] father

paesaggio m [pa-aysaj-jo] landscape

paese m [pa-ayzay] country; town; village

pag. (pagina) p., pp.

pagamento m payment

pagare [pagaray] to pay

pagare alla cassa pay at the desk

pagare qui pay here

pagina f [pajeena] page

Pagine Gialle fpl [pajeenay jal-lay] Yellow Pages

paio m [pa-yo] pair

palazzo m [palatzo] palace

palazzo comunale [komoonalay] town hall

palco m box (in theatre)

paletta f spade (beach); dustpan

palla f ball

pallacanestro f basketball

pallamano f handball

pallavolo f volleyball

pallone m [pal-lonay] ball

palude f [palooday] marsh, swamp

panetteria f [panet-tairee-ya] baker's

paninoteca f [paneenotayka] bar selling sandwiches

panne: restare in panne [restaray een pan-nay] to break down

panno m cloth

pannolino m nappy, diaper

pantaloni mpl trousers, (US) pants

pantofole fpl [pantofolay] slippers

papà m dad

parabrezza m [parabretza] windscreen

paracadutismo m [parakadooteezmo] parachuting

paralume m [paraloomay] lampshade

paraurti m [para-oortee] bumper, fender

parcheggiare [parkej-jaray] to park

parcheggio m [parkej-jo] car park, parking lot; parking

parcheggio a giorni alterni parking on alternate days

parcheggio a pagamento paying car park/parking lot

parcheggio custodito car park/parking lot with attendant

parcheggio incustodito unattended car park/parking lot

parcheggio privato private parking

parcheggio riservato agli

ospiti dell'albergo parking reserved for hotel guests only

parchimetro m parking meter

parco m park

parecchi [parek-kee], parecchie [parek-yay] several

parete f [paraytay] wall

Parigi f [pareejee] Paris

parità f [pareeta] equality

parlamento m parliament

parlare [parlaray] to talk; to speak

parola f word

parrucchiere m [par-rook-yairay], parrucchiera f hairdresser

parte f [partay] part

a parte except

d'altra parte however

da qualche altra parte [kwalkay] elsewhere

da qualche parte somewhere

una parte (di) a part (of), a share of

partecipare (a) [partecheeparay] to take part in

partenza f [partentza] departure

partire [parteeray] to leave

partita f match (sport)

partito politico m political party

Pasqua f [paskwa] Easter

passaggio a livello m [passaj-jo a leevel-lo] level/grade crossing

passaggio pedonale [pedonalay] pedestrian crossing

passante m/f [pas-santay]

passer-by

passaporto m passport

passatempo m pastime

passeggero m [pas-sej-jairo], **passeggera** f passenger

passeggiata f [pas-sej-jata] walk; stroll

passeggino m [pas-sej-jeeno] pushchair

passo m pass; step

passo carrabile carraio driveway

pasticceria f [pasteechairee-a] cake shop

pastificio m [pasteefeecho] fresh pasta shop

pastiglie per la gola fpl [pasteel-yay pair] throat pastilles

pastiglie per la tosse [tos-say] cough sweets

pasto m meal

patatine [patateenay] crisps, (US) potato chips

patente f [patentay] driving licence

patria f [patr-ya] native land

pattinaggio su ghiaccio m [pat-teenaj-jo soo g-yacho] ice skating

pattinare [pat-teenaray] to skate

pattini mpl skates

pattumiera f [pat-toom-yaira] dustbin, trashcan

paura f [powra] fear

pavimento m floor

paziente (m/f) [patz-yentay] patient

pazzia f [patz-ee-a] madness

pazzo [patzo] mad

sei pazzo? [say] you must be crazy!

peccato: è un peccato it's a pity

pecora f sheep

pedaggio m [pedaj-jo] toll

pedale m [pedalay] pedal

pedalò m pedal boat

pedata f kick

pedoni mpl pedestrians

peggio [pej-jo] worse

peggiori [pej-joree], **peggiore** [pej-joray] worst; worse

pelle f [pel-lay] skin; leather

pelle scamosciata f [skamoshata] suede

pelletteria f [pel-let-tairee-a] leather goods

pellicceria f [pel-leechairee-a] furrier

pellicola (a colori) f (colour) film

pendolare m/f [pendolaray] commuter

pendolino m [pendoleeno] special fast train, first class only

pene m [paynay] penis

penicillina f [peneecheel-leena] penicillin

penisola f [peneezola] peninsula

penna f [pen-na] pen

penna a sfera [sfaira] ballpoint pen

pennarello m [pen-narel-lo] felt-tip pen

penna stilografica f fountain pen

pennello m paint brush

pensare [pensaray] to think

pensilina f bus shelter

pensionato m [pens-yonato], pensionata f pensioner

pensione f [pens-yonay] guesthouse

pensione completa [komplayta] full board

pentola f saucepan

pentolino f [pentoleeno] small saucepan

per [pair] for; by; through; in order to

per aprire svitare unscrew to open

per cento [chento] per cent

perché [pairkay] because

perché? why?

perciò [percho] therefore

percorso m [pairkorso] route

perdere [pairdairay] to lose

perdere un treno to miss a train

perdita f leak

per favore [pair favoray] please

perfetto perfect

perfino even

pericolo m danger

pericolo di valanghe [valangay] danger of avalanches

pericoloso: è pericoloso sporgersi it is dangerous to lean out of the window

periferia f [paireefairee-a] suburbs, outskirts

periodo di validità:... valid for/until:...

permanente f [pairmanentay] perm

permesso (m) permit; allowed; excuse me

permettere [pairmet-tairay] to allow

però [pairo] but

per piacere [pair p-yachairay] please

persiane fpl [pairs-yanay] shutters

persino even

perso lost

persona f person

persuadere [pairswadairay] to persuade

pertosse f [pairtos-say] whooping cough

per tutte le altre destinazioni all other destinations

per uso esterno for external use

per uso interno for internal use

per uso veterinario for veterinary use

p. es. (per esempio) e.g.

pesante [pezantay] heavy

pesare [pezaray] to weigh

pesca f [payska] fishing; peach

pesce m [peshay] fish

pescecane m [peshaykanay] shark

pescheria f [peskairee-a] fishmonger's

peso m [payzo] weight

peso netto net weight

peso netto sgocciolato dry net weight

pettegolare [pet-tegolaray] to gossip

Pe

pettinarsi to comb one's hair

pettine m [**pet**-teenay] comb

petto m chest; breast

pezzi di ricambio **mpl** [**pet**zee dee reek**amb**-yo] spare parts

pezzo m [**pet**zo] piece

piacere (m) [p-yach**air**ay] pleasure; to like

per piacere [**pair**] please

piacere di conoscerla [konosh**air**la] pleased to meet you

piacevole [p-yach**e**volay] pleasant

pianerottolo m landing

pianeta m [p-yan**ay**ta] planet

piangere [p-y**an**jairay] to cry

piano (m) floor, storey; quietly; slowly

piano di sopra upstairs

piano di sotto downstairs

piano superiore [soopair-y**o**ray] upper floor

pianoterra m ground floor, (US) first floor

pianta f plant; map

pianterreno m [p-yantair-**ray**no] ground floor, (US) first floor

pianura f plain

pianura padana Po valley

piastrella f tile

piatti: lavare i piatti to do the washing-up

piattino m saucer

piatto (m) plate; dish; flat (adj)

piatto di portata serving dish

piatto fondo soup plate

piatto piano plate

piazza f [p-y**at**za] square

piccante [peek-k**an**tay] spicy

piccolo small

piede m [p-y**ay**day] foot

andare a piedi [p-y**ay**dee] to walk

a piedi on foot

in piedi standing

Piemonte m [p-yaym**on**tay] Piedmont

pieno [p-y**ay**no] full

pietra f stone

pigiama m [peej**a**ma] pyjamas

pigrizia f [peegr**ee**tz-ya] laziness

pigro lazy

pila f torch

pillola f pill

pilota m pilot

pinacoteca f gallery

pinne **fpl** [**peen**-nay] flippers

pinze **fpl** [**peen**tzay] pliers

pinzette **fpl** [peentzet-tay] tweezers

pioggia f [p-y**oj**-ja] rain

piove [p-y**o**vay] it's raining

piovere [p-y**o**vairay] to rain

pipa f pipe

piscina f [peesh**ee**na] swimming pool

piscina coperta indoor swimming pool

piscina per bambini paddling pool

piscina scoperta open-air swimming pool

pista f slope; rink; track; runway

pista ciclabile [cheekl**a**beelay] cycle path

pista da fondo cross-country

ski track

pista da pattinaggio [pat-tee-naj-jo] ice rink

pista da sci [shee] ski slope

pista difficile [deef-feecheelay] difficult slope

pista facile [facheelay] easy slope

pista per slitte [sleet-tay] toboggan run

pistola f gun

pittore m [peet-toray], pittrice f [peet-treechay] painter

pittura f painting

più [p-yoo] more

non... più ... no more

più grande [granday] bigger

più o meno [mayno] more or less

piumino m [p-yoomeeno] duvet

piuttosto [p-yoot-tosto] rather

pizzicheria f [peetzeekairee-a] delicatessen

plastica f plastic

platea f [platay-a] stalls

p.le (piazzale) Sq., Square

pneumatico m [pnay-oomateeko] tyre

po': un po' (di) a little bit (of)

poca few

pochi [pokee], poche [pokay] few

pochino: un pochino [pokeeno] a little bit

poco few

fra poco in a little while

poesia f [po-ezee-a] poetry; poem

poi [poy] then

politica f politics

politico m, politica f politician

politico political

polizia f [poleetzee-a] police

polizia stradale [stradalay] traffic police

poliziotta f [poletz-yot-ta] policewoman

poliziotto m policeman

polleria f [pol-lairee-a] butcher's specializing in poultry

pollice m [pol-leechay] thumb

pollivendolo m butcher specializing in poultry

polmoni mpl lungs

polmonite f [polmoneetay] pneumonia

polso m wrist

poltrona f seat in stalls; armchair

pomata f cream

pomata cicatrizzante [cheekatreetzantay] healing cream for cuts

pomeriggio m [pomaireej-jo] afternoon

ponte m [pontay] bridge; deck

pontile m [ponteelay] landing pier, jetty

popolazione f [popolatz-yonay] population

popolo m the people

porca miseria! [meezair-ya] bloody hell!

porcellana f [porchel-lana] porcelain; china

porta f door

portabagagli m [portabagal-yee] porter (in station)

portacenere m [portachenairay] ashtray(s)

porta d'ingresso f [deengres-so] front door

portafoglio m [portafol-yo] wallet

portamonete m [portamonaytay] purse

portapacchi m [portapak-kee] roof rack

portare [portaray] to carry; to take; to bring

portatile [portateelay] portable

porte-enfant m [port-anfan] carry-cot

portiere (di notte) m [port-yairee dee not-tay] (night) porter, janitor

portinaio m [porteena-yo], portinaia f caretaker

porto m harbour

porzione per bambini f [porz-yonay pair] children's portion

posare [posaray] to put down

posate fpl [pozatay] cutlery

possiamo* we can

posso* I can

possono they can

posta f mail

posta aerea [a-airay-a] airmail

posta centrale [chentralay] main post office

postagiro m [postajeero] postal giro

posteriore: sedile posteriore m [saydeelay postairee-oray] back seat

posti a sedere mpl seats

posti in piedi standing room

postino m postman

posto m place; seat; space; job, post

posto di polizia [poleetzee-a] police station

posto di telefono pubblico public telephone

posto prenotato [prenotato] reserved seat

posto riservato a mutilati e invalidi seat reserved for disabled persons only

postumi della sbornia mpl [zborn-ya] hangover

potabile [potabeelay] drinkable acqua potabile [akwa] drinking water

potere* (m) [potairay] to be able, can; power

potete* [potaytay] you can

potuto* been able to

povero poor

povertà f poverty

PP.TT. (Poste e Telecomunicazioni) fpl Italian Post Office

pranzo m [prandzo] lunch

prato m [prato] lawn; meadow

prato all'inglese [al-leenglayzay] lawn

precedenza f [prechedentza] right of way

precipitarsi (in) [precheepeetarsee] to rush in

preferire [prefaireeray] to prefer

preferito favourite

prefisso m dialling code, area code

pregare [pregaray] to request

si prega di (non)... please do (not) ...

si prega di non fumare please refrain from smoking

si prega di ritirare lo scontrino please get your receipt first

prego [praygo] please; pardon; you're welcome; after you

prego? pardon?, pardon me?

prelevamenti withdrawals

prelevare dei soldi [prelevaray day] to withdraw money

prelievo m [prel-yayvo] withdrawal

premere [praymairay] to press

premio m [praym-yo] prize

prenda take

prendere* [prendairay] to take; to catch

prendere il sole [solay] to sunbathe

prendere in affitto to rent

prendersi: da prendersi a digiuno to be taken on an empty stomach

da prendersi dopo/prima dei pasti to be taken after/before meals

da prendersi secondo la prescrizione medica to be taken according to doctor's prescription

da prendersi tre volte al giorno to be taken three times a day

prenotare [prenotaray] to book, to reserve

prenotato reserved

prenotazione f [prenotatz-yonay]

reservation, booking

prenotazione obbligatoria [ob-bleegator-ya] reservation compulsory

preoccuparsi per [pray-ok-kooparsee pair] to worry about

preparare [prepararay] to prepare

prepararsi to get ready

prepararsi a scendere [shendairay] get ready to alight

presa f [praysa] socket

presa multipla adaptor

presentare [prezentaray] to introduce

presente [prezentay] present

preservativo m condom

preside m/f [prayseeday] headmaster; headmistress

preso* [prayzo] taken

pressione gomme f [pres-yonay gom-may] tyre pressure

prestare [prestaray] to lend

farsi prestare (da) to borrow (from)

prestito: prendere in prestito [presteeto] to borrow

presto soon; early

prete m [praytay] priest

pretendere [pretendairay] to claim; to demand

previsioni del tempo mpl [preveez-yonee] weather forecast

prezzo m [pretzo] price

prezzo intero full price

prezzo ridotto reduced price

prigione f [preejonay] prison

prima f first; first gear
  prima di before
prima classe [klas-say] first
  class
prima colazione f [kolatz-yonay]
  breakfast
prima qualità high quality
primavera f spring
prima visione first release/
  showing
primo m first
primo piano m first floor, (US)
  second floor
primo tempo m first half
principale [preencheepalay]
  main
principe m [preencheepay]
  prince
principessa f [preencheepes-sa]
  princess
principiante m/f [preencheep-
  yantay] beginner
privato [preevato] private
probabilmente [probabeelmentay]
  probably
prodotto artigianalmente
  [arteejanalmentay] made by
  craftsmen
professore (Prof.) m teacher;
  professor
professoressa (Prof.essa) f
  teacher; professor
profondo deep
profumeria f [profoomairee-a]
  perfume shop
profumo m perfume
pro loco f tourist office in
  small town
prolunga f extension lead

promettere [promet-tairay] to
  promise
pronto ready; hello (on
  telephone)
pronto intervento m
  emergency service
pronto soccorso m first aid;
  casualty
pronunciare [pronooncharay] to
  pronounce
proprietario m [propr-yetar-yo],
  proprietaria f owner
proprio exactly; just; really;
  own
prosa f [proza] theatre drama
  compagnia di prosa theatre
  company
prossimo next
proteggere [protej-jairay] to
  protect
protestare [protestaray] to
  protest
provare [provaray] to try (on)
  prova! just try!
provincia f [proveencha] district
prudente [proodentay] cautious
prudenza f [proodentza] caution
prurito m itch
P.S. (Pubblica Sicurezza) f
  Police
P.T. (Poste e Telecomunicazioni)
  fpl Italian Post Office
pubblico (m) public; audience
pugilato m [poojeelato] boxing
pugno m [poon-yo] fist; punch
  un pugno (di) a handful (of)
pulire [pooleeray] to clean
pulito clean
pulitura f dry-cleaner's

pullman m coach, long-distance bus

pungere [**poo**njairay] to sting

punire [poo**nee**ray] to punish

punteggio m [poontej-jo] score

punto di vista m point of view

puntuale [poontwalay] on time

puntura f [poont**oo**ra] bite; injection

può* [pwo] he/she/it can; you can

può darsi maybe, perhaps

puoi* [pwoy] you can

pura lana vergine pure virgin wool

pura seta pure silk

puro cotone pure cotton

puro lino pure linen

puzzle m jigsaw

puzzo m [**poo**tzo] stink

p.zza (piazza) Square

Q

qua [kwa] here

di qua (over) here, this way

quaderno m [kwada**ir**no] exercise book

quadrato m [kwa**dr**ato] square

quadro m [kwa**d**ro] painting; picture

qualche [**kwal**kay] some, a few

qualcosa [kwalk**o**za] something; anything

qualcos'altro [kwalk**o**zaltro] something else

qualcuno [kwalk**oo**no] somebody

quale [**kwa**lay] which

qualità f [kwal**ee**ta] quality

quando [**kwa**ndo] when

quanta? [**kwa**nta] how much?

quanti? [**kwa**ntee], **quante?** [**kwa**ntay] how many?

quantità f [kwant**ee**ta] quantity

quanto? [**kwa**nto] how much?

quaranta [kwa**ra**nta] forty

quarta f [**kwa**rta] fourth (gear)

quartiere m [kwart-y**ai**ray] quarter, area

quarto (m) [**kwa**rto] quarter, fourth

tre quarti mpl three quarters

quasi [kwa**zee**] almost, nearly

quattordici [kwat-**tor**-deechee] fourteen

quattro [**kwa**t-tro] four

quello [kwel-lo] that (one)

quello lì that (one)

questa [kw**e**sta] this (one)

queste [kw**e**stay] these

questi [kw**e**stee] these

questo [kw**e**sto] this (one)

questo qui [kwee] this (one)

qui [kwee] here

quindi [kw**ee**ndee] therefore

quindici [kw**ee**n-deechee] fifteen

quinta f [kw**ee**nta] fifth (gear)

quinto (m) [kw**ee**nto] fifth

R

racc. recorded delivery

racchetta (da tennis) f [rak-ket-ta] (tennis) racket

raccomandata f recorded delivery (mail)

raccomandata con ricevuta di

ritorno [reecheev**oo**ta] recorded-delivery mail with card sent back to sender on delivery

raccomandata espresso recorded-delivery express mail

raccordo autostradale m [owto-strad**a**lay] motorway junction, highway intersection

radersi to shave

radiosveglia f [rad-yosv**a**yl-ya] radio alarm

raffreddore m [raf-fred-d**o**ray] cold (illness)

ragazza f [rag**a**tza] girl; girlfriend

ragazza alla pari au pair girl

ragazzo m [rag**a**tzo] boy; boyfriend

raggio m [raj-jo] spoke

raggi X mpl [raj-jee eeks] X-ray

ragionevole [rajon**a**yvolay] reasonable

ragno m [ran-yo] spider

RAI-TV (Radiotelevisione italiana) f [ra-eeteev**oo**] Italian radio and television

rallentare [ral-lent**a**ray] reduce speed, slow down

rampe [r**a**mpay] ramps

rappresentante m/f [rap-prezent**a**ntay] agent

raramente [raram**e**ntay] seldom

raro rare

rasoio m [raz**oy**-o] razor; shaver

ratto m rat

razza di idiota! [r**a**tza] stupid idiot!

re m [ray] king

recinto m [rech**ee**nto] fence

reclamare [reklam**a**ray] to complain

reclamo m complaint

regalo m present

reggiseno m [rej-jees**a**yno] bra

regina f [rej**ee**na] queen

regionale m [rejon**a**lay] local train stopping at all stations

registratore (a cassette) m [rejeestrat**o**ray a kas-set-tay] tape/cassette recorder

Regno Unito m [ren-yo] United Kingdom

remare [rem**a**ray] to row

remo m [r**a**ymo] oar

rene m [r**a**ynay] kidney (in body)

Rep. (repubblica) f republic

reparto m department; ward

respirare [respeer**a**ray] to breathe

respiratore (a tubo) m [respeerat**o**ray a t**oo**bo] snorkel

responsabile [responsab**ee**lay] responsible

restituire [resteetw**ee**ray] to give back

resto m rest; change (money)

il resto (di) m the rest (of)

rete f [r**a**ytay] net; goal; network

retromarcia f [retrom**a**rcha] reverse gear

riagganciare [ree-ag-ganch**a**ray] to hang up

ribassato reduced

ricambi mpl spare parts

ricamo m embroidery

ricco [**reek**-ko] rich

ricetta f [reechet-ta] recipe; prescription

ricevere [reechay**vair**ay] to receive

ricevitore m [reecheveeto**ray**] receiver

ricevuta f [reechev**oo**ta] receipt

ricevuta di ritorno acknowledgement of receipt

ricevuta fiscale [feeska**lay**] bill, (US) check (from a restaurant, bar etc)

ricominciare (da capo) [reekomeench**ar**ay] to start again

riconoscere [reekono**shai**ray] to recognize

ricordarsi (di) to remember

ridere [**ree**dairay] to laugh

ridicolo ridiculous

ridiscendere [redeeshen**dair**ay] to go back down

ridotto reduced

ridurre [reed**oor**-ray] to reduce

riduttore m [reedoot-to**ray**] adaptor

riduzione f [reedootz-yo**nay**] reduction

riempire [r-yemp**eer**ay] to fill (in)

rientrare [r-yentr**ar**ay] to go/come back (in/home)

rifiuti mpl [reef-y**oo**tee] rubbish

rilassarsi [reelas-sar**see**] to relax

rimandare [reeman**dar**ay] to send back

rimanere [reeman**air**ay] to stay, to remain

rimborsare [reembor**sar**ay] to refund

rimorchio m [reem**ork**-yo] trailer

rimozione forzata illegally parked vehicles removed at owner's expense

rinfresco m reception

ringraziare [reengratz-ya**ray**] to thank

rione m [ree-o**nay**] neighbourhood

riparare [reepar**ar**ay] to repair

riparazioni fpl [reeparatz-y**onee**] repairs

riparo m shelter

ripartire [reepart**eer**ay] to set off again

ripetere [reepay**tair**ay] to repeat

ripido steep

riposarsi to have a rest

riposo m [reep**o**zo] rest

risata f [reesata] laugh

riscaldamento m heating

riscuotere un assegno [reeskwo**tair**ay oon as-**sen**-yo] to cash a cheque

riserva f [reesa**irv**a] reserve
di riserva spare

riservato [reesair**vato**] reserved

riservato ai clienti dell'albergo for hotel guests only

riservato ai non fumatori non-smokers only

riservato carico loading only

riservato polizia police only

riservato scarico (merci) unloading (of goods) only

riservato tram, taxi, bus trams,

taxis, buses only

riservato viacard for magnetic toll card holders only

risparmi mpl savings

rispedire [reespedeeray] to send back

rispondere [reespondairay] to reply

risposta f answer

ristorante m [reestorantay] restaurant

risultato m result

ritardo m delay

essere in ritardo to be late

in ritardo delayed

ritirata f toilet/rest room (on train)

ritiro bagagli m [bagal-yee] baggage claim

ritornare [reetornaray] to return, to come/go back

ritorni go back

ritorno m return

riva f shore

rivista f magazine

rivoltante [reevoltantay] disgusting

roccia f [rocha] rock; rock climbing

romano Roman

romanzo m [romandzo] novel

rompere [rompairay] to break

rosa (f) rose; pink

rosolia f [rozolee-a] German measles

rossetto m lipstick

rosso red

rosticceria f [rosteechairee-a] take-away selling hot meat

dishes

rotaie fpl [rota-yay] tracks, rails

rotondo round

rotto broken

roulotte f [roolot] caravan, (US) trailer

rovesciarsi [rovesharsee] to capsize

rovine fpl [roveenay] ruins

R.R. (ricevuta di ritorno) return receipt for registered mail

R.U. (Regno Unito) m UK

rubare [roobaray] to steal

rubinetto m tap, faucet

rubrica f address book

rullino m film

rumore m [roomoray] noise

rumoroso [roomorozo] noisy

ruota f [rwota] wheel

ruscello m [rooshel-lo] stream

S

S. (santo/santa) St., Saint

sabato m Saturday

sabbia f [sab-ya] sand

sacchetto (di plastica) m [sak-ket-to] (plastic) bag

sacco a pelo m [paylo] sleeping bag

sagra f feast; (open air) festival

sala f living room

sala da pranzo [prandzo] dining room

sala d'aspetto waiting room

sala d'attesa [dat-taysa] waiting room

sala d'imbarco [deembarko]

departure lounge
salato savoury; salty
saldi mpl sale
saldi di fine stagione [feenay stajonay] end of season sales
sali da bagno mpl [ban-yo] bath salts
saliera f [sal-yaira] salt cellar
salire [saleeray] to go up; to get on/in
salita f slope; entry
  in salita uphill
salone per uomo [womo] men's hairdresser
salotto m living room, lounge
saltare [saltaray] to jump
salto m jump
salumaio m [salooma-yo] delicatessen
salumeria f [saloomairee-a] delicatessen
salumiere m [saloom-yairay] delicatessen
salute f [salootay] health
  (alla) salute! cheers!
  in salute in good health
  salute! bless you!
salvagente m [salvajentay] rubber ring
salve! [salvay] hi!
salvietta f [salv-yet-ta] napkin
sandali mpl [sandalee] sandals
sangue m [sangway] blood
sanguinare [sangweenaray] to bleed
sano healthy
sapere [sapairay] to know
sapone m [saponay] soap
sapore m [saporay] flavour

Sardegna f [sardayn-ya] Sardinia
sartoria f [sartoree-a] tailor's; dressmaker's
S.A.U.B. (Struttura Amministrativa Unificata di Base) f Italian national health service, Italian health care
sbagliato [zbal-yato] wrong
sbaglio m [zbal-yo] mistake
sbarcare [sbarkaray] to disembark
sbrigarsi [zbreegarsee] to hurry
  sbrigati! [zbreegatee] hurry up!
sbucciare [zboocharay] to peel
scacchi mpl [skak-kee] chess
scadenza f [skadentza] expiry date; deadline
scaffali mpl shelves
scala f ladder
scala mobile [mobeelay] escalator
scale fpl [skalay] stairs
scalo m stop-over
  fare scalo to stop over
scandaloso [skandalozo] shocking
scandinavo Scandinavian
scapolo m bachelor
scarpe fpl [skarpay] shoes
scarpe da ginnastica [jeen-nasteeka] trainers
scarponi da sci mpl [da shee] ski boots
scatola f box
  la scatola priva del talloncino non può essere venduta

without a coupon this box
cannot be sold

scatola del cambio [kamb-yo]
gearbox

scatto m unit

scavi mpl [skavee] excavations

scegliere [shayl-yairay] to
choose

scendere [shendairay] to go
down; to get off

scendere le scale [skalay] to
go/come downstairs

scheda f [skayda] card

scheda telefonica phonecard

scherzo m [skertzo] joke

schiaffo m [sk-yaf-fo] slap

schiena f [sk-yayna] back (of
body)

schifo: che schifo! [kay skeefo]
it's disgusting!

schifoso [skeefozo] foul

schiuma da barba f [sk-yooma]
shaving foam

schizzare [skeetzaray] to splash

sci m [shee] ski; skiing

sciacquare [shakwaray] to rinse

sci acquatico m [shee
akwateeko] waterski;
waterskiing

sciampo m [shampo] shampoo

sciare [shee-aray] to ski

andare a sciare to go skiing

sciarpa f [sharpa] scarf

sciatore m [shee-atoray] skier

sciatrice f [shee-atreechay] skier

sci d'acqua m [shee dakwa]
water-skiing

sci di fondo cross-country
skiing

scienza f [shee-entza] science

sciocco (m) [shok-ko] silly;
idiot

scivolare [sheevolaray] to skid

scivoloso [sheevolozo] slippery

scodella f bowl

scogliera f [skol-yaira] cliff

scoglio m [skol-yo] rock

scolara f schoolgirl

scolaro m schoolboy

scommessa f bet

scommettere [skom-met-tairay]
to bet; to stake

scomodo uncomfortable

scomparire [skompareeray] to
disappear

scompartimento m
compartment

scontento unhappy

sconto m discount

scontrino m receipt

scontro m crash

scopa f broom

scorciatoia f [skorchatoy-a]
shortcut

scorso: l'anno scorso last year

scotch m Sellotape®, Scotch
tape®

scottarsi to get sunburnt

scottatura f [skot-tatoora]
sunburn; burn

Scozia f [skotzee-a] Scotland

scozzese (m/f) [skotzayzay]
Scottish; Scot

scrittura f [skreet-toora] writing

scrivere [skreevairay] to write

scrivere a macchina [mak-
keena] to type

scultura f sculpture

scuola f [skwola] school
scuola di lingue [leengway] language school
scuola di sci [shee] ski school
scuola elementare [elementaray] primary school
scuola media inferiore [mayd-ya eenfair-yoray] junior secondary school
scuola media superiore [soopair-yoray] senior secondary school
scuotere [skwotairay] to shake
scuro dark
scusa f [skooza] apology; excuse
  scusa! sorry!
scusarsi [skoozarsee] to apologize
scusi! [skoozee] sorry!
  come, scusi? [komay] pardon?, pardon me?
sdraiarsi [zdra-yarsee] to lie down
se [say] if
sé [say] himself; herself; itself; oneself; themselves
sebbene [seb-baynay] although
sec. (secolo) century
seccante [sek-kantay] annoying
secchiello m [sek-yel-lo] bucket
secchio m [sek-yo] bucket
secco dry
secolo m [saykolo] century
seconda f second (gear)
seconda classe f [klas-say] second class
seconda visione f second

release/showing
secondo (m) second
secondo tempo m second half
sedere m [saydairay] bottom (of person)
sedersi to sit down
sedia f [sayd-ya] chair
sedia a rotelle [rotel-lay] wheelchair
sedia a sdraio [zdra-yo] deck chair
sedici [say-deechee] sixteen
sedile m [saydeelay] seat; bench
seduto sitting, seated
seg. (seguente) following
sega f [sayga] saw
seggiola f [sej-jola] chair
seggiovia f [sej-jovee-a] chairlift
segnale m [sen-yalay] signal
segnale d'allarme [dal-larmay] alarm
segnaletica in rifacimento road signs being redone
segnaletica orizzontale in allestimento road signs being painted
segreteria telefonica f [segretairee-a] answering machine
segreto [segrayto] secret
seguire [segweeray] to follow
  segua [saygwa] follow
sei* [say] you are
sei [say] six
selezionare il numero dial the number
sella f saddle
semaforo m traffic lights

sembrare [sembraray] to seem

semiasse m [semee-assay] axle; shaft

seminterrato m basement

semplice [sempleechay] simple

sempre [sempray] always
sempre d(i)ritto straight ahead, straight on

seno m [sayno] breast

sensato sensible

sensibile [senseebeelay] sensitive

senso: di buon senso [bwon] sensible

senso dell'umorismo m [del-loomoreezmo] (sense of) humour

senso unico one way

sentiero m [sent-yairo] path

sentire [senteeray] to feel; to hear; to smell

sentirsi (bene) [baynay] to feel (well)

sentirsi poco bene to feel unwell

senza [sentza] without
senza dubbio [doob-yo] undoubtedly

senza conservanti no preservatives

separatamente [separatamentay] separately

separato separate

sera f [saira] evening
alle 8 di sera at 8 p.m.
la/di sera in the evening

serbatoio m [sairbatoy-o] tank

serio [sair-yo] serious
sul serio [sool] seriously;

really

serpente m [sairpentay] snake

serratura f lock

servire [sairveeray] to serve
servitevi help yourselves
serviti help yourself
si serva help yourself

servire freddo serve chilled

servizi [sairveetzee] toilets, rest room

servizio m [sairveetz-yo] service
il servizio è gratuito free service

servizio a bordo in-flight service

servizio autotraghetto [owtotraget-to] car ferry

servizio compreso [kompray-zo] service charge included

servizio escluso not including service charge

servizio guasti faults service

servizio in camera room service

servizio traghetto [traget-to] passenger ferry

sessanta sixty

sessista sexist

sesso m sex

sesto (m) sixth

seta f [sayta] silk

sete: avere sete [avairay saytay] to be thirsty

settanta seventy

sette [set-tay] seven

settembre m [set-tembray] September

settimana f week
alla settimana per week

due settimane [doo-ay set-teemanay] fortnight

settimo (m) seventh

sfacciato [sfachato] cheeky

sfinito exhausted

sfortunatamente [sfortoonatamentay] unfortunately

sgabello m [zgabel-lo] stool

sgarbato [zgarbato] rude

sgradevole [zgradayvolay] unpleasant

si [see] himself; herself; itself; themselves

si [see] yes

siamo* we are

siccome [seek-komay] as, since

sicuro safe; sure

siete* [s-yaytay] you are

sigaretta f cigarette

sigaro m cigar

Sigg. (signori) Messrs

sigillare [seejeel-laray] to seal

significare [seen-yeefeekaray] to mean

signor (Sig.) [seen-yor] Mr; Sir

signora (Sig.a) (f) [seen-yora] lady; Mrs; madam

signore m [seen-yoray] gentleman

signore fpl ladies' toilet, rest room

signori mpl gents' toilet, rest room

signorina (Sig.na) [seen-yoreena] Miss

silenzio m [seelentz-yo] silence

simile [seemeelay] similar

simpatico nice

sinagoga f synagogue

sincero [seenchairo] sincere, frank

singhiozzo m [seeng-yotzo] hiccups

sinistra f [seeneestra] left

a sinistra on/to the left

siringa f syringe

s.l.m. (sul livello del mare) above sea level

slogarsi [zlogarsee] to sprain

smalto per le unghie m [zmalto pair lay oong-yay] nail polish

smettere [zmet-tairay] to stop

snello [znel-lo] slim

so: non (lo) so I don't know

sobborghi mpl [sob-borgee] suburbs

soccorso m help; assistance

soccorso alpino mountain rescue

soccorso stradale [stradalay] breakdown service

società f [sochayta] society; company

soffitta f loft

soffitto m ceiling

soggiorno m [soj-jorno] stay; lounge

sognare [son-yaray] to dream

sogno m [son-yo] dream

soldi mpl [soldee] money

sole m [solay] sun

soleggiato [solej-jato] sunny (place)

solito [soleeto] usual

di solito usually

sollevare [sol-levaray] to lift

solo alone; only

solo il sabato/la domenica Saturdays/Sundays only

solo servizio cuccette e letti sleepers/sleeping cars only

soltanto only

soluzione salina per lenti a contatto f [solootz-yonay – pair] soaking solution for contact lenses

somministrazione per via orale to be taken orally

sonnecchiare [son-nek-yaray] to doze

sonnifero m sleeping pill

sonno: avere sonno to be sleepy

sono* I am; they are

sopra on; above

di sopra upstairs

sopracciglio m [sopracheel-yo] eyebrow

soprammobile m [sopram-mobeelay] ornament

soprannome m [sopran-nomay] nickname

sordo deaf

sorella f sister

sorgente f [sorjentay] spring

sorpassare [sorpas-saray] to overtake

sorpasso fast lane, lane for overtaking

sorprendente [sorprendentay] surprising

sorpresa f [sorpraysa] surprise

sorridere [sor-reedairay] to smile

sorriso m smile

sosta autorizzata... parking

permitted for ...

sosta vietata no parking

sostenere [sostenairay] to maintain; to uphold

sottile [sot-teelay] thin

sotto under; below

di sotto downstairs

sottolineare [sot-toleenay-aray] to emphasize

sottopassaggio m [sot-topas-sajjo] underpass

SP (strada provinciale) f secondary road

Spagna f [span-ya] Spain

spagnolo (m) [span-yolo], **spagnola (f)** Spanish; Spaniard

spago m string

spalla f shoulder

sparare [spararay] to shoot

sparire [spareeray] to disappear

sparisci! [spareeshee] get lost!

spartirsi to share

spaventoso [spaventozo] appalling, dreadful

spazzare [spatzaray] to sweep

spazzola f [spatzola] brush

spazzolino m [spatzoleeno] brush

specchietto retrovisore m [spek-yet-to retroveezoray] rearview mirror

specchio m [spek-yo] mirror

specialista m/f [spech-yaleesta] specialist

specialità f [spech-yaleeta] speciality, specialities

specialmente [spech-yalmentay] especially

spedire [spedeeray] to send; to post, to mail

spedire per posta to post, to mail

spegnere [spen-yairay] to switch off

spegnere il motore switch off engine

spendere [spendairay] to spend

sperare [speraray] to hope

spesa f [spaysa] shopping

spesso often

spettacolo m performance, show

spia f gauge

spiace: mi spiace [spee-achay] I'm sorry

spiaggia f [sp-yaj-ja] beach

spiccioli mpl [speecholee] (small) change

spiegare [sp-yaygaray] to explain

spilla f brooch

spilla di sicurezza [seekooretza] safety pin

spillo m pin

spina f plug (electrical); thorn

spingere [speenjairay] to push

spiritoso [speereetozo] witty

spogliarsi [spol-yarsee] to undress

spogliatoi mpl [spol-yatoy] changing rooms

spolverare [spolvairaray] to dust

sponda f shore; riverbank

sporco dirty

sporco maschilista m [maskeeleesta] male chauvinist pig

sporgersi (da) [sporjairsee] to lean (out)

sportello m counter; door (on train)

sportello automatico [owtomateeko] cash dispenser, automatic teller

sportello pacchi parcels counter

sport invernali mpl winter sports

sposato married

spugna f [spoon-ya] sponge

spuntata f trim

spuntino m snack

squadra f [skwadra] team

squalo m [skwalo] shark

SS (strada statale) f main road, national road

sta: come sta? [komay] how are you?

stadio m [stad-yo] stadium

stagione f [stajonay] season

stagno m [stan-yo] pond

stagnola f [stan-yola] silver foil

stai: come stai? [komay sta-ee] how are you?

stamattina this morning

stampa f Press

stampe printed matter

stampelle fpl [stampel-lay] crutches

stanco tired

stanotte [stanot-tay] tonight

stanza f [stantza] room

stare [staray] to be; to stand; to be located; to stay, to remain; to suit

stare bene [baynay] to be well

stare poco bene to be unwell

starter **m** choke

statale [statalay] national; state

state: come state? [komay statay] how are you?

Stati Uniti **mpl** [statee ooneetee] United States

stato* (**m**) been; state

statua **f** [statwa] statue

stazione **f** [statz-yonay] station

stazione degli autobus [daylyee **ow**toboos] bus station

stazione della metropolitana underground, (US) subway station

stazione delle corriere [del-lay cor-yairay] coach station

stazione di servizio [sairveetz-yo] petrol/gas station, service station

stazione ferroviaria railway station

steccato **m** fence

stella **f** star

stendersi to lie down

sterlina **f** pound (sterling)

sterzo **m** [stertzo] steering; steering wheel

stesso, stessa, stessi, stesse [stes-say] same

stile **m** [steelay] style

stirare [steeraray] to iron

stirarsi [steerarsee] to stretch out

stitico [steeteeko] constipated

stivali **mpl** [steevalee] boots

stoffa **f** material, fabric

stomaco **m** stomach

storia **f** [stor-ya] story; history

storia dell'arte **f** [del-lartay] history of art

stoviglie **fpl** [stoveel-yay] crockery

straccio **m** [stracho] rag; cloth; duster;

strada **f** road

strada a fondo cieco blind alley

strada camionabile route for heavy vehicles

strada dissestata uneven road surface

strada ghiacciata ice on road

strada interrotta road blocked

strada privata private road

strada provinciale secondary road

strada sdrucciolevole slippery road

strada secondaria secondary road

strada senza uscita no thoroughfare, dead end

strada statale main road

straniero **m** [stran-yairo], straniera **f** foreigner

straniero foreign

strano strange

straordinario [stra-ordeenar-yo] exceptional

stretto narrow

strillare [streel-laray] to scream

strisce pedonali **fpl** [streeshay] pedestrian crossing

strofinaccio (da cucina) **m** [strofeenacho (da koocheena)] tea towel

stronzo **m** bastard

studente m [stoodentay] student

studentessa f student

studiare [stood-yaray] to study

studio m study

studioso [stood-yozo] studious

stufa f heater

stupefacente [stoopayfachentay] astonishing

stupefacenti mpl drugs

stupendo! brilliant!

stupro m rape

su [soo] on; up

sua* [soo-a] his; her(s); its; your(s)

subito [soobeeto] immediately

succedere [soochaydairay] to happen

sud m south

Sudafrica f South Africa

sudafricano (m), sudafricana (f) South African

sudare [soodaray] to sweat

sud-ovest m [sood-ovest] south-west

sue* [soo-ay] his; her(s); its; your(s)

sul [sool], sulla, sullo, sui [soo-ee], sugli [sool-yee], sulle* [sool-lay] on the

suo* [soo-o] his; her(s); its; your(s)

suocera f [swochaira] mother-in-law

suocero m [swochairo] father-in-law

suoi* [swoy] his; her(s); its; your(s)

suola f [swola] sole (of shoe)

suonare [swonaray] to play

(instrument); to ring; please ring

superficie f [soopairfeechay] surface; area

supermercato m supermarket

superstrada f motorway/highway without toll

supplementare [soop-plementaray] extra

supplemento 3o letto third bed supplement payable

supplemento rapido [rapeedo] supplement for fast train

supporre [soop-por-ray] to assume

surf m surfboard; surfing

surgelati mpl [soorjelatee] frozen food

surgelato frozen

sussurrare [soos-soor-raray] to whisper

svedese (m/f) [zvedayzay] Swedish; Swede

sveglia f [zvayl-ya] alarm clock

svegliare [zvayl-yaray] to wake

svegliarsi [zvayl-yarsee] to wake up

sveglio [zvayl-yo] alert; awake

svendita f [zvendeeta] sale

svenire [zveneeray] to faint

Svezia f [zvetzee-a] Sweden

sviluppare [zveeeloop-paray] to develop

svitato [zveetato] cracked, nutty

Svizzera f [zveetzaira] Switzerland

svizzero (m), svizzera (f) Swiss

svuotare [zvwotaray] to empty

T

T (tabaccheria) tobacconist's
tabaccaio m [tabak-ka-yo] tobaconnist's
tabaccheria f [tabak-kair**ee**-a] tobacconist's
tabacchi mpl [tabak-k**ee**] tobacco goods
tabacco m tobacco
tabellone m indicator board
taccuino m [tak-kw**ee**no] notebook
tachimetro m speedometer
taglia f [tal-ya] size
tagliando di controllo m [tal-yando] coupon guaranteeing quality; proof of purchase
tagliare [tal-ya**ray**] to cut
tagliaunghie m [tal-ya-**oong**-yay] nail clippers
taglio m [tal-yo] cut
taglio di capelli haircut
taglio e cucito [ay kooch**ee**to] dressmaking
talco m talcum powder
tallone m [tal-lonay] heel
tanta a lot; so much
tanti, tante [tantee, tantay] many, lots of
tanti auguri [owg**oo**ree] best wishes
tanto a lot; so much
tapparella f blind
tappeto m [tap-payto] carpet
tappezziere m [tap-petz-yairay] decorator; upholsterer
tappo m cap; plug; cork

tardi late
  a più tardi [p-yoo] see you later
targa f number plate
tariffa f fare; charge
tariffa interna [eentairna] inland postage
tariffe postali internazionali fpl [tareef-fay – eentairnatz-yonalee] international postage rates
tariffe postali nazionali [natz-yonalee] national postage rates
tasca f pocket
tassa f tax
tassista m/f taxi driver
tasso di cambio m [kamb-yo] exchange rate
tasso di interesse [eentaires-say] interest rate
taverna f inn, tavern
tavola f [tavola] table
tavola a vela [vayla] sailboard
tavola calda snack bar
tavolino m coffee table
tavolo m table
tazza f [tatza] cup
tazzina da caffè f [tatzeena] espresso coffee cup
T.C.I. (Touring Club Italiano) m Italian touring club
te* [tay] you
tè m [tay] tea
teatro m [tay-atro] theatre
teatro lirico opera house
tedesco (m/f) [tedesko] German
TEE m Trans-Europe-Express train

tegame f [tegamay] pan

teglia f [tayl-ya] casserole dish

teiera f [tay-yaira] teapot

telefonare [telefonaray] to phone

telefonata f phone call

telefono m [telayfono] telephone

telefono a gettoni [jet-tonee] phone that takes tokens

telefono a scatti phone which counts time-units used for which you pay at end of call

telefono a schede [skayday] cardphone

Telepass® electronic toll charge system on motorway

telo da bagno m [ban-yo] bath towel

temperino m penknife

tempesta f storm

tempo m time; weather

tempo libero free time, leisure

tempo limite di accettazione latest check-in time

temporale m [temporalay] thunderstorm

tenda f curtain; tent

tenere [tenayray] to hold; to keep

tenere lontano dalla portata dei bambini keep out of the reach of children

tenere rigorosamente la destra keep to the right

tergicristallo m [tairjeekreestal-lo] windscreen wiper

terminare [tairmeenaray] to end

termometro m thermometer

termosifone m [termoseefonay] radiator

terra f earth, soil

terrazzo m [tair-ratzo] (large) balcony; patio

terza f [tairtza] third (gear)

terzo (m) third

tessera di abbonamento f season ticket

tesserino m travel card

tessuto m material, fabric

testa f head

testa del treno front of the train

tetto m roof

Tevere m [tevairay] Tiber

ti* [tee] you; yourself; to you

tiepido [t-yaypeedo] lukewarm

tifoso m, tifosa f fan (supporter)

timbro m rubber stamp; postmark

timido shy

tinello m small dining room

tintoria f [teentoree-a] drycleaner's

tirare [teeraray] to pull

tiro m shooting

titolo m title

tizio m [teetz-yo] bloke, guy

toccare [tok-karay] to touch

tocca a me [tok-ka a may] this round's on me; it's my turn

togliere [tol-yairay] to take away; to remove

togliersi: togliti! [tol-yeetee] get out of the way!

toilette f [twalet] toilet(s), rest room; dressing table(s)

tonnellata f [ton-nel-lata] tonne

tonsillite f [tonseel-leetay] tonsillitis

topo m mouse

torcia elettrica f [torcha] torch, flashlight

Torino f Turin

tornare [tornaray] to return, to come back

tornare a casa to go home; to come home

torneo m [tornay-o] tournament, competition

toro m bull

torre f [tor-ray] tower

torrefazione f [tor-refatz-yonay] shop selling coffee

Toscana f Tuscany

tosse f [tos-say] cough

tossire [tos-seeray] to cough

tostapane m [tostapanay] toaster

tostare [tostaray] to toast

tovagliolo m [toval-yolo] serviette

tra among; between

tradizionale [tradeetz-yonalay] traditional

tradurre [tradoor-ray] to translate

traduzione f [tradootz-yonay] translation

traffico m traffic

traghetto m [traget-to] ferry

tragitto m [trajeet-to] route; journey

tramonto m sunset

trampolino m diving board; ski jump; trampoline

tranne [tran-nay] except

tranquillo [trankweel-lo] quiet

transito con catene o pneumatici da neve chains or snow tyres compulsory

tranviere m [tranv-yairay] tram driver

trapano m drill

trapunta f quilt

trascinare [trasheenaray] to drag

trasferimento bancario m [bankar-yo] bank transfer

trasmissione f [trasmees-yonay] transmission; TV/radio programme

trattoria f [trat-toree-a] restaurant

traversata f crossing (sea)

tre [tray] three

tredici [tray-deechee] thirteen

treni feriali/festivi trains on weekdays/holidays

treno m [trayno] train

treno diretto through train

treno espresso long-distance express train

treno interregionale long-distance, stopping train

treno merci freight train

treno metropolitano city/ suburban train

treno regionale local train, stopping at all stations

trenta thirty

tribunale m [treeboonalay] law courts

tricolore m [treekoloray] Italian flag

trimestre m [treemestray] term

triplo triple, treble
triste [treestay] sad
tritatutto m food processor
troppo too; too much
trovare [trovaray] to find
truccarsi to put on one's
  make-up
trucco m make-up
tu* [too] you
tua* [too-a] your(s)
tubo m [toobo] pipe
tubo di scappamento exhaust
  pipe
tue* [too-ay] your(s)
tuffarsi to dive
tuffo m dive
tuo [too-o], tuoi* [twoy] your(s)
tuono m [twono] thunder
turismo m [tooreezmo] tourism
turista m/f tourist
tuta da ginnastica f [jeen-
  nasteeka] tracksuit
tutta all; everything
  tutta la... all the ...; the
    whole ...
tuttavia however

tutte [toot-tay] all; every;
  everybody
  tutte le direzioni all routes
  tutte le/tutti i... all the ...
    every ...
tutti all; every; everybody
  tutti e due [ay doo-ay] both of
    them
tutto all; everything
  in tutto altogether
  tutto il... all the ...; the whole
    ...
tutto compreso all inclusive

U

ubriaco drunk
uccello m [oochel-lo] bird
uccidere [oocheedairay] to kill
UE (Unione Europea) f [oo-ay]
  EU (European Union)
ufficio m [oof-feecho] office
ufficio cambi [kambee] bureau
  de change
ufficio del turismo [tooreezmo]
  tourist office
ufficio di informazioni
  turistiche [eenformatz-
  yonee tooreesteekay] tourist
  information centre
ufficio informazioni tourist
  information
ufficio postale [postalay] post
  office
ufficio prenotazioni [prenotatz-
  yonee] reservations
ufficio prenotazioni merci
  reservations office for goods
ufficio prenotazioni passeggeri
  reservations office for
  passengers
ufficio turistico tourist office
uguaglianza f [oogwal-yantza]
  equality
uguale [oogwalay] equal, same
ultimo [oolteemo] last
umido [oomeedo] wet
umore m [oomoray] mood
umorismo m [oomoreezmo]
  humour
un, una* [oona] a; one
undici [oon-deechee] eleven

Ungheria f [oongairee-a] Hungary

unghia f [oong-ya] fingernail

unguento m [oongwento] ointment

unico single

Unione Europea f [oon-yonay ay-ooropay-a] European Union

unità socio-sanitaria locale f local health centre(s)

università f [ooneevairseeta] university, universities

uno* [oono] a; one

uomini mpl [womeenee] men; gents' (toilet), mens' rest room

uomo m [womo] man

urlare [oorlaray] to yell

urtare [oortaray] to hit, to knock

usare [oozaray] to use

uscire [oosheeray] to go out
uscire di casa to leave the house
uscire di nuovo [nwovo] to go/come back out

uscita f [oosheeta] exit, way out; gate (airport)

uscita automezzi vehicle exit

uscita camion works exit

uscita d'emergenza emergency exit

uscita di sicurezza emergency exit

uscita operai workers' exit

uso e dosi use and dosage

U.S.S.L. (Unità Socio-Sanitaria Locale) f local health centre(s)

utensili da cucina mpl [koocheena] cooking utensils

utile [ooteelay] useful

V

v. (vedi) see

va he/she/it goes; you go **come va?** [komay] how are things?
va bene! [baynay] that's fine!, it's OK!; that's right
va' a farti friggere! [freej-jairay] go to hell!
va' a quel paese! [kwel pa-ayzay] get lost!

vacanze fpl [vakanzay] holidays, vacation

vacanze di Natale [natalay] Christmas holidays/vacation

vacanze di Pasqua [paskwa] Easter holidays/vacation

vacanze estive [esteevay] summer holidays/vacation

vaccinazione f [vacheenatz-yonay] vaccination

vaccino m [vacheeno] vaccination

vada via... [oltray] go past the ...

vado* I go

vaffanculo! fuck off!

vaglia internazionale m [val-ya eentairnatz-yonalay] international money order(s)

vaglia postale [postalay] money order(s)

vaglia telegrafico telegram

money order(s)

vagone m [vagonay] carriage, car

vagone bagagliaio [bagal-ya-yo] luggage/baggage van

vagone letto sleeper, sleeping car

vagone ristorante [reestorantay] restaurant car

vai* [va-ee] you go

valanghe [valangay] avalanches

validità f validity

valigia f [valeeja] suitcase
disfare le valigie [deesfaray lay valeejay] to unpack

valle f [val-lay] valley

valore: di valore [dee valoray] valuable

valuta f currency

valvola f [valvola] valve

vanga f spade

vanitoso [vaneetozo] vain

vanno* they go

vaporetto m passenger ferry

varechina f [varaykeena] bleach

variabile [varee-abeelay] changeable

vasca da bagno f [ban-yo] bathtub

vasellame m [vazel-lamay] crockery

vaso m [vazo] vase; pot

vassoio m [vas-soy-o] tray

vattene! [vat-tenay] go away!

vecchia (f) [vek-ya] old; old woman

vecchio (m) old; old man

vedere [vedairay] to see
fare vedere to show

vedere data sul coperchio/sul retro see date on lid/back

vedi foglio illustrativo see illustrated instructions leaflet

vedova f [vaydova] widow

vedovo m widower

vegetariano (m) [vejetar-yano], **vegetariana (f)** vegetarian

veicoli lenti crawler lane

veicolo m [vay-eekolo] vehicle

vela f [vayla] sail; sailing

veleno m [velayno] poison

veliero m [vel-yairo] sailing ship

veloce [velochay] fast

velocemente [velochaymentay] quickly

velocità f [velocheeta] speed

vendere [vendairay] to sell

vendesi for sale

vendita f sale

venerdì m Friday

Venezia f [venetzee-a] Venice

veneziane fpl [venetz-yanay] Venetian blinds

veneziano [venetz-yano] Venetian

vengo* I come

vengono* they come

veniamo* we come

venire* [veneeray] to come

venite* [veneetay] you come

venti twenty

ventilatore m [venteelatoray] fan (electrical)

vento m wind

venuto* come

veramente [vairamentay] really

verde [vairday] green

al verde broke

vernice f [vairneechay] paint

vernice fresca wet paint

vero [vairo] true

vero cuoio [kwo-yo] real leather

versamenti deposits

versamento (bancario) m payment; (bank) giro

versare dei soldi [vairsaray day] to pay in money

vescica f [vaysheeka] bladder; blister

vespa f wasp

vestaglia f [vestal-ya] dressing gown

vestire [vesteeray] to dress

vestirsi to get dressed

vestito m dress

vetro m glass (material)

vetta f summit, peak

vettura f coach, carriage

VF (Vigili del Fuoco) mpl fire brigade

vi* [vee] you; yourselves; to you; each other

via (f) [vee-a] road, street; way; away

via aerea f [a-airay-a] airmail

viacard® f motorway/ highway magnetic card

viaggiare [v-yaj-jaray] to travel

viaggio m [v-yaj-jo] journey, trip; tour

fare un viaggio to go on a journey

viaggio d'affari business trip

viaggio organizzato [organeedzato] package tour

viale m [vee-alay] avenue, boulevard

vialetto m [v-yalet-to] path

vicino m [veecheeno], vicina f neighbour

vicino (a) near; nearby

vicolo m alleyway

vicolo cieco [chayko] cul-de-sac; dead end

videoregistratore m [veeday-o-rejeestratoray] video recorder

viene* [v-yaynay] he/she/it comes; you come

vieni* [v-yaynee] you come

vietato [v-yaytato] forbidden

vietato accendere fuochi no campfires

vietato ai minori di 14 anni no admittance to children under 14

vietato attraversare i binari do not cross the tracks

vietato bagnarsi no bathing

vietato campeggiare no camping

vietato entrare no entry

vietato fumare no smoking

vietato gettare oggetti dal finestrino do not throw objects out of the window

vietato l'ingresso no entry; no admittance

vietato l'uso dell'ascensore ai minori di anni 12 non accompagnati unaccompanied children under 12 must not use the lift/elevator

vietato pescare no fishing

vietato sporgersi dal finestrino do not lean out of the window

vietato sputare no spitting

vietato tuffarsi no diving

vietato usare la toilette durante le fermate e nelle stazioni do not use the toilet/rest room when the train has stopped or is in the station

vigili del fuoco **mpl** [veejeelee del fwoko] fire brigade

vigili urbani **mpl** traffic police

vigna f [veen-ya] vineyard

villaggio **m** [veel-laj-jo] village

villetta f small detached house

vincere [veenchairay] to win

vincitore **m** [veencheetoray] winner

vincitrice f [veencheetreechay] winner

viola [v-yola] purple

violenza f [v-yolentza] violence

visita f [veezeeta] visit

visita guidata [gweedata] guided tour

visitare [veezeetaray] to visit

vista f view

visto **m** visa

vita f life; waist

vitamine **fpl** vitamins

vitaminico vitamin (-enriched)

vite f [veetay] screw

vivere [veevairay] to live

vivo alive

v.le (viale) **m** avenue

voce f [vochay] voice

voglia: ho voglia di... [o vol-ya] I feel like ...

vogliamo* [vol-yamo] we want

voglio* [vol-yo] I want

vogliono* [vol-yono] they want

voi* [voy] you

volante m [volantay] steering wheel

volare [volaray] to fly

voler dire [deeray] to mean

volere* (m) [volairay] to want; will, wish

volete* [volaytay] you want

volgare [volgaray] coarse

voli internazionali mpl [eentairnatz-yonalee] international flights

voli nazionali [natz-yonalee] domestic flights

volo m flight

volo a vela [vayla] gliding

volo di linea [leenay-a] scheduled flight

volo diretto direct flight

volta f time

qualche volta [kwalkay] sometimes

una volta once

una volta scongelato il prodotto non deve essere ricongelato do not refreeze once thawed

voltarsi to turn round

volutamente [volootamentay] deliberately

voluto* wanted

vomitare [vomeetaray] to vomit, to be sick

vorrei [vor-ray] I would like

vostro, vostra, vostri, vostre*
[**vo**stray] your(s)
vs. (vostro) your(s)
vulcano m [voolk**a**no] volcano
vuoi* [vwoy] you want
vuole* [vwo**la**y] he/she/it
wants; you want
   vuole...? [vwo**la**y] do you
   want ...?
vuotare [vwot**a**ray] to empty
vuoto [vwo**o**to] empty
vuoto a perdere no deposit
(on bottle)
vuoto a rendere returnable
(bottle)

W

W (viva...!) long live ...!
water m [vat**ai**r] W.C.
windsurf m windsurfing;
windsurfing board

Z
---

zaino m [dz**a**-eeno] rucksack
zanzara f [dzandz**a**ra] mosquito
zerbino m [dzairb**ee**no] doormat
zia f [tz**ee**-a] aunt
zio m uncle
zitto [tz**ee**t-to] quiet; silent
   zitto! shut up!
zona f [dz**o**na] area
zona a traffico limitato
restricted traffic area
zona disco parking discs only
zona pedonale pedestrian
precinct

Menu Reader:
Food

Essential Terms

bread	il pane	[panay]
butter	il burro	[boor-ro]
cup	la tazza	[tatza]
dessert	il dessert	[des-sair]
fish	il pesce	[peshay]
fork	la forchetta	[forket-ta]
glass	il bicchiere	[beek-yairay]
knife	il coltello	
main course	la portata principale	
meat	la carne	[karnay]
menu	il menù	[menoo]
pepper	il pepe	[paypay]
plate	il piatto	[p-yat-to]
salad	l'insalata f	
salt	il sale	[salay]
set menu	il menù fisso	[menoo]
soup	la minestra, la zuppa	[tzoop-pa]
spoon	il cucchiaio	[kook-ya-yo]
starter	l'antipasto m	
table	il tavolo	

another ..., please ancora ..., per favore [pair favoray]

excuse me! (to call waiter/waitress) mi scusi [mee skoozee]

could I have the bill, please? il conto, per favore

abbacchio alla romana [ab-bak-yo] spring lamb

acciughe [achoogay] anchovies

acciughe sott'olio [sot-tol-yo] anchovies in oil

aceto [acheto] vinegar

affettato misto variety of cold, sliced meats such as salami, ham etc

affogato al caffè [kaf-fay] ice cream with hot espresso poured over it

affumicato smoked

aglio [al-yo] garlic

agnello [an-yel-lo] lamb

agnello al forno roast lamb

agnolotti al burro e salvia [an-yolot-tee – ay salv-ya] meat-filled pasta shapes served with butter and sage

agoni alla graticola grilled long, narrow fish from Lake Como

albicocca apricot

alloro laurel

anacardi cashew nuts

ananas pineapple

ananas al maraschino [maraskeeno] pineapple with sweet liqueur

anatra duck

anatra all'arancia [arancha] duck à l'orange

anello di riso e piselli rice and peas cooked in a ring-shaped mould

anguilla al forno [angweel-la] baked eel

anguria water melon

antipasti starters, hors d'oeuvres

antipasti caldi hot starters

antipasti freddi cold starters

antipasti misti variety of starters

antipasti misti toscani croutons with liver pâté, salami and cured ham

antipasto di pesce assortito [peshay] mixed seafood starter

arachidi [arakeedee] peanuts

aragosta spiny lobster

arancia [arancha] orange

arancini [arancheenee] fried rice balls

aringa herring

arista di maiale al forno [my-alay] roast chine of pork

arrosto roast

asiago [az-yago] full-fat white cheese

asparagi [asparajee] asparagus

astice [asteechay] lobster

avocado all'agro avocado pears with oil, lemon and vinegar dressing

baccalà dried cod

baccalà alla vicentina [veechenteena] dried salted cod cooked with onions, olive oil, milk, anchovies, parsley and parmesan and served with polenta

bagnacauda [ban-yakowda] vegetables, usually raw in an oil, garlic and anchovy sauce barbabietole [barbab-**yay**tolay] beetroot

basilico [ba**zee**leeko] basil

bastoncini di pesce [baston**chee**nee dee pe**shay**] fish fingers

bavarese [bavar**ay**zay] (ice-cream) cake with cream

Bel Paese [pa-**ay**zay] soft, full-fat white cheese

besciamella [beshamel-la] béchamel sauce, white sauce

bignè [been-**yay**] cream puff

biscotti e verduzzo [ay vaird**oo**tzo] home-made biscuits served with a glass of dry white wine

biscotto biscuit

bistecca steak

bistecca alla fiorentina [f-yoren**tee**na] large charcoal-grilled beef steak

bistecca di manzo [**ma**ndzo] beef steak

bistecca di cavallo horsemeat steak

bocconcini di manzo e vitello [bok-konch**ee**nee dee **ma**ndzo ay] chopped beef and veal

bollito boiled

bollito misto assorted boiled meats with vegetables

bomba ice cream bombe; doughnut

bombolone [bombol**o**nay] doughnut

bra full-fat white cheese

braciola di maiale [brach**o**la dee my-**a**lay] pork chop

branzino al forno [brant**zee**no] baked sea bass

brasato [bra**za**to] braised; braised beef with herbs

brasato al Barolo braised beef cooked in Barolo wine

bresaola [breza-ola] dried, salted beef sliced thinly and eaten cold

brioche [bree-**o**sh] croissant

broccoletti all'aglio [al-lal-yo] broccoli cooked in garlic

brodetto fish casserole

brodo clear broth

brodo di pollo chicken broth

brodo vegetale [vejay**ta**lay] clear, vegetable broth

bruschetta alla romana [broosk**et**-ta] toasted bread rubbed with garlic and sprinkled with olive oil

bucatini al pomodoro pasta similar to spaghetti (only thicker and with a hole through it) with tomato sauce

budino pudding

burro butter

caciotta [kach**o**t-ta] type of creamy, white, medium-soft cheese

caciotta toscana slightly mature, medium-soft cheese from Tuscany

caciucco alla livornese [kach**oo**k-ko **a**l-la leevorn**ay**zay] soup made from seafood, tomato and wine served with home-made bread

calamari fritti fried squid

calamari in umido stewed squid

calamaro squid

calzone [kaltzonay] folded pizza with tomato and mozzarella or ricotta and ham, or other fillings inside

calzone all'amalfitana calzone with cottage cheese, egg, ham and grana cheese

canestrato hard ewes milk cheese

cannella cinnamon

cannelloni al forno rolls of pasta filled with meat and baked in a sauce

cannoli alla siciliana [seecheel-yana] cylindrical pastries filled with ricotta and candied fruit

cannoncini alla crema [kan-noncheenee] cylindrical pastries filled with custard

cantuccini [kantoocheenee] almond biscuits

caponata di melanzane [melandzanay] fried aubergines/eggplants and celery cooked with tomato, capers and olives

cappelle di funghi porcini alla griglia [kap-pel-lay dee foongee porcheenee al-la greel-ya] grilled boletus mushroom tops

cappelletti small, filled pasta parcels

capperi capers

cappone lesso [kap-ponay] boiled capon

capretto al forno roast kid

caprino fresh, soft goat's cheese

capriolo in salmì roe deer venison in game sauce

caramella sweet

carciofi [karchofee] artichokes

carciofini sott'olio [karcho-feenee sot-tol-yo] baby artichokes preserved in oil

carne [karnay] meat

carne macinata [macheenata] minced meat

carote [karotay] carrots

carpaccio [karpacho] finely sliced raw beef fillets with oil, lemon and grated Parmesan

carré di maiale al forno [kar-ray dee my-alay] roast loin of pork

carrello dei dolci [dolchee] dessert trolley

cassata siciliana [seecheel-yana] Sicilian ice-cream cake with candied fruit, chocolate and ricotta

castagnaccio alla toscana [kastan-yacho] tart from Tuscany made with chestnut flour

castagne [kastan-yay] chestnuts

catalogna [katalon-ya] type of chicory with large leaves

cavoletti di Bruxelles [brooksel] Brussels sprouts

cavolfiore [kavolf-yoray] cauliflower

cavolo cabbage

cavolo rosso red cabbage

cazzuola alla milanese
[katzwola al-la meelanayzay]
spicy pork sausage, pork and
beans stewed in gravy

ceci [chaychee] chickpeas

cefalo [chefalo] mullet

cernia [chairn-ya] grouper (fish)

cervella al burro [chairvel-la]
brains cooked in butter

cetriolo [chetree-olo] cucumber

charlotte [sharlot] ice-cream
cake with cream, biscuits
and fruit

chiacchiere [k-yak-yairay] sweet
pastries fried in lard and
sprinkled with fine sugar

chiodi di garofano [k-yodee]
cloves

ciambella [chambel-la] ring-
shaped cake

cicoria [cheekoree-a] chicory

cicorino [cheekoreeno] small
chicory plants

ciliege [cheel-yay-jay] cherries

cima alla piemontese [cheema
al-la p-yaymontayzay] baked
veal stuffed with chicken and
chopped vegetables, served
cold

cime di rapa [cheemay] young
leaves of turnip plant

cinghiale in salmì [cheeng-yalay]
wild boar in game sauce

cioccolata [chok-kolata]
chocolate

cioccolata al latte [lat-tay] milk
chocolate

cioccolata fondente [fondentay]

plain chocolate

cioccolato [chok-kolato]
chocolate

cipolle [cheepol-lay] onions

cocktail di gamberetti prawn
cocktail

coda alla vaccinara
[vacheenara] oxtail diced and
stewed with vegetables

colomba pasquale [paskwalay]
dove-shaped cake with
candied fruit eaten at Easter

conchiglie alla marchigiana
[konkeel-yay al-la markeejana]
pasta shells in tomato sauce
with celery, carrot, parsley
and ham

condimento per l'insalata
salad dressing

coniglio [koneel-yo] rabbit

coniglio in salmì rabbit in
game sauce

cono gelato [jelato] ice-cream
cone

contorni vegetable side dishes

coperto cover charge (usually
includes bread)

coperto pane e grissini cover
charge includes bread and
breadsticks

coppa cured neck of pork,
finely sliced and eaten cold

cornetto croissant

cosciotto di agnello al forno
[koshot-to dee an-yel-lo] baked
leg of lamb

costata alla fiorentina
[f-yorenteena] Florentine
entrecôte

costata (di manzo) [mandzo] beef entrecôte

costoletta chop

costoletta di vitello alla griglia [greel-ya] grilled veal chop

cotechino [kotekeeno] spiced pork sausage, usually boiled

cotoletta veal cutlet

cotoletta alla milanese [meelanayzay] veal escalope in breadcrumbs

cotoletta alla valdostana veal chop with ham and cheese cooked in breadcrumbs

cotolette di agnello [an-yel-lo] lamb chops

cotolette di maiale [kotolet-tay dee my-alay] pork chops

cotto cooked

cozze [kotzay] mussels

cozze alla marinara mussels in marinade sauce

crauti [krowtee] white cabbage cut in strips, cooked in vinegar and white wine

crema [krayma] custard

crema al caffè [kaf-fay] coffee custard pudding

crema al cioccolato [chok-kolato] chocolate custard pudding

crema alla vaniglia [vaneel-ya] vanilla-flavoured custard pudding

crema di ... cream of ... soup

crema pasticciera [pasteechaira] confectioner's custard

crêpe [krep] pancake

crêpe suzette flambéed pancake with orange sauce

crescente [kreshentay] type of flat, fried Emilian bread

crescenza [kreshentza] soft, creamy white cheese

crescione [kreshonay] watercress

crespelle [krespel-lay] savoury pancakes

crocchette di patate [krok-ket-tay dee patatay] potato croquettes

crocchette di pesce [peshay] fish croquettes

crocchette di riso rice croquettes

crostata casalinga [cazaleenga] home-made lattice pie with jam or custard

crostata di frutta fruit tart

crostata di mele [maylay] apple pie

crostini ai funghi [a-ee foongee] croutons with mushrooms cooked in oil with garlic and parsley

crostini toscani croutons with liver pâté

crostoni di mozzarella [dee motzarel-la] mozzarella and tomato sauce served hot on home-made bread

crudo raw

dadi stock cubes

datteri dates

dentice al forno [denteechay] baked dentex (type of sea bream)

dolce [dolchay] dessert

dolci [dolchee] cakes, gâteaux, desserts etc

dolci della casa home-made cakes

endivia belga [endeev-ya] Belgian endive

entrecôte (di manzo) [mandzo] beef entrecôte

erbe aromatiche [airbay aromateekay] herbs

fagiano [fajano] pheasant

fagioli [fajolee] beans

fagioli alla messicana type of chili con carne

fagioli all'olio [al-lol-yo] beans with salt, pepper, oil and vinegar

fagioli borlotti in umido fresh borlotti beans cooked in vegetables, herbs and tomato sauce

fagiolini [fajoleenee] green beans

fagiolini lessi [les-see] boiled French beans

faraona [fara-ona] guinea fowl

farina flour

fatto in casa [kaza] home-made

fegatini di pollo chicken livers

fegato [faygato] liver

fegato alla veneta [venayta] liver cooked in butter with onions

ferri: ai ferri [a-ee] grilled

fetta biscottata slices of crispy toast-like bread

fettuccine [fet-toocheenay] ribbon-shaped pasta

fichi [feekee] figs

filetti di merluzzo [mairlootzo] fillets of cod

filetti di pesce persico [peshay pairseeko] fillets of perch

filetto fillet

filetto ai ferri [a-ee] grilled fillet of beef

filetto al cognac fillet of beef in cognac

filetto al pepe verde [paypay vairday] fillet of beef with green pepper

filetto al sangue [sangway] rare fillet of beef

filetto a media cottura [maydya] medium-done fillet beef

filetto ben cotto well-done fillet of beef

filetto di manzo [mandzo] fillet of beef

filone (di pane) [feelonay dee panay] large French stick

finocchi gratinati [feenok-kee] fennel with melted grated cheese

finocchio [feenok-yo] fennel

fiori di zucca fritti [f-yoree dee tzook-ka] fried pumpkin flowers

flan di spinaci [speenachee] spinach flan

focaccia [fokacha] flat bread sprinkled with olive oil and baked or grilled

foglie di vite alla greca [fol-yay

dee **vee**tay] Greek-style vine leaves

fondue Bourguignonne [boorgeen-**yon**] cubes of fillet steak fried in oil and dipped in various sauces

fonduta fondue made with cheese, milk and eggs

fontina soft, mature cheese often used in cooking

formaggi misti [formaj-jee] selection of cheeses

formaggio [form**aj**-jo] cheese

forno: al forno roast

fragole [**frag**olay] strawberries

fricassea di coniglio [freekas-**say**-a dee kon**ee**l-yo] chopped rabbit cooked in butter and aromatic herbs

frico e polenta [ay] fried latteria cheese with polenta

frittata type of omelette

frittelle di banane [freet**el**-lay dee ban**a**nay] banana fritters

frittelle di mele [**may**lay] apple fritters

fritto fried

fritto misto mixed seafood in batter

frittura di pesce [p**e**shay] variety of fried fish

frutta fruit

frutta alla fiamma [f-**yam**-ma] flambéd fruit

frutta fresca di stagione [staj**o**nay] seasonal fruit

frutta secca dried fruit; nuts

frutti di bosco mixture of forest fruits

frutti di mare [m**a**ray] seafood

frutti di mare gratinati seafood au gratin

funghi [**foo**ngee] mushrooms

funghi porcini [porch**ee**nee] boletus mushrooms

funghi trifolati mushrooms fried in garlic and parsley

fusilli al pomodoro [fooz**ee**l-lee] pasta twirls with tomato sauce

galantina di pollo chicken with spices and herbs served in gelatine

gallina chicken

gamberetti shrimps

gamberetti in salsa rosa [**ro**za] shrimps in mayonnaise and ketchup sauce

gamberi crayfish; prawns

gamberoni king prawns

gelatina [jelate**ee**na] gelatine

gelato [j**e**lato] ice cream

gelato di crema vanilla ice cream

gelato di frutta fruit-flavoured ice cream

ghiacciolo [g-yach**o**lo] ice lolly

giardiniera di verdure [jardeen-y**a**ira dee vaird**oo**ray] diced, mixed vegetables, cooked and pickled

gnocchetti verdi [n-yok-k**et**-tee v**air**dee] small flour, potato and spinach dumplings sometimes served with melted gorgonzola

gnocchi [n-**yok**-kee] small flour and potato dumplings

gnocchi ai formaggi [a-ee formaj-jee] potato dumplings with gorgonzola, fontina, mascarpone and Parmesan

gnocchi alla romana small semolina dumplings baked in butter

gnocchi al ragù dumplings with minced meat and tomato sauce

gorgonzola strong, soft blue cheese from Lombardy or Piedmont

grana generic name of cheeses similar to Parmesan

grana padano cheese similar to Parmesan

grancevola [granch**ay**vola] spiny spider crab

granchio [gr**an**k-yo] crab

grasso fat

gratin di patate [grat**ee**n dee patatay] potatoes with grated cheese

griglia: alla griglia [al-la gr**eel**-ya] grilled

grigliata di pesce [greel-yata di p**e**shay] grilled fish

grigliata mista mixed grill (meat or fish)

grissini breadsticks

gruviera [groov-y**ai**ra] Gruyère cheese

gulash ungherese [oongar**ay**zay] Hungarian goulash

impanato breaded, in breadcrumbs

indivia [eend**ee**v-ya] endive

insalata salad

insalata caprese [kapr**ay**zay] sliced tomatoes, mozzarella and oregano

insalata di carne [**kar**nay] meat salad

insalata di mare [**ma**ray] seafood salad

insalata di nervetti sinewy, chopped boiled beef or veal, served cold with beans and pickles

insalata mista mixed salad

insalata russa Russian salad

insalata verde [**vai**rday] green salad

involtini small beef olives

involtini di prosciutto [pro-sh**oo**t-to] small rolls of sliced ham filled with Russian salad

krapfen doughnut

lamponi raspberries

lardo al pepe [**pay**pay] fatty ham with pepper

lasagne al forno [laz**an**-yay] lasagne

latteria [lat-tair**ee**-a] full-fat white cheese

lattuga lettuce

legumi pulses

lenticchie [lent**ee**k-yay] lentils

lepre [**le**pray] hare

lesso boiled

limone [leem**o**nay] lemon

lingua [**lee**ngwa] tongue

lingua salmistrata ox tongue marinaded in brine and then cooked

linguine al pesto [leengweenay] kind of flat spaghetti with crushed basil, garlic, oil and Parmesan dressing

lombatina di vitella ai ferri [a-ee] grilled loin of veal

lonza di maiale al latte [lontza dee my-alay al lat-tay] pork loin cooked in milk

maccheroni alla siciliana [mak-kaironee al-la seecheel-yana] macaroni with tomato sauce and grated Sicilian ricotta cheese

maccheroni al ragù macaroni in a minced beef and tomato sauce

macedonia di frutta [machedon-ya] fruit salad

macedonia di frutta al maraschino [mara-skeeno] fruit salad in Maraschino liqueur

maggiorana [maj-jorana] marjoram

maiale [my-alay] pork

maionese [my-onayzay] mayonnaise

mandarancio [mandarancho] clementine

mandorle [mandorlay] almonds

mantovana almond cake from Prato

manzo [mandzo] beef

marinato marinated, soused, pickled

marmellata jam

marmellata d'arance [daranchay] marmalade

marroni chestnuts

marzapane [martzapanay] marzipan

mascarpone [maskarponay] full-fat, cream cheese, often used in desserts

medaglioni di vitello [medal-yonee] round pieces of veal

mela [mayla] apple

mela flambé flambéd apple

melanzane [melandzanay] aubergines/eggplants

melanzane alla piastra [p-yastra] grilled aubergines/eggplants

melanzane alla siciliana [seecheel-yana] baked aubergine/eggplant slices with parmesan, tomato sauce and egg

melone [melonay] melon

melone al porto melon with port

menta mint

menu fisso set menu

menu turistico tourist menu

meringata meringue pie

meringhe con panna [maireengay] meringues with cream

merluzzo [mairlootzo] cod

merluzzo alla pizzaiola [peetza-yola] cod in tomato sauce with anchovies, capers and parsley

213

merluzzo in bianco [b-yanko] boiled cod with oil and lemon

messicani in gelatina [jelateena] rolls of veal in gelatine

miele [m-yaylay] honey

millefoglie [meel-lefol-yay] custard slice

minestra di orzo [ortzo] barley soup

minestra di riso e prezzemolo (in brodo) [pretzaymolo] parsley and rice soup

minestra di verdure [vairdooray] vegetable soup

minestra in brodo soup with vegetables and pasta or rice

minestre [meenestray] soups

minestrone [meenestronay] thick vegetable broth with rice or thin pasta

mirtilli [meerteel-lee] bilberries

montasio [montaz-yo] full-fat white cheese

Montebianco [monteb-yanko] puréed chestnut and whipped cream pudding

more [moray] mulberries, blackberries

mortadella large, mild-flavoured cured sausage, usually served in thin slices

mostarda di Cremona preserve made from candied fruit in grape must or sugar with mustard

mousse al cioccolato [chok-kolato] chocolate mousse

mozzarella [motzarel-la] white, mild, slightly rubbery buffalo milk cheese

mozzarella in carrozza [een kar-rotza] slices of bread and mozzarella coated in flour and fried

nasello [nazel-lo] hake

naturale: al naturale [natooralay] plain, natural

nervetti con cipolla [cheepol-la] chopped, sinewy beef and veal with onions

nocciole [nocholay] hazelnuts

noccioline [nocholeenay] peanuts

noce di cocco [nochay] coconut

noce di vitello ai funghi [a-ee foongee] veal with mushrooms

noce moscata nutmeg

noci [nochee] walnuts

nodino veal chop

oca goose

olio [ol-yo] oil

olio di semi [saymee] vegetable oil

olio d'oliva olive oil

oliva olive

omelette omelette

orata al forno baked gilthead (fish)

orecchiette al sugo (di pomodoro) [orek-yet-tay] small pasta shells with tomato sauce

orecchiette con cime di rapa

[cheemay] orecchiette with turnip tops

origano oregano

orzo [ordzo] barley

ossobuco stewed shin of veal

ostriche [ostreekay] oysters

paglia e fieno [pal-ya ay f-yayno] mixture of ordinary and green tagliatelle

pagnotta [pan-yot-ta] round loaf

paillard di manzo [pa-yar dee mandzo] slices of grilled beef

paillard di vitello slices of grilled veal

pancetta [panchet-ta] bacon

pancotto stale bread cooked with tomatoes etc

pan di Spagna [span-ya] sponge cake

pandoro kind of sponge cake eaten at Christmas

pane [panay] bread

pane bianco [b-yanko] white bread

pane integrale [eentegralay] wholemeal bread

pane tostato toast

pane casereccio [kazairecho] home-made bread

pane di segale [saygalay] rye bread

pane e coperto cover charge including bread

pane in cassetta sliced bread

pane nero [nairo] wholemeal bread

panettone [panet-tonay] dome-shaped cake with sultanas and candied fruit eaten at Christmas

panforte [panfortay] nougat-type spiced delicacy from Siena

panini sandwiches; filled rolls

panna cream

panna cotta kind of pudding typical of Tuscany

panna montata whipped cream

panna per cucinare [pair koocheenaray] cream for cooking

panzanella [pantzanel-la] Tuscan dish of bread with fresh tomatoes, onions basil and olive oil

papaia [papa-ya] papaw, papaya

pappa col pomodoro tomato soup with toasted home-made bread typical of Tuscany

parmigiana di melanzane [parmeejana dee melandzanay] baked dish of layers of aubergines/eggplants, tomato sauce, mozzarella and Parmesan

parmigiano reggiano [parmeejano rej-jano] Parmesan cheese

passato di patate [patatay] cream of potato soup

passato di verdure [vairdooray] cream of vegetable soup

pasta pasta; cake; pastry

215

pasta al forno pasta baked in white sauce with grated cheese

pasta alla frutta fruit pastry

pasta e fagioli [ay fajolee] very thick soup with blended borlotti beans and small pasta

pasta e piselli pasta with peas

pasticcino [pasteecheeno] small cake

pasticcio di fegato d'oca [pasteecho dee faygato] baked, pasta-covered dish with goose liver

pasticcio di lepre [lepray] baked, pasta-covered dish with hare

pasticcio di maccheroni [makkaironee] baked macaroni

pastiera napoletana [past-yaira] flaky pastry with wheat, ricotta and candied fruit

pastina in brodo noodle soup

patate [patatay] potatoes

patate al forno baked potatoes

patate arrosto roast potatoes

patate fritte [freet-tay] chips, French fries

patate in insalata potato salad

patate prezzemolate [pretzemolatay] boiled potatoes with oil and parsley

patate saltate [saltatay] sautéed potatoes

patatine [patateenay] crisps, (US) potato chips

patatine fritte [freet-tay] chips, French fries

pâté di carne [karnay] pâté

pâté di fegato [faygato] liver pâté

pâté di pesce [peshay] fish pâté

pecorino strong, hard ewe's milk cheese

pecorino sardo hard, mature Sardinian ewes cheese

pelati peeled tinned tomatoes

penne [pen-nay] pasta quills

penne ai quattro formaggi [a-ee kwat-tro formaj-jee] penne with sauce made from four cheeses

penne all'arrabbiata [ar-rabyata] penne with tomato and chili pepper sauce

penne rigate [reegatay] penne with ridges

pepe [paypay] pepper (spice)

peperonata peppers cooked in olive oil with onion, tomato and garlic

peperoncino [pepaironcheeno] chilli pepper

peperone [pepaironay] pepper (vegetable)

peperoni ripieni (di carne) [reep-yaynee dee karnay] stuffed peppers (filled with meat)

peperoni sott'olio [sot-tol-yo] peppers in oil

pera [paira] pear

pernice [pairneechay] partridge

pernice alla cacciatora [kachatora] stewed spiced partridge

pesca [peska] peach

pesce [peshay] fish

pesce al cartoccio [kartocho]

fish baked in foil with herbs

pesce in carpione [karp-yonay] soused fish

pesce spada swordfish

pesche sciroppate [peskay sheerop-patay] peaches in syrup

petti di pollo alla bolognese [bolon-yayzay] chicken breasts in breadcrumbs with tomato sauce

petti di pollo impanati chicken breasts in breadcrumbs

piatti di carne [p-yat-tee dee karnay] meat dishes

piatti di pesce [peshay] fish dishes

piatto unico freddo [p-yat-to] cold sliced meat with pickles

piccata di vitello al limone [leemonay] veal in sour lemon sauce

piccione [peechonay] pigeon

piccione arrosto roast pigeon

piedini di maiale [p-yaydeenee dee my-alay] pigs' trotters

pinoli pine nuts

pinzimonio [peentzeemon-yo] selection of whole, raw vegetables eaten with oil and vinegar dressing

piselli peas

piselli al prosciutto [proshoot-to] fresh peas cooked in clear broth, with butter, ham and basil

pistacchi [peestak-kee] pistachios

pizza ai porcini [porcheenee] pizza with boletus

mushrooms

pizza ai quattro formaggi [kwat-tro formaj-jee] pizza with four cheeses – mozzarella, gorgonzola, latteria, grana

pizza agli asparagi [al-yee asparajee] asparagus pizza

pizza alla diavola [d-yavola] pizza with spicy salami

pizza alla marinara pizza with tomato, oregano, garlic and anchovies

pizza alla zingara [tzeengara] pizza with aubergines/ eggplants, peppers, mushrooms and olives

pizza al S. Daniele [san dan-yaylay] pizza with cured ham

pizza campagnola [kampan-yola] pizza with mushrooms and peppers

pizza capricciosa [kapreechosa] pizza with tomato, ham, mushrooms and artichokes

pizzaiola [peetza-ee-ola] slices of cooked beef in tomato sauce, oregano and anchovies

pizza Margherita [margaireeta] pizza with tomato and mozzarella

pizza napoletana pizza with tomato, mozzarella and anchovies

pizza nordica pizza with chopped salami and frankfurters

pizza orchidea [orkeeday-a] pizza with peppers and egg

pizza pugliese [pool-yayzay] tomato and onion pizza

pizza quattro stagioni [stajonee] pizza with ham, mushrooms, artichokes and anchovies

pizza romana pizza with tomato, mozzarella, anchovies and oregano

pizza siciliana [seecheel-yana] pizza with anchovies, capers, olives and oregano

pizzetta [peetzet-ta] small pizza

pizzoccheri alla Valtellinese [peetzok-kairee al-la valtel-leenayzay] thin, pasta strips with green vegetables, melted butter and cheese

polenta yellow cornmeal porridge, left to set and cut in slices, can be fried or baked

polenta concia [koncha] sliced polenta baked with garlic, cheese and butter

polenta e osei [ozay-ee] small birds served with polenta

polenta e uccellini [oo-chel-leenee] small birds served with polenta

polenta fritta fried polenta

polenta pasticciata [pasteechata] layers of polenta, tomato sauce and cheese

pollame [pol-lamay] poultry

pollo chicken

pollo alla cacciatora [kachatora] chicken chasseur – pieces of fried chicken in a white wine and mushroom sauce

pollo alla diavola [dee-avola] chicken pieces pressed and fried

polpette [polpet-tay] meatballs

polpettone [polpet-tonay] meatloaf

polpi alla veneziana [venetz-yana] chopped boiled octopus, seasoned with garlic, lemon juice and parsley

polpo octopus

pomodori tomatoes

pomodori alla maionese [my-onay-zay] tomatoes with mayonnaise

pomodori pelati peeled tinned tomatoes

pomodori ripieni di riso [reep-yaynee] tomatoes stuffed with rice

pomodoro tomato

pompelmo grapefruit

porchetta [porket-ta] roast sucking pig

porchetta allo spiedo [sp-yaydo] sucking pig on the spit

porro leek

portata course (of meal)

prezzemolo [pretzaymolo] parsley

primi piatti [p-yat-tee] first courses

prosciutto [proshoot-to] ham

prosciutto al madera ham with madeira

prosciutto cotto cooked ham

prosciutto crudo dry-cured ham

prosciutto crudo di S. Daniele [san dan-**yay**lay] finest quality prosciutto crudo from S. Daniele

prosciutto di Praga type of dry-cured ham

provolone [provo**lo**nay] oval-shaped cheese, with a slight smoked and spicy flavour

prugne [pr**oo**n-yay] plums

punte di asparagi all'agro [**poo**ntay dee asparajee] asparagus tips in oil and lemon dressing

purè di patate [p**oo**ray dee pat**a**tay] creamed potatoes

quaglie [kw**a**l-yay] quails

radicchio [rad**ee**k-yo] chicory

ragù sauce made with minced beef and tomatoes

rapa type of white turnip with flavour similar to radish

ravanelli radishes

ravioli egg pasta filled with meat or cheese

ravioli al pomodoro ravioli in tomato sauce

razza [r**a**tza] skate

resta di Como speciality of Como, pastry rolled around a stick and baked

ribollita vegetable soup with toasted home-made bread, typical of Tuscany

ricotta soft white cheese, similar to cottage cheese

ricotta piemontese [p-yay-mont**ay**zay] similar to ricotta romana

ricotta romana soft, white cheese often used in desserts

ricotta siciliana [seecheel-**ya**na] slightly mature and salty ricotta

rigatoni al pomodoro short, ridged pasta shapes with tomato sauce

ripieno [reep-**yay**no] stuffed

risi e bisi risotto with peas and small pieces of ham

riso rice

riso alla greca boiled rice with olives, cheese and tomato

riso in brodo rice in clear broth

riso pilaf rice cooked slowly in the oven with butter and onion

risotto rice simmered slowly in clear broth

risotto al Barolo risotto with Barolo wine

risotto alla castellana risotto with mushroom, ham, cream and cheese sauce

risotto alla marinara seafood risotto

risotto alla milanese (allo zafferano) [meelan**ay**zay al-lo tzaf-fair**a**no] risotto with saffron

risotto al nero di seppia [n**ai**ro dee s**e**p-ya] risotto with cuttlefish ink

risotto al salto sautéed saffron risotto

risotto con la salsiccia [salseecha] risotto with pork sausage

roast-beef all'inglese [eenglayzay] thin slices of roast beef served cold with lemon

robiola [rob-yola] soft cheese from Lombardy

rognone trifolato [ron-yonay] small pieces of kidney in garlic, oil and parsley

rombo turbot

rosetta kind of roll

rosmarino rosemary

rucola rocket

Saint-Honoré [santonoray] tart with soft, pastry base and small cream éclairs

salame [salamay] salami

salame di cioccolato [dee chok-kolato] mixture of broken biscuits and chocolate in the shape of a salami

salatini [salateenee] tiny salted crackers, crisps and peanuts (eaten with aperitifs)

sale [salay] salt

salmone [salmonay] salmon

salsa sauce

salsa cocktail mayonnaise and ketchup sauce, served with fish and seafood

salsa di pomodoro tomato sauce

salsa tartara tartar sauce

salsa vellutata white sauce

made with clear broth instead of milk

salsa verde [vairday] sauce made from chopped parsley, anchovies and oil, served with meat

salsiccia [salseecha] sausage

saltimbocca alla romana slices of veal rolled up with ham and sage and fried

salvia [salv-ya] sage

sangue: al sangue [sangway] rare

sarago [sarago] white bream

sarde ai ferri [sarday a-ee] grilled sardines

scaloppine [skalop-peenay] veal escalopes

scaloppine al Marsala veal escalopes in Marsala

scamorza affumicata [skamortza] smoked, soft, oval-shaped cheese

scamorza alla griglia [greel-ya] grilled soft cheese

scampi crayfish, scampi

scarola type of endive

schiacciata toscana [skee-achata] bread with fresh oil and rosemary

scorfano scorpion fish

scorpena [skorpayna] scorpion fish

scorzonera al burro [skortzonaira] type of root cooked in butter

secondi (piatti) [p-yat-tee] main courses, second courses

sedano [saydano] celery

sedano di Verona Veronese celery

sella di cervo [chairvo] rump of venison

selvaggina [selvaj-jeena] game

semifreddo ice cream and sponge dessert

senape [senapay] mustard

seppie in umido [sep-yay] stewed cuttlefish

sfogliata agli spinaci [sfol-yata a-yee speenachee] flaky pastry with spinach filling

sfogliata al salmone [sal-monay] flaky pastry with salmon filling

sofficini al formaggio [sof-feecheenee al formaj-jo] Findus® crispy pancakes with cheese filling

sogliola [sol-yola] sole

sogliola alla mugnaia [moon-ya-ya] sole cooked in flour and butter

sorbetto sorbet; soft ice cream

sottaceti [sot-tachaytee] pickles

soufflé al formaggio [formaj-jo] cheese soufflé

soufflé al prosciutto [pro-shoot-to] ham soufflé

spaghetti alla carbonara spaghetti with egg, cheese and diced bacon sauce

spaghetti alla marinara spaghetti with seafood

spaghetti all'amatriciana [amatree-chana] spaghetti with bacon, onions and tomato sauce

spaghetti alla puttanesca spaghetti with anchovies, capers and black olives in tomato sauce

spaghetti all'arrabbiata [al-lar-rab-yata] spaghetti with tomato and chilli sauce

spaghetti alle noci [nochee] spaghetti with fresh cream, grated nuts and cheese

spaghetti alle vongole [vongolay] spaghetti with clams

spaghetti al nero di seppia [nairo dee sep-ya] black spaghetti flavoured with cuttlefish ink

spaghetti al pesto spaghetti in crushed basil, garlic, oil and Parmesan dressing

spaghetti al ragù spaghetti with minced beef and tomato sauce

spalla di maiale al forno [my-alay] shoulder of roast pork

speck type of dry-cured, smoked ham

spezie [spaytz-yay] spices

spezzatino di vitello [spetzateeno] veal stew

spiedini [sp-yaydeenee] small pieces of a variety of meat or fish roasted on a spit

spiedo: allo spiedo [sp-yaydo] on a spit

spigola sea bass

spinaci [speenachee] spinach

221

spinaci all'agro spinach with oil and lemon

spuma di salmone [spooma dee salmonay] salmon mousse

spuntino snack

stoccafisso dried cod

stracchino [strak-keeno] soft cheese from Lombardy

stracchino alle fragole [al-lay fragolay] dessert of strawberries and whipped cream liquidized and frozen

stracciatella [stracha-tel-la] vanilla ice cream with chocolate chips; beaten eggs cooked in boiling, clear broth

strangolapreti [strangolapraytee] little spinach and potato balls

strozzapreti al basilico e pomodoro [strotzapraytee al bazeeleeko ay] small dumplings with tomato and basil

strudel di mele [maylay] apple strudel

stufato stewed

stufato con verdure [vairdooray] meat stewed with vegetables and herbs

sugo al tonno tomato sauce with garlic, tuna and parsley

svizzera [zveetzaira] hamburger

tacchino [tak-keeno] turkey

tagliata [tal-yata] finely-cut beef fillet

tagliatelle [tal-yatel-lay] thin, flat strips of egg pasta

tagliatelle alla bolognese [bolon-yayzay] tagliatelle with minced beef and tomato sauce

tagliatelle al ragù tagliatelle with minced beef and tomato sauce

tagliatelle rosse [ros-say] tagliatelle with chopped red peppers

tagliatelle verdi [vairdee] tagliatelle with chopped spinach

taglierini al tartufo [tal-yaireenee] very thin pasta strips with truffles

taglierini gratinati thin pasta strips au gratin

tagliolini [tal-yoleenee] thin, soup noodles

tagliolini verdi panna e prosciutto [vairdee – ay proshoot-to] thin green noodles with cream and ham sauce

taleggio [talej-jo] full-fat, semi-mature, mild, soft cheese from Northern Italy

tartine [tarteenay] canapés

tartufo round ice cream sprinkled with cocoa or chocolate powder; truffle (edible fungi)

tavola calda snack bar serving hot dishes

testina di vitello head of small calf

timballo di riso alla finanziera [fee-nantz-yaira] type of rice pie filled with chicken entrails and crests

timo thyme

tiramisù dessert made of coffee-soaked sponge, eggs, Marsala wine, mascarpone cheese and cocoa powder

toast [tost] toasted sandwich

tomini sott'olio [sot-tol-yo] cheese with pepper marinated in oil and herbs

tonno tuna fish

torrone [tor-ronay] nougat

torta cake; tart; flan

torta della nonna tart with cream and pine nuts

torta di mele [maylay] apple tart

torta di noci [nochee] walnut tart

torta di ricotta type of cheesecake

torta gelato [jelato] ice-cream tart

torta lorenese [lorenayzay] quiche lorraine

torta pasqualina [paskwaleena] flaky pastry with spinach, cheese, ham and hard-boiled eggs

tortelli home-made ravioli filled with ricotta and spinach

tortelli di patate [patatay] home-made ravioli filled with mashed potato and nutmeg

tortellini small pasta filled with pork loin, ham, Parmesan and nutmeg

tortellini al ragù tortellini with minced beef and tomato sauce

tortelloni di magro pasta filled with cheese, parsley and vegetables

tortelloni di ricotta pasta filled with cheese, parsley and vegetables

tortino di asparagi [asparajee] asparagus pie

tortino di patate [patatay] potato pie

tournedos [toornaydo] round, thick slice of beef fillet

tramezzino [tramedzeeno] sandwich

trancio di coda di rospo [trancho] angler fish cutlet

trancio di palombo smooth hound slice (fish)

trancio di pesce spada [peshay] swordfish steak

trenette col pesto [trenet-tay] type of flat spaghetti with crushed basil, garlic, oil and cheese sauce

triglia [treel-ya] mullet

trippa tripe

trota trout

uccelletti [oochel-let-tee] small birds wrapped in bacon on cocktail sticks

umido stewed

uova [wova] eggs

uova affogate [af-fogatay] poached eggs

uova all'occhio di bue [ok-yo dee boo-ay] fried eggs

uova al tegamino con pancetta [panchet-ta] eggs and bacon

uova farcite [farcheetay] eggs stuffed with tuna, capers and mayonnaise

uova in camicia [kameecha] poached eggs

uova in cocotte [kokot] eggs cooked in a cast-iron pan

uova strapazzate [strapatzatay] scrambled eggs

uovo [wovo] egg

uovo alla coque [kok] boiled egg

uovo sodo hard-boiled egg

uva grapes

uva bianca white grapes

uva nera [naira] black grapes

valigette verdi al gorgonzola [valeejet-tay vairdee] large green ravioli filled with gorgonzola cheese

vaniglia [vaneel-ya] vanilla

vellutata di piselli creamed peas with egg yolks

vellutata al pomodoro cream of tomato soup with fresh cream

vellutata di asparagi [asparajee] creamed asparagus with egg yolks

veneziana [venetz-yana] type of small panettone cake sprinkled with sugar

verdura [vairdoora] vegetables

verdura di stagione [stajonay] seasonal vegetables

verdure fresche di stagione [vairdooray freskay] seasonal vegetables

vermicelli [vairmeechel-lee] pasta thinner than spaghetti

vitello veal

vitello tonnato sliced veal in blended tuna, anchovy, oil and lemon sauce

vol-au-vent alla crema di formaggio [krayma dee formaj-jo] cream cheese vol-au-vent

vongole [vongolay] clams

würstel [voorstel] frankfurter

zabaglione/zabaione [tzabal-yonay] dessert made from beaten eggs, sugar and Marsala

zafferano [tzaf-fairano] saffron

zampone con lenticchie [tzamponay kon lenteek-yay] stuffed pig's trotters with lentils

zucca [tzook-ka] pumpkin

zucchero [tzook-kairo] sugar

zucchine [tzook-keenay] courgettes

zucchine al pomodoro chopped courgettes in tomato, garlic and parsley sauce

zuccotto [tzook-kot-to] ice-cream cake with sponge, fresh cream and chocolate

zuppa [tzoop-pa] soup

zuppa inglese [eenglayzay]
trifle
zuppa pavese [pavayzay] soup
with home-made bread,
grated cheese and an egg

Menu Reader: Drink

Essential Terms

beer	la birra	[**beer**-ra]
bottle	la bottiglia	[bot-**teel**-ya]
brandy	il brandy	
coffee	il caffè	[kaf-**fay**]
cup	la tazza	[**tatza**]
a cup of ...	una tazza di...	
gin	il gin	
gin and tonic	un gin tonic	
glass	il bicchiere	[beek-**yai**ray]
a glass of ...	un bicchiere di...	
milk	il latte	[**l**at-tay]
mineral water	l'acqua minerale **f**	[**a**kwa meen-air**a**lay]
orange juice	il succo d'arancia	[**s**ook-ko d'ar**a**ncha]
port	il porto	
red wine	il vino rosso	
rosé	il rosé	
soda (water)	il seltz	
soft drink	la bibita (analcolica)	
sugar	lo zucchero	[**t**zook-kairo]
tea	il tè	[**tay**]
tonic (water)	l'acqua tonica **f**	[**a**kwa]
vodka	la vodka	
water	l'acqua **f**	[**a**kwa]
whisky	il whisky	
white wine	il vino bianco	[b-**y**anko]
wine	il vino	
wine list	la lista dei vini	[**day**]

another ..., please   ancora ..., per favore [pair fav**o**ray]

acqua [akwa] water

acqua minerale [meenairalay] mineral water

acqua minerale gassata sparkling mineral water

acqua minerale non gassata still mineral water

acqua naturale [natooralay] still mineral water

acqua tonica tonic water

alcol alcohol

alcolici [alkoleechee] alcoholic drinks

Amaretto liqueur made from apricot kernels, giving it a strong almond-type flavour

amaro dark, bitter, herbal digestive liqueur

analcolici [analkoleechee] non-alcoholic drinks

aperitivo aperitif

aranciata [aranchata] orangeade

Asti Spumante [spoomantay] sparkling sweet white wine from Asti in Piedmont

Barbaresco dry red wine, typical of the Piedmont region

Barbera [barbaira] dark dry red wine from Piedmont

Bardolino dry red wine from area around Verona

Bardolino secco dry red wine from the Veneto region

Barolo dark dry red wine from Piedmont

bevande drinks

bianco [b-yanko] white

Bianco dei Castelli secco dry white wine from Lazio

bibita analcolica soft drink

birra [beer-ra] beer

birra alla spina draught beer

birra chiara [k-yara] amber-coloured light beer, lager

birra grande [granday] large beer (40 cl, approx. 1 pint)

birra in bottiglia [bot-teel-ya] bottled beer

birra media [mayd-ya] medium beer (30 cl)

birra piccola small beer (20cl, approx. 1/2 pint)

birra rossa darker, maltier beer

birra scura [skoora] beer similar to bitter, darker than birra rossa

bitter bitter-tasting red or orange alcoholic aperitif

Brachetto [braket-to] sweet sparkling red wine from Marche or Acqui, Piedmont

Brunello di Montalcino [montalcheeno] expensive dry red wine, from Montalcino, Tuscany

Cabernet [kabairnay] dry red wine from Veneto

cacao [kaka-o] cocoa

caffè [kaf-fay] coffee(s); café(s)

caffè corretto espresso coffee with a dash of liqueur or spirit

caffellatte [kaf-fel-lat-tay] half espresso, half milk

caffè lungo weak black coffee

caffè macchiato [mak-yato] espresso coffee with a dash of milk

caffè ristretto extra-strong espresso coffee

caffè solubile [soloobeelay] instant coffee

camomilla camomile tea

cappuccino [kap-poocheeno] espresso coffee with foaming milk, sprinkled with cocoa/ chocolate powder

Cartizze [karteetz-zay] sparkling dry white wine from Veneto

Chianti [k-yantee] dark red Tuscan wine

china [keena] liqueur made from chinchona bark

chinotto [keenot-to] sparkling, dark soft drink

cioccolata calda [chok-kolata] hot chocolate

Cirò [cheero] slightly sweet, delicate red, rosé or white wine

Coca Cola® Coke®

Cortese [kortayzay] dry Piedmontese wine

Corvo di Salaparuta dry Sicilian red wine

cubetto di ghiaccio [g-yacho] ice cube

degustazione (di vini) [degoostatz-yonay] wine tasting

denominazione di origine controllata mark

guaranteeing the quality of a wine

digestivo [deejesteevo] digestive liqueur

D.O.C. (Denominazione di Origine Controllata) certifies the origin of a wine

D.O.C.G. (Denominazione di Origine Controllata e Garantita) guarantees the quality of a wine

Dolcetto [dolchet-to] dry red wine from Piedmont area

espresso strong black coffee

Est-Est-Est dry or sweet white wine from around Montefiascone area in Lazio

frappé [frap-pay] whisked milkshake or fruit drink with crushed ice

frappé al cioccolato [chok-kolato] chocolate milkshake with crushed ice

frappé alla banana banana milkshake with crushed ice

frappé alla fragola strawberry milkshake with crushed ice

Frascati dry white wine from area around Rome

Freisa [frayza] dry red wine from Piedmont region

frizzante [freedzantay] fizzy

frullato di frutta milkshake with fruit and crushed ice

gazzosa [gatz-zoza] clear lemonade

ghiaccio [g-ya**ch**o] ice
granita drink with crushed ice
granita di caffè [kaf-f**ay**] coffee granita
granita di caffè con panna coffee and fresh cream granita
granita di limone [leem**o**nay] lemon granita
grappa very strong, clear spirit distilled from grape husks
Grignolino [green-yol**ee**no] dry red wine, light in colour
Grumello dry, red wine with slight strawberry flavour

Inferno dry red wine from Lombardy

Lambrusco sweet red or white sparkling wine from Emilia Romagna area
latte [**l**at-tay] milk
latte macchiato con cioccolato [mak-y**a**to kon chok-kol**a**to] foaming milk with a sprinkling of cocoa or chocolate powder
Lemonsoda® sparkling lemon drink
limonata lemonade; lemon juice
liquore [leekw**o**ray] liqueur
lista dei vini [day] wine list

Malvasia [malvaz**ee**-a] dry white wine, sometimes

slightly sparkling, from Sardinia or Friuli
Marsala thick, very sweet wine similar to sherry
Merlot [mair**lo**] very dark red wine with slightly herby flavour, of French origin
Moscato sweet, sparkling fruity wine

Nebbiolo [neb-y**o**lo] dry red wine from Piedmont region

Oransoda® sparkling orange drink
Orvieto [orvee-**ay**to] crisp white wine, usually dry

Pinot [peen**o**] light, dry white wine from the north
Pinot bianco [b-y**a**nko] dry slightly sparkling white wine from the north
Pinot grigio [gree**j**o] dry white wine from the north
Pinot nero [**na**iro] dry red wine from the north
porto port
prodotto e imbottigliato da... produced and bottled by ...
Prosecco sparkling or still white wine from Veneto, can be either sweet or dry

Recioto [rech**o**to] sweet sparkling red wine from Veneto
Refosco dry red wine from Friuli

Riesling [**ree**zling] dry white wine form various Northern regions

rosatello [roza**tel**-lo] dry rosé wine

rosato [ro**za**to] dry rosé wine

rosé [ro**zay**] rosé wine

rosso red

Sambuca (con la mosca) aniseed-flavoured liqueur (served with a coffee bean in the glass)

Sangiovese [sanjova**yzay**] heavy, dry red wine

Sassella dry, delicate red wine from Vatellina area

Sauvignon [soveen-**yon**] dry white wine from Veneto

sidro cider

Soave [so-**avay**] light, dry white wine from region around Lake Garda

spremuta d'arancia [da**rancha**] freshly squeezed orange juice

spremuta di limone [leem**o**nay] freshly squeezed lemon juice

spumante [spoo**man**tay] sparkling wine, like champagne

Strega® [**stray**ga] sweet liqueur made from a secret recipe

succo [**sook**-ko] juice

succo d'arancia [da**rancha**] orange juice

succo di albicocca apricot juice

succo di pera pear juice

succo di pesca peach juice

succo di pompelmo grapefruit juice

tè [tay] tea

tè al latte [**lat**-tay] tea with milk

tè al limone [leem**o**nay] lemon tea

Terlano dry white wine from area around Bolzano

Tocai [tok-a-ee] dry white wine from Veneto and Friuli

Valpolicella [valpolee**chel**-la] dry red wine from Veneto region

Verdicchio [vair**deek**-yo] dry white fruity wine from Marche

Vermentino dry wine from Liguria and Sardinia

Vernaccia di S. Gimignano [vair**na**cha dee san jeemeen-**ya**no] dry white wine from Tuscany

vino wine

vino bianco [b-**yan**ko] white wine

vino da dessert [des-**sair**] dessert wine

vino da pasto table wine

vino da tavola table wine

vino della casa house wine

Vino Nobile di Montepulciano [**no**beelay dee montepool**chano**]

high-class Tuscan red wine
vino rosato [roz**a**to] rosé wine
vino rosé [roz**ay**] rosé wine
vino rosso red wine
Vin Santo type of dessert wine
from Tuscany

How the
Language
Works

Pronunciation

In this phrase book, the Italian has been written in a system of imitated pronunciation so that it can be read as though it were English bearing in mind the notes on pronunciation given below:

ay	as in m**ay**	ow	as in n**ow**
e	as in g**e**t	y	as in **y**es
g	always hard as in **g**oat		

Letters given in bold type indicate the part of the word to be stressed.

When double consonants are given in the pronunciation such as j-j, t-t and so on, both consonants should be pronounced, for example **formaggio** [formaj-jo], **biglietto** [beel-yet-to].

Abbreviations

adj	adjective	**m**	masculine
f	feminine	**mpl**	masculine plural
fpl	feminine plural		

Notes

In the English-Italian section, when two forms of the verb are given in phrases such as: 'can you ...?' **puoi/può...?**, the first is the familiar form and the second the polite form (see the entry for **you** in the dictionary).

In other cases, when two forms are given as in expressions like: 'a few' **alcuni/alcune**, the first form is masculine and the second feminine (see **How the Language Works** page XXX).

An asterisk (*) next to a word in the English-Italian or Italian-English means that you should refer to the **How the Language Works** section for further information.

Nouns

Italian nouns have one of two genders – masculine or feminine. Generally, nouns ending in **-o** are masculine:

il traghetto
eel trag**et**-to
the ferry

lo zaino
lo tza-**ee**no
the rucksack

Nouns ending in **-a** are usually feminine:

la macchina
la m**a**k-keena
the car

la benzina
la bentz**ee**na
petrol

Nouns ending in **-e** can be either masculine or feminine:

il ristorante
eel reestor**a**ntay
the restaurant

la chiave
la k-y**a**vay
the key

A number of nouns ending in **-a** are used to refer to both men and women:

l'autista m / f
lowt**ee**sta
the driver

l'artista m / f
lart**ee**sta
the artist

la guida f
la gw**ee**da
the guide

il / la centralinista
eel / la chentraleen**ee**sta
the switchboard operator

Plural Nouns

Generally, to form the plural of a noun:

singular	plural
-o	-i
-a	-e
-e	-i

il biglietto	**i biglietti**
eel beel-**yet**-to	ee beel-**yet**-tee
the ticket	the tickets
la strada	**le strade**
la st**ra**da	lay st**ra**day
the road	the roads
il dolce	**i dolci**
eel d**o**lchay	ee d**o**lchee
the dessert	the desserts

The following variations are common:

singular	plural
-ca, -ga,	-che, -ghe,
-co, -go	-chi, -ghi
-io	-i
-cia, -gia	-ce, -ge

il parco	**i parchi**
eel p**a**rko	ee p**a**rkee
the park	the parks
l'albicocca	**le albicocche**
lalbeek**o**k-ka	lay albeek**o**k-kay
the apricot	the apricots
il negozio	**i negozi**
eel neg**o**tz-yo	i neg**o**tzee
the shop	the shops

l'arancia
larancha
the orange

le arance
lay aranchay
the oranges

Nouns ending in **-i**, **-u**, a stressed vowel or a consonant do not change in the plural:

il taxi / i taxi
the taxi / the taxis

lo sport / gli sport
the sport / the sports

il film / i film
the film / the films

il tram / i tram
the tram / the trams

il caffè / i caffè
eel kaf-**fay** / ee kaf-**fay**
the coffee / the coffees

la città / le città
la cheet-**ta** / lay cheet-**ta**
the city / the cities

A few other common nouns don't change their ending in the plural:

il cinema / i cinema
eel **chee**nema / ee **chee**nema
the cinema / the cinemas

la radio / le radio
la **rad**-yo / lay **rad**-yo
the radio / the radios

Further common exceptions to the above rules are:

il braccio
eel bra**ch**o
the arm

le braccia
lay bra**ch**a
the arms

il ciclista
eel cheekl**ee**sta
the cyclist

i ciclisti
ee cheekl**ee**stee
the cyclists

il dito
eel d**ee**to
the finger

le dita
lay d**ee**ta
the fingers

l'uomo
lw**o**mo
the man

gli uomini
l-yee w**o**meenee
the men

l'uovo	le uova
lwovo	lay wova
the egg	the eggs

Articles

The words for articles ('the' and 'a') in Italian vary according to three elements:

> the gender of the noun
> the first letter of the noun
> whether the noun is singular or plural

Masculine articles:

il, un (the, a)
lo, uno (the, a) before **s** + consonant, before **gn**, **ps** and **z**
l', un (the, a) before a vowel

il / un treno	**l'albergo / un albergo**
eel / oon tra**y**no	lalb**ai**rgo / oon alb**ai**rgo
the / a train	the hotel / a hotel
lo / uno scontrino	**lo / uno specchio**
lo / **oo**no skontr**ee**no	lo / **oo**no spek-yo
the / a receipt	the / a mirror

lo / uno zaino
lo / **oo**no tza-**ee**no
the / a rucksack

Feminine articles:

la, una (the, a)
l', un' (the, a) before a vowel

la / una stanza	**l'autostrada / un'autostrada**
la / **oo**na st**a**ntza	lowtostr**a**da / oonowtostr**a**da
the / a room	the motorway / a motorway

Plural Articles

Masculine plural articles correspond to the singular as follows:

singular	plural	
il, un	i, dei	(the, some)
lo, uno	gli, degli	(the, some)
l', un	gli, degli	(the, some)

i / dei pomodori
ee / day pomod**o**ree
the / some tomatoes

i / dei biglietti
ee / day beel-y**e**t-tee
the / some tickets

gli / degli sbagli
l-yee / d**a**yl-yee sba-yee
the / some mistakes

gli / degli scompartimenti
l-yee / d**a**yl-yee skomparteem**e**ntee
the / some compartments

gli / degli adolescenti
l-yee / d**a**yl-yee adolesh**e**ntee
the / some teenagers

Feminine plural articles correspond to the singular as follows:

singular	plural	
la, una	le, delle	(the, some)
l', un'	le, delle	(the, some)

le / delle stanze
lay / d**e**l-lay st**a**ntzay
the / some rooms

le / delle arance
lay / d**e**l-lay ar**a**nchay
the / some oranges

le / delle automobili
lay / d**e**l-lay owtom**o**beelee
the / some cars

Prepositions

When used with certain prepositions the article changes its form. Some common examples are:

	il	lo	la	i	gli	le
a (at, to)	al	allo	alla	ai	agli	alle
da (from)	dal	dallo	dalla	dai	dagli	dalle
di (of)	del	dello	della	dei	degli	delle
in (in)	nel	nello	nella	nei	negli	nelle
su (on)	sul	sullo	sulla	sui	sugli	sulle

alla stazione
al-la statz-yonay
at / to the station

alle terme
al-lay tairmay
to the thermal baths

nella casa
nel-la kaza
in the house

nei treni
nay traynee
in the trains

Adjectives and Adverbs

Adjectives must agree in gender and number with the noun they refer to. In the English-Italian section of this book, all adjectives are given in the masculine singular form. Adjectives ending in **-o** change as follows:

	singular	plural
m	piccolo	piccoli
f	piccola	piccole

Adjectives ending in **-e** change as follows:

	singular	plural
m	grande	grandi
f	grande	grandi

In Italian, adjectives are generally placed after the noun:

un ristorante caro
oon reestorantay karo
an expensive restaurant

i biglietti cari
i beel-yet-tee karee
the expensive tickets

una mostra interessante
oona mostra eentaires-santay
an interesting exhibition

una camera singola
a single room

delle scarpe italiane
del-lay skarpay eetal-yanay
some Italian shoes

Some common adjectives sometimes precede the noun:

bello beautiful
brutto ugly
giovane jovanay young
vecchio vek-yo old
nuovo nwovo new
largo wide

stretto narrow
grande granday big
piccolo small
breve brayvay short
lungo long
antico ancient

l'antico duomo
lanteeko dwomo
the ancient cathedral

una grande fetta di torta
oona granday fet-ta dee torta
a large slice of cake

A few adjectives are invariable (i.e. the ending never changes):

un vestito blu / rosa
oon vesteeto bloo / roza
a blue / pink dress

una camicia blu / rosa
oona kameecha bloo / roza
a blue / pink shirt

Comparatives

The comparative is formed by placing **più** (more) or **meno** (less) before the adjective and **di** (than) after it:

grande
granday
large

più grande
p-yoo granday
larger

rumoroso	meno rumoroso
roomoro**zo**	**may**no roomoro**zo**
noisy	less noisy

questo albergo è più / meno caro di quello
kw**e**sto alb**ai**rgo ay p-yoo / **may**no k**a**ro dee kw**e**l-lo
this hotel is more / less expensive than that one

è più tranquillo qui
ay p-yoo trankw**ee**l-lo kwee
it's quieter here

Superlatives

Superlatives are formed by placing one of the following before the adjective:

il / la più the most	**il / la meno** the least
i / le più	**i / le meno**

questo itinerario è il meno pericoloso
kw**e**sto eeteenair**a**r-yo ay eel **may**no paireekol**o**zo
this route is the least dangerous

la pizzeria Napoli è la più popolare
la peetzair**ee**-a n**a**polee ay la p-yoo popol**a**ray
the Napoli pizza restaurant is the most popular

piazza San Marco è la piazza più famosa di Venezia
p-y**a**tza san m**a**rko ay la p-y**a**tza p-yoo fam**o**za dee ven**e**tz-ya
St Mark's Square is the most famous square in Venice

'As ... as' is translated as follows:

questo ristorante è tanto caro quanto quello
kw**e**sto reestor**a**ntay ay t**a**nto k**a**ro kw**a**nto kw**e**l-lo
this restaurant is as expensive as that one

la città non è interessante come pensavo
la cheet-t**a** non ay eentaires-s**a**ntay k**o**may pens**a**vo
this town is not as interesting as I thought

Note also:

> **è venuto il più in fretta possibile**
> ay venooto eel p-yoo een fret-ta pos-seebeelay
> he came as soon as he could

The superlative form ending in **-issimo** indicates that something is 'very / extremely ...' without comparing it to something else:

bello	**bellissimo**
beautiful	very beautiful
vecchio	**vecchissimo**
vek-yo	vek-kees-seemo
old	very old

The following two adjectives have irregular comparatives and superlatives:

buono	**migliore**	**il migliore**	**ottimo**
bwono	meel-yoray	eel meel-yoray	ot-teemo
good	better	the best	excellent
cattivo	**peggiore**	**il peggiore**	**pessimo**
kat-teevo	pej-joray	eel pej-joray	pes-seemo
bad	worse	the worst	extremely bad

Adverbs

If the adjective ends in **-o**, take the feminine form and add **-mente** to form the adverb:

esatto	**esattamente**
esat-to	esat-tamentay
exact	exactly

If the adjective ends in **-e**, add **-mente** to form the adverb:

veloce	**velocemente**
velochay	velochementay
fast, quick	quickly

Possessive Adjectives

Possessive adjectives, like other Italian adjectives, agree with the noun in gender and number:

	singular			
	m		**f**	
my	**il mio**	eel **mee**-o	**la mia**	la **mee**-a
your (fam)★	**il tuo**	**too**-o	**la tua**	**too**-a
his / her / its / your (pol)★	**il suo**	**soo**-o	**la sua**	**soo**-a
our	**il nostro**	**no**stro	**la nostra**	**no**stra
your (pl)★	**il vostro**	**vo**stro	**la vostra**	**vo**stra
their	**il loro**	**lo**ro	**la loro**	**lo**ro

	plural			
	m		**f**	
my	**i miei**	ee mee-**yay**	**le mie**	lay **mee**-ay
your (fam)★	**i tuoi**	too-**oy**	**le tue**	**too**-ay
his / her / its / your (pol)★	**i suoi**	soo-**oy**	**le sue**	**soo**-ay
our	**i nostri**	**no**stree	**le nostre**	**no**stray
your (pl)★	**i vostri**	**vo**stree	**le vostre**	**vo**stray
their	**i loro**	**lo**ro	**le loro**	**lo**ro

★see **Personal Pronouns** page 248.

la sua stanza
la **soo**-a **stan**tza
his / her / your room

il suo biglietto
eel **soo**-o beel-**yet**-to
his / her / your ticket

i miei soldi
ee **mee**-yay **sol**dee
my money

il vostro appartamento
eel **vo**stro ap-parta**men**to
your flat (plural)

If when using **il suo / la sua** etc, it is unclear whether you mean 'his', 'her' or 'your', you can use the following instead:

il biglietto di lui
eel beel-**yet**-to dee **loo**-ee
his ticket

il biglietto di lei
eel beel-**yet**-to dee lay
her ticket

247

When talking about members of your family, the article is always omitted if the noun is singular:

mio marito è malato
mee-o mareeto ay malato
my husband is ill

questi sono i miei genitori
kwestee sono ee mee-yay jeneetoree
these are my parents

Possessive Pronouns

To translate 'mine', 'yours', 'theirs' etc, use the same forms as in the table of possessive adjectives on page 247:

ho già ordinato il mio antipasto
o ja ordinato eel mee-o anteepasto
I've already ordered my starter

ho già ordinato il mio
I've already ordered mine

Personal Pronouns

Subject Pronouns

io	**ee**-o	I
tu[1]	too	you
Lei[2]	lay	you
lui	**loo**-ee	he, it
lei[2]	lay	she, it
noi	noy	we
voi[3]	voy	you
loro	**lo**ro	they

[1] **tu** is used when speaking to one person and is the familiar form generally used when speaking to family, friends and children

[2] **Lei** is the polite form of address, which is also the same form as the feminine third person singular **lei**; it takes the third person singular of verbs, see **Verbs** page 252.

3 **voi** is both the familiar and polite form used when speaking to more than one person

In Italian, the subject pronoun is usually omitted:

vorrei la ricevuta
vor-**ray** la reechev**oo**ta
I'd like a / the receipt

è partito
ay part**ee**to
he has left

although it may be retained for emphasis or to avoid confusion:

sono io!
sono **ee**-o
it's me!

siamo noi!
s-y**a**mo noy
it's us!

io pago i panini, tu le birre
ee-o pago ee pan**ee**nee, too lay b**ee**r-ray
I'll pay for the sandwiches, you pay for the beers

lui è inglese e lei è americana
loo-ee ay eengl**ay**zay ay lay ay amaireek**a**na
he is English and she is American

Object Pronouns

me / mi	may / mee	me
te / ti	tay / tee	you
Lei / la*	lay / la	you
lui / lo*	**loo**-ee / lo	him, it
lei / la*	lay / la	her, it
noi / ci	noy / chee	us
voi / vi	voy / vee	you
loro / li	**lo**ro / lee	them

* These become l' when preceding a vowel or silent h:

l'ha vista ieri?
la **vee**sta y**ai**ree
did he see her yesterday?

Object pronouns generally precede the verb. The first form given in the table above is used for emphasis and with prepositions:

la riconosco	**conosco lei, non lui**
la reekon**o**sko	kon**o**sko lay non l**oo**-ee
I recognize her	I know her, not him
questa pizza è per me	**non ti sento**
kw**e**sta p**ee**tza ay pair may	non tee s**e**nto
this pizza is for me	I can't hear you
dallo a lui	**vengo con Lei**
d**a**l-lo a l**oo**-ee	v**e**ngo kon lay
give it to him	I'm coming with you

When used with infinitives, pronouns are added to the end of the infinitive and the final **-e** of the infinitive is dropped:

portare to take

può portarmi all'aeroporto?
pwo port**a**rmee all-airop**o**rto
can you take me to the airport?

If you are using an object pronoun to mean 'to me', 'to you' etc (although 'to' might not always be necessary in English), you generally use the following:

mi	mee	(to) me
ti	tee	(to) you
Le	lay	(to) you
gli	l-yee	(to) him, (to) it
le	lay	(to) her, (to) it
ci	chee	(to) us
vi	vee	(to) you
loro	l**o**ro	(to) them

ci porti dell'acqua, per favore
chee p**o**rtee d**e**l-lakwa, pair fav**o**ray
please bring us some water

> **Carla gli ha dato i soldi**
> karla l-yee a dato ee soldee
> Carla has given him the money

Note that when followed by

lo, la, l', li and le
mi, ti, ci and vi change to
me, te, ce and ve:

> **Carla me l'ha dato**
> karla may la dato
> Carla has given it to me

and **gli + lo, la, l', li or le** becomes **glielo, gliela, gliel', glieli, gliele:**

> **Carla glielo ha dato**
> karla l-yee-elo a dato
> Carla has given it to him

Some verbs taking a direct object in English take an indirect object in Italian: e.g. **telefonare, credere** BUT some verbs taking an indirect object in English take a direct object in Italian: e.g. **ascoltare** to listen to, **aspettare** to wait for, etc:

gli telefono domani	**ascoltami!** (direct object)
l-yee telayfono domanee	askoltamee
I'll phone him tomorrow	listen to me!

Reflexive Pronouns

These are used with reflexive verbs like **lavarsi** 'to wash (one-self), to have a wash':

mi	mee	(used with 'I')
ti	tee	(used with familiar 'you')
si	see	(used with he / she / it and formal 'you')
ci	chee	(used with 'we')
vi	vee	(used with plural 'you')
si		(used with 'they')

chiamarsi to be called

mi chiamo...
mee k-ya mo
my name is ..., I am called ...

divertirsi to enjoy oneself

mi sono divertito / divertita*
mee so no deevairteeto / deevairteeta
I enjoyed myself

ci siamo divertiti / divertite*
chee s-ya mo deevairteetee / deevairteetay
we enjoyed ourselves

* masculine / feminine plural forms of the past participle (see page 255)

■ Verbs

There are three verb types, recognizable by their endings – -are, -ere and -ire, for example:

portare to carry **chiedere** to ask **partire** to leave

Present Tense

The present tense corresponds to 'I leave' and 'I am leaving' in English. To form the present tense for the three main types of verb, remove the endings -are, -ere and -ire and add the endings as given below:

portare to carry, also to bring, to wear

porto	porto	I carry
porti	portee	you carry
porta	porta	he / she / it carries, you carry
portiamo	port-yamo	we carry
portate	portatay	you carry
portano	portano	they carry

chiedere to ask

chiedo	k-**yay**do	I ask
chiedi	k-**yay**dee	you ask
chiede	k-**yay**day	he / she / it asks, you ask
chiediamo	k-yayd-**ya**mo	we ask
chiedete	k-yayd**ay**tay	you ask
chiedono	k-**yay**dono	they ask

partire to leave

parto	**par**to	I leave
parti	par**tee**	you leave
parte	par**tay**	he / she / it leaves, you leave
partiamo	part-**ya**mo	we leave
partite	part**ee**tay	you leave
partono	**par**tono	they leave

See the section on **Subject Pronouns** page 248 for the use of the different words for 'you'.

Some common verbs are irregular:

avere to have		**essere** to be	
ho	o	sono	**so**no
hai	i	sei	say
ha	a	è	ay
abbiamo	ab-**ya**mo	siamo	s-**ya**mo
avete	av**ay**tay	siete	s-**yay**tay
hanno	**an**-no	sono	**so**no

andare to go		**venire** to come	
vado	**va**do	vengo	**ven**-go
vai	vi	vieni	v-**yay**nee
va	va	viene	v-**yay**nay
andiamo	and-**ya**mo	veniamo	ven-**ya**mo
andate	and**a**tay	venite	ven**ee**tay
vanno	**van**-no	vengono	**ven**-gono

fare to do, to make

faccio	facho
fai	fi
fa	fa
facciamo	fachamo
fate	fatay
fanno	fan-no

dovere to have to

devo	dayvo
devi	dayvee
deve	dayvay
dobbiamo	dob-yamo
dovete	dovaytay
devono	dayvono

sapere to know

so	so
sai	si
sa	sa
sappiamo	sap-yamo
sapete	sapaytay
sanno	san-no

bere to drink

bevo	bayvo
bevi	bayvee
beve	bayvay
beviamo	bev-yamo
bevete	bevaytay
bevono	bayvono

dire to say

dico	deeko
dici	deechee
dice	deechay
diciamo	deechamo
dite	deetay
dicono	deekono

potere to be able

posso	pos-so
puoi	pwoy
può	pwo
possiamo	pos-yamo
potete	potaytay
possono	pos-sono

volere to want

voglio	vol-yo
vuoi	vwoy
vuole	vwolay
vogliamo	vol-yamo
volete	volaytay
vogliono	vol-yono

dare to give

do	do
dai	di
dà	da
diamo	d-yamo
date	datay
danno	dan-no

Past Tense: Perfect Tense

To describe an action that has taken place in the past, use the present tense of either **avere** or **essere** (see page 253) followed by the past participle of the verb to form the perfect tense. The past participle is formed by taking the stem (i.e. the verb minus the -are, -ere or -ire ending) of the infinitive and adding the endings as follows:

portare to carry	**vedere** to see	**partire** to leave
portato carried	**veduto** seen	**partito** left

Most verbs take **avere** in the perfect tense:

l'ha venduto
la vend**oo**to
he / she has sold it

ha finito
a feen**ee**to
he / she has finished

non l'ho vista (or veduta)
non lo v**ee**sta (or ved**oo**ta)
I haven't seen her

Some verbs take **essere**, for example, some verbs of motion like **andare** 'to go' and all reflexive verbs like **alzarsi** 'to get up'. When **essere** is used, the past participle agrees according to whether the subject of the sentence is masculine, feminine or plural:

è partito
ay part**ee**to
he left

è partita
ay part**ee**ta
she left

sono andati / andate** a Firenze la settimana scorsa
sono and**a**tee / and**a**tay a feer**e**ntzay la set-teem**a**na sk**o**rsa
they went to Florence last week

ci siamo alzati / alzate** alle sette
chee s-y**a**mo altz**a**tee / altz**a**tay **a**l-lay s**e**t-tay
we got up at seven o'clock

sono andato / andata* all'ufficio postale ieri

sono andato / andata al-loofeecho postalay yairee

I went to the post office yesterday

* = feminine singular form
** = feminine plural form

The following common verbs use essere to form the perfect tense:

andare	to go	sono andato / andata
arrivare	to arrive	sono arrivato / arrivata
cadere	to fall	sono caduto / caduta
entrare	to enter	sono entrato / entrata
nascere	to be born	sono nato / nata
partire	to leave	sono partito / partita
passare	to pass	sono passato / passata
ritornare	to return	sono ritornato / ritornata
salire	to go up	sono salito / salita
scendere	to go down	sono sceso / scesa
venire	to come	sono venuto / venuta

Some common verbs have irregular past participles:

aprire	to open	aperto
bere	to drink	bevuto
chiedere	to ask	chiesto
chiudere	to close	chiuso
comprendere	to include	compreso
correre	to run	corso
dire	to say	detto
essere	to be	stato
fare	to do, to make	fatto
leggere	to read	letto
mettere	to put	messo
offrire	to offer	offerto
perdere	to lose, to waste	perso or perduto
prendere	to take	preso

ridere	to laugh	riso
scendere	to go down	sceso
scrivere	to write	scritto
spingere	to push	spinto
togliere	to take off	tolto
vedere	to see	visto or veduto
venire	to come	venuto
vivere	to live	vissuto

Imperfect Tense

This is used to describe an action in the past which was repeated, habitual, or often taking place over a period of time. To form the imperfect, change the verb endings as follows:

portare	portavo	portavo	I carried, I was carrying,
	portavi	portavee	I used to carry etc
	portava	portava	
	portavamo	portavamo	
	portavate	portavatay	
	portavano	portavano	
vedere	vedevo	vedayvo	I saw, I was seeing,
	vedevi	vedayvee	I used to see etc
	vedeva	vedayva	
	vedevamo	vedevamo	
	vedevate	vedevatay	
	vedevano	vedevano	
partire	partivo	parteevo	I left, I was leaving,
	partivi	parteevee	I used to leave
	partiva	parteeva	
	partivamo	parteevamo	
	partivate	parteevatay	
	partivano	parteevano	

quando ero studente, vivevo a Padova
kwando **ai**ro stoodentay, veev**ay**vo a **pa**dova
when I was a student, I used to live in Padua

com'era il tempo in Sicilia?
kom**ai**ra eel **te**mpo een seech**eel**-ya
what was the weather like in Sicily?

Essere is irregular in the imperfect tense:

ero	**ai**ro	I was, I used to be etc
eri	**ai**ree	
era	**ai**ra	
eravamo	aira**va**mo	
eravate	aira**va**tay	
erano	**ai**rano	

Future Tense

For verbs ending in **-ere** and **-ire**, the future tense is formed by removing the final **-e** from the infinitive and adding the endings as in the tables below:

chiedere to ask

chiederò	k-yaydair**o**	I will ask etc
chiederai	k-yaydair**i**	
chiederà	k-yaydair**a**	
chiederemo	k-yaydair**ay**mo	
chiederete	k-yaydair**ay**tay	
chiederanno	k-yaydairan-no	

partire to leave

partirò	parteer**o**	I will leave etc
partirai	parteer**i**	
partirà	parteer**a**	
partiremo	parteer**ay**mo	
partirete	parteer**ay**tay	
partiranno	parteeran-no	

With verbs ending in **-are**, the **-a-** in the stem changes to **-e-**:

portare to bring

porter**ò**	portair**o**	I will bring etc
porter**ai**	portair**i**	
porter**à**	portair**a**	
porter**emo**	portair**aymo**	
porter**ete**	portair**aytay**	
porter**anno**	portair**an-no**	

comprerò una bottiglia di vino rosso
komprair**o oo**na bot-**teel**-ya dee **vee**no **r**os-so
I'll buy a bottle of red wine

For some irregular verbs, these same endings are added to a modified verb stem:

andare	to go	**andrò**	I will go etc
avere	to have	**avrò**	
bere	to drink	**berrò**	
dovere	to have to	**dovrò**	
essere	to be	**sarò**	
fare	to do, to make	**farò**	
potere	to be able	**potrò**	
sapere	to know	**saprò**	
stare	to stay	**starò**	
tenere	to hold	**terrò**	
vedere	to see	**vedrò**	
venire	to come	**verrò**	
vivere	to live	**vivrò**	
volere	to want	**vorrò**	

sarà necessario?
sar**a** neches-**sar**-yo
will it be necessary?

Frequently in Italian, the present tense can be used instead of the future to refer to a future action (as is often the case in English):

partiamo domani
part-ya**mo doma**nee
we leave tomorrow

When an action is imminent, Italian often uses the present tense where English uses the future:

vengo subito da te
vengo s**oo**beeto da tay
I'll come to your place straight away

Sometimes the Italian future tense is used to indicate probability:

sarà vero
sa**rà** vai**ro**
it might be true

Negatives

To make a sentence negative, place **non** in front of the verb or pronoun:

capisco	non capisco
kap**ee**sko	non kap**ee**sko
I understand	I don't understand

mi piace il gelato / non mi piace il gelato
mee p-y**a**chay eel jel**a**to / nonne mee p-y**a**chay eel jel**a**to
I like ice cream / I don't like ice cream

sono stato a Roma / non sono stato a Roma
I have been to Rome / I have not been to Rome
abbiamo mangiato bene / non abbiamo mangiato bene
ab-y**a**mo manj**a**to b**ay**nay
we've eaten well / we've not eaten well

When there is no verb, **non** is used as follows:

non molto	**non troppo**
non **mo**lto	non **tro**p-po
not much	not too much

non nuovo	**non per me, grazie**
non n**wo**vo	non pair may gr**a**tzee-ay
not new	not for me, thanks

In other expressions, when translating words like 'nothing / anything' or 'nobody / anybody', Italian uses double negatives:

non c'è nessuno	**non ne so niente**
non chay nes-**soo**no	non nay so n-y**e**ntay
there's nobody there	I don't know anything about it
there isn't anybody there	I know nothing about it

non ne voglio nessuno
non nay **vo**l-yo nes-s**oo**no
I don't want any

Imperative

The imperative mood is used to express a command (such as 'come here!', 'let's go' etc). Generally, the imperative forms are similar to those of the present tense. Remove the **-are**, **-ere** or **-ire** ending of the verb and add the endings as below:

	tu	Lei	noi	voi
portare to bring	porta	porti	portiamo	portate
chiedere to ask	chiedi	chieda	chiediamo	chiedete
partire to leave	parti	parta	partiamo	partite

fate presto!	**prenda un opuscolo, è gratis**
f**a**tay pr**e**sto	pr**a**ynda oon op**oo**skolo ay gr**a**tees
hurry up! (plural)	take a leaflet, it's free (polite)

Pronouns are generally added to the end of the imperative form (although in some cases they precede the imperative):

aspettami!
aspet-tamee
wait for me! (familiar)

mi aspetti!
mee aspet-tee
wait for me! (polite)

The following commonly used imperatives are irregular:

vieni qui!
vyaynee kwee
come here!
(familiar)

venga qui!
venga kwee
come here!
(polite)

va' a casa!
va a kaza
go home!

dimmi la verità!
deem-mee la vaireeta
tell me the truth!

fa' presto!
fa presto
hurry up!

da' questo a Gigi
da kwesto a jee-jee
give this to Gigi

The negative form of the imperative is obtained by placing **non** before the verb; for the **tu** form, however, the verb changes to the infinitive:

non parlare così in fretta!
non parlaray cosee een fret-ta
don't speak so fast! (familiar)

non parli così in fretta!
non parlee cosee een fret-ta
don't speak so fast! (polite)

non fate rumore!
non fatay roomoray
don't be noisy!
don't make any noise! (plural)

Questions

Often word order remains the same in a question, but the intonation changes – the voice should be raised at the end of the question:

parla inglese?
parla eenglayzay
do you speak English?

Word order can also be inverted to form a question. This is always the case when a question word is used:

quando chiude il museo?
kwando k-yooday eel moozay-o
when does the museum close?

è arrivato il pacco?
ay ar-reevato eel pak-ko
has the parcel arrived?

Dates

Use the numbers on pages 265-266 to express the date, except for the first when the ordinal **il primo** should be used:

il primo settembre [eel preemo set-tembray] the first of September
il tre marzo [eel tray martzo] the third of March
il ventuno giugno [eel ventoono yoon-yo] the twenty-first of June

Days

Monday	lunedì	loonedee
Tuesday	martedì	martedee
Wednesday	mercoledì	mairkoledee
Thursday	giovedì	jovedee
Friday	venerdì	venairdee
Saturday	sabato	sabato
Sunday	domenica	domayneeka

Months

January	gennaio	jen-**na**-yo
February	febbraio	feb-**bra**-yo
March	marzo	**mar**tzo
April	aprile	a**pree**lay
May	maggio	**ma**j-jo
June	giugno	**yoo**n-yo
July	luglio	**loo**l-yo
August	ag**o**sto	
September	settembre	set-**tem**bray
October	ottobre	ot-**to**bray
November	novembre	no**vem**bray
December	dicembre	deech**em**bray

Time

■ what time is it? che ore sono? [kay **o**ray sono]
one o'clock l'una [**loo**na]
two o'clock le due [lay d**oo**-ay]
it's one o'clock è l'una [ay **loo**na]
it's two o'clock sono le due [**so**no lay d**oo**-ay]
it's ten o'clock sono le dieci [**so**no lay dee-**e**chee]
five past one l'una e cinque [**loo**na ay ch**een**kway]
ten past two le due e dieci [lay d**oo**-ay ay dee-**e**chee]
quarter past one l'una e un quarto [**loo**na ay oon kw**ar**to]
quarter past two le due e un quarto [lay d**oo**-ay]
half past ten le dieci e mezza [lay dee-**e**chee ay m**e**dza]
twenty to ten le dieci meno venti [lay dee-**e**chee m**ay**no v**e**ntee]
quarter to two le due meno un quarto [lay d**oo**-ay m**ay**no oon kw**ar**to]
at eight o'clock alle **o**tto
at half past four alle quattro e mezza [**al**-lay kw**a**t-tro ay m**e**dza]
14.00 le quattordici [lay kwat-**to**rdeechee]
17.30 le diciassette e trenta [lay deechas-**se**t-tay ay tr**e**nta]

2 a.m. le due di notte [lay doo-ay dee not-tay]
2 p.m. le due del pomeriggio [pomereej-jo]
6 a.m. le sei del mattino [lay say]
6 p.m. le sei di sera [dee saira]
noon mezzogiorno [medzojorno]
midnight mezzanotte [medzanot-tay]
an hour un'ora [ora]
a minute un minuto [meenooto]
a second un secondo [sekondo]
a quarter of an hour un quarto d'ora [kwarto dora]
half an hour mezz'ora [medzora]
three quarters of an hour tre quarti d'ora [tray kwartee dora]

Numbers

0	zero [tzairo]
1	uno [oono]
2	due [doo-ay]
3	tre [tray]
4	quattro [kwat-tro]
5	cinque [cheenkway]
6	sei [say]
7	sette [set-tay]
8	otto [ot-to]
9	nove [no-vay]
10	dieci [dee-aychee]
11	undici [oon-deechee]
12	dodici [doh-deechee]
13	tredici [tray-deechee]
14	quattordici [kwat-tor-deechee]
15	quindici [kween-deechee]
16	sedici [say-deechee]
17	diciassette [deechas-set-tay]
18	diciotto [deechot-to]
19	diciannove [deechan-no-vay]

20	venti [**ventee**]
21	ventuno [vent-**oo**no]
22	ventidue [ventee-**doo**-ay]
23	ventitré [ventee-**tray**]
30	trenta [**trenta**]
31	trentuno [trent**oo**no]
40	quaranta [kwar**a**nta]
50	cinquanta [cheenkw**a**nta]
60	sessanta [ses-**santa**]
70	settanta [set-**tanta**]
80	ottanta [ot-**tanta**]
90	novanta [nov**a**nta]
100	cento [**chento**]
110	centodieci [chento-dee-**ay**chee]
200	duecento [doo-ay-ch**e**nto]
300	trecento [tray-ch**e**nto]
1,000	mille [**mee**lay]
2,000	duemila [doo-ay-m**ee**la]
5,000	cinquemila [cheenkway-m**ee**la]
5,720	cinquemilasette-centoventi [cheenkway-m**ee**la-set-tay-chento-ventee]
10,000	diecimila [dee-echeem**ee**la]
10,550	diecimilacinque-centocinquanta [dee-echeem**ee**la-cheenkway-ch**e**nto-cheenkw**a**nta]
20,000	ventimila [venteem**ee**la]
50,000	cinquantamila [cheenkwantam**ee**la]
100,000	centomila [chentom**ee**la]
1,000,000	un milione [oon meel-y**o**nay]

In Italian, thousands are written with a full stop instead of a comma, e.g. 1.000, 10.000. Decimals are written with a comma, e.g. 3.5 would be 3,5 in Italian.

Ordinals

1st	primo	[**pree**mo]
2nd	secondo	[sek**o**ndo]
3rd	terzo	[**tairt**zo]
4th	quarto	[k**war**to]
5th	quinto	[k**wee**nto]
6th	sesto	
7th	settimo	[**set**-teemo]
8th	ottavo	[ot-**ta**vo]
9th	nono	
10th	decimo	[**day**cheemo]

Conversion Tables

1 centimetre = 0.39 inches	1 inch = 2.54 cm
1 metre = 39.37 inches = 1.09 yards	1 foot = 30.48 cm
1 kilometre = 0.62 miles = 5/8 mile	1 yard = 0.91 m
	1 mile = 1.61 km

km	1	2	3	4	5	10	20	30	40	50	100
miles	0.6	1.2	1.9	2.5	3.1	6.2	12.4	18.6	24.8	31.0	62.1

miles	1	2	3	4	5	10	20	30	40	50	100
km	1.6	3.2	4.8	6.4	8.0	16.1	32.2	48.3	64.4	80.5	161

1 gram = 0.035 ounces	1 kilo = 1000 g = 2.2 pounds

g	100	250	500	1 oz = 28.35 g
oz	3.5	8.75	17.5	1 lb = 0.45 kg

kg	0.5	1	2	3	4	5	6	7	8	9	10
lb	1.1	2.2	4.4	6.6	8.8	11.0	13.2	15.4	17.6	19.8	22.0

kg	20	30	40	50	60	70	80	90	100
lb	44	66	88	110	132	154	176	198	220

lb	0.5	1	2	3	4	5	6	7	8	9	10	20
kg	0.2	0.5	0.9	1.4	1.8	2.3	2.7	3.2	3.6	4.1	4.5	9.0

1 litre = 1.75 UK pints / 2.13 US pints

1 UK pint = 0.57 litre	1 UK gallon = 4.55 litre
1 US pint = 0.47 litre	1 US gallon = 3.79 litre

centigrade / Celsius $°C = (°F - 32) \times 5/9$

°C	-5	0	5	10	15	18	20	25	30	36.8	38
°F	23	32	41	50	59	64	68	77	86	98.4	100.4

Fahrenheit $°F = (°C \times 9/5) + 32$

°F	23	32	40	50	60	65	70	80	85	98.4	101
°C	-5	0	4	10	16	18	21	27	29	36.8	38.3